An Etiquette Book with an Exciting New Look

This book has been designed especially to meet the needs of today's busy family.

Presented in a simple question-and-answer form, cross-indexed and fully illustrated with diagrams, it contains all the information you will ever need about marriage, birth, death, engagements, showers, formal and informal weddings, birth announcements, christenings, funerals, introductions, letters, table manners, tipping, etiquette for club and church members.

Included is a special section devoted to manners for children and teen-agers, along with sound advice on dating.

There is also a detailed guide to all kinds of entertaining—formal and informal, at home or in a public place.

Written in a refreshingly down-to-earth and witty style, *Modern Manners* is today's most readable and practical guide to graceful contemporary living.

Crest books are designed to bring to a larger reading public, at small cost, reprints of outstanding books previously published at much higher prices.

MODERN MANNERS

Etiquette for All Occasions

By CAROLYN HAGNER SHAW

A Crest Reprint

FAWCETT PUBLICATIONS, INC., *Greenwich Conn.*

MODERN MANNERS was originally published by E. P. Dut-
ton & Company, Inc., and is reissued at 50¢ in this new CREST
edition through arrangement with that company.

First CREST printing, April 1960

DEDICATION

To my daughter and son, Jean and John

CREST BOOKS are published by
FAWCETT WORLD LIBRARY
67 West 44th Street, New York 36, N. Y.

Printed in the United States of America

CONTENTS

INTRODUCTION

SINCE the cave-man era, manners have been based on one principle only—consideration for the other fellow. Customs that have come down through the ages have naturally been modified as our ways of living have changed, but the reasons behind it all haven't.

We don't eat with our fingers or pick our teeth in public because it is unsightly to the beholder. We learn to observe the everyday courtesies, the "thank you's" and the "pleases," and to follow the easy rules that make our contacts with others more pleasant for them, and, incidentally, ourselves.

"Minding our manners" need not be an unpleasant chore. Learn a few simple rules, be thoughtful toward others, and you can't go wrong.

This book is written to help you accomplish relaxed, easy manners in your everyday way of life. It is designed for today's families. It is concerned with the amenities of everyday living, and includes the more formal observances that mark the special events that come into all our lives, from birth to death. The questions, and their answers, are geared to the life of the average family as lived today. The "do's" and "do nots" are presented with one idea in mind: To bring the assurance and poise that come from not only knowing WHAT to do—but what NOT to do.

To those who pretend to disdain the accepted customs in dealing with others, I might point out that to cultivate good manners is actually being selfish in the best sense of the word. Like bread cast upon the waters, "minding your manners" with ease and thoughtfulness will come back to you twofold in the respect and friendship that will be received from all with whom you come in contact.

CAROLYN HAGNER SHAW

ACKNOWLEDGMENT

With deep appreciation for the assistance of John Farr Simmons, former Chief of Protocol of the State Department; Ruth Crane Schaefer of Washington, and Horace Richardson, specialist on invitation forms.

FACTS OF LIFE

FACTS OF LIFE — ENGAGEMENTS

Should a man obtain permission from the father of the girl before presenting his hand and heart to the young lady herself?

In years gone by, yes. Today, no. Now a couple usually makes the decision on their own before announcing it to their respective parents (as if they hadn't already guessed!). After this, it is the considerate man who has a conference with his fiancée's dad to discuss his own background and plans for the future.

What is expected of the parents of the couple?

If the parents of the man live in the same city as those of the girl, they should call immediately, within three days if possible, on the girl and her parents. By all means the mother, at least, should definitely do so. Should they live in another city, a letter, usually from the mother of the man, should be written to the girl to welcome her into their family.

Is anything expected of the couple before the formal announcement of the engagement?

Yes. A few days before the formal announcement is made, the couple should call or write all close relatives and any intimate friends, telling them the glad tidings.

REMINDER: Don't forget to mention that they should not give away the secret before it is announced publicly.

Is it a hard-and-fast rule that an engagement ring must be presented to the bride to be before the formal announcement?

Goodness, no! Many a young couple cannot afford, and certainly do not need, such a material expression of their love. It is a mistaken idea that a ring must be given to plight the troth. It is nice if it can be done, but if it can't, better wait until you can afford it.

When should the formal announcement be made?

It is wise, as life is rather uncertain, never to do so more than six months before the wedding is to take place, never less than two months. The ideal time is three or four months before the ceremony. Except in unusual circumstances, long engagements should be avoided.

Is it proper to issue a printed or engraved announcement?

Never. A personal note to relatives and close friends may be written before the formal announcement in the newspapers, but never an engraved or printed announcement before or after.

What procedure is followed when issuing the announcement?

Do not telephone to the newspapers. Always write, preferably on a typewriter, to avoid mistakes. The date you wish it to appear should be carefully indicated.

EXAMPLE: "For release, Sunday, September 5."

The same date is given to all newspapers. A photograph of the prospective bride may or may not accompany the story. Some newspapers do not use engagement photographs.

Who makes this announcement?

The parents or relatives of the girl, never those of the man or any of his relatives.

What information should the announcement contain?

EXAMPLE: "Mr. and Mrs. John Richard Green announce the engagement of their daughter, Elizabeth Mary, to Mr. James Philip Gray, son of Mr. and Mrs. Albert James Gray." Pertinent facts relative to the background of both families may be included, as well as a brief résumé of the schools attended by the couple, and if the man has had a military service this may also be mentioned. If the date of the wedding has already been decided, if it is not more than four months away, it should be included in the announcement of the engagement. If more than four months, a later announcement of the date should be sent to the newspapers.

If there are complicated relationships in the girl's family, who makes the announcement under those conditions?

If one parent is deceased, the survivor does so, mentioning that she is the daughter of the late Mr. or Mrs. So-and-So. If both parents are deceased, the nearest relative—an aunt, uncle, older sister, brother, cousin, or guardian. If alone in the world, the girl herself may announce the engagement.

EXAMPLE: "Miss Mary Ann Powell, daughter of the late

Mr. and Mrs. James Lincoln Powell, announces her engagement to," etc.

When parents are separated but not divorced, if amicable decision can be reached—and it should be—they would announce it jointly. If not, the parent with whom the girl lives should do so. If parents are divorced, and neither has remarried, the one with whom the girl makes her home.

EXAMPLE: "Mrs. Warren Smith announces the engagement of her daughter," etc.

It should be mentioned in the article that Miss Smith is the daughter of Mr. John Samuel Smith.

If parents are divorced, and one or more has remarried, again in this case the one with whom the girl lives.

EXAMPLE: "Mr. and Mrs. Nelson John Brown announce the engagement of her daughter, Alice May Terry, to," etc.

You will note that the bride's surname has been used in this case, as it is different now from that of her mother, and also in this announcement should be included that Miss Terry is the daughter of Mr. George Terry. If Dad is making the announcement and Mother has remarried, it would be "Miss Terry is the daughter of Mrs. Nelson John Brown."

When a widow remarries, is it proper for the engagement to be announced?

Age comes into this. If she is young, say under thirty-five years of age, an announcement may properly be made by her parents, as follows:

"Mr. and Mrs. Robert John Dean announce the engagement of their daughter, Mrs. Rebecca Dean Brown, to," etc.

It may be mentioned that Mrs. Brown is the widow of Mr. John Francis Brown, if she wishes to do so. Should she be more than thirty-five, a formal announcement of the engagement is usually not made. When the wedding takes place, an announcement should then be sent to the newspapers, and an engraved announcement mailed to the relatives and friends on the day the ceremony takes place.

If the girl has been adopted, should this fact be mentioned when announcing her engagement?

Not if, when the child was adopted, the couple legally gave her their surname and brought her up as their own. Mentioning that she is adopted is certainly not necessary and is in bad taste. The announcement should be made as for any daughter. Only in the case where the child has not assumed the surname of those who adopted her (and this is rare) is it necessary to clarify. The wording would then be, "Mr. and Mrs. Henry John Green announce the engagement of their adopted daughter, Phyllis Smith, to," etc.

Is an engagement announcement party a "must"?

No. It is entirely up to the individual. If a party is given, however, it should be before the formal announcement to the newspapers, and is usually held a day or two ahead of this.

What forms of entertainment are best?

Usually on the informal side. It may take the form of a luncheon, late-afternoon get-together, dinner, buffet supper, or an evening party.

Who should be invited?

Members of both families.

REMINDER: Don't forget to include all of the members of the family of the bridegroom to be. Not to do so can start everything off on the wrong foot! Then, of course, close friends of the couple are included.

How should invitations be issued?

If the group is to be small, a telephone call is the easiest way. For a larger group, a short note may be written by either the bride or her mother. Care must be taken in both cases not to give away the reason for the party, or your big secret will be a surprise to no one.

How should the news be broken to the assembled guests? And by whom?

No rules govern this. Do, however, guard against over-stepping the bounds of good taste by being too facetious or "clever" in the mode of announcement. Table decorations may tell the news and the father of the girl should propose a toast such as, for example, "To my Janie and Dick Phillips. May great happiness be theirs."

How do guests congratulate the couple?

Express wishes for future happiness to the girl—never congratulate her! The gentleman is the recipient of the congratulations.

Is it necessary to take a gift to such a party?

No. After all, when you attend the party, you are not supposed to know it is the announcement of an engagement. Therefore, why should you take a gift?

After the engagement is known, is a gift from relatives and close friends considered obligatory?

No. It is entirely up to the individual whether or not he will present a gift. Usually it is not done.

Who may properly give a bridal shower?

Never, under any circumstances, should a relative (close or far away) of either the bride or the bridegroom ever entertain at a shower for the girl. REASON: relatives should not invite guests (who are expected to bring gifts) when the recipient is one of their own. Any close feminine friend, often one of those who will attend the bride on her wedding day, should be hostess.

What form does such an affair take?

Any type of informal get-together, as in the case of the engagement party. Every effort is usually made to make it a surprise for the bride to be.

How do you send out invitations to a party of this type?

The hostess may either telephone or write a note. It should be stated whether it is to be a general gift party or one of a specific kind, such as lingerie and linen, or maybe silver, or kitchenware.

Must each guest bring a gift?

Definitely yes. It need not be expensive, but it is a "must."

If invited to several showers for the same bride, must one take gifts to each?

If you want to go to all of the showers you're invited to, one gift, the first one, can be as important as you care to make it; later gifts may be "token" gifts, suitable to the kind of shower but costing as little as $1.00. If you don't attend, send a gift or not as you wish; a regret to the hostess is sufficient.

Are men ever included in showers?

Usually not. If the party is in the evening, the men may be asked to join the girls after the gifts have been opened.

Are showers given for the second-time bride?

Not usually. No rule against it, though.

If a formal announcement of an engagement has been made and the couple decide later that marriage just wouldn't work for them, what then?

If the engagement is broken before the wedding invitations

go out, the less said the better. No formal notice in the news-papers is necessary. Quietly telling family and friends is suf-ficient. No details, either. That's the couple's business. Only the most heartless person will infringe by asking the whys and wherefores.

If wedding invitations have gone out before the engagement is broken, how can those invited be notified?

A small engraved card should be sent to all those to whom invitations were sent. The wording on the card would be as follows: "Mr. and Mrs. John Henry Brown announce that the marriage of their daughter, Mary Ann, to Mr. David William Gray, will not take place."

An announcement using the same wording may be sent to the society department of the newspapers. This, however, is not necessary, and is advised against.

Should any shower or wedding gifts that have been received be returned to the donors?

Yes. Immediately. A short handwritten note, written by the girl, should accompany each one. It is only necessary to express appreciation of the thought, and the bare statement that the wedding is not going to take place is all that has to be said. No detailed explanation should ever be gone into, as it is ex-tremely bad taste.

FACTS OF LIFE — WEDDINGS

What is the difference between the formal, semi-formal, and informal wedding?

The first is more elaborately and expensively planned in all details than any other wedding. The bride always wears a formal wedding gown, with a veil and a train.

The semi-formal follows much the same pattern, only on a less elaborate and expensive scale. The bride may wear the formal gown with veil and train, or one of ballerina length with a veil, but of course no train.

The informal limits the guests to a fairly small group of relatives and friends, and the bride is attired in an afternoon gown or suit.

What is the first step when planning a wedding?

The family of the bride must decide the type of wedding it is to be, based, of course, on what the budget will stand. The following will help make this decision.

Who pays for what?

The bride's trousseau is a tradition stemming from the olden days when the bride carried a "trusse" or "little bundle" with her when she went to the home of her new husband. This was the age of marriage by purchase when the bridegroom bought his bride from her father. Today Dad still pays: for the invitations and the preparation for their mailing; all floral decorations, either in the church or the home and wherever the reception is held; the bride's bouquet (the bridegroom may pay for this if he wishes); the bridesmaids' bouquets and a gift to each; church expenses, including the aisle canvas, canopy, music, and the sexton; transportation of bridal party to and from church; the wedding breakfast or reception in its entirety. The bridegroom never should pay any of these expenses under any circumstances.

What does the bridegroom pay for?

The bridegroom is virtually a guest at his own wedding.

He is only responsible for the following:

He pays for the wedding ring (as it is an unending circle, this ring has symbolized a marriage for eternity ever since the Egyptians started the custom centuries ago. So whether it costs $5.00 or $500, this is really a "must," but note that if it is a double-ring ceremony, the bride pays for her bridegroom's ring); the marriage license; a gift for the bride, always for her personal adornment; the bride's bouquet (if he wishes); boutonnières for himself, best man, and ushers; a going-away corsage for his bride, and one for each mother; gloves and ties for the best man and ushers, and a gift for each; any hotel bills incurred by them while serving him at the wedding; his bachelor dinner if any; the clergyman's fee ($10.00 being considered the minimum—very minimum).

Granted this is the time to splurge a little, going beyond your means won't make the marriage any happier. A wedding built around gracious simplicity can be a treasured memory just as much, if not more so, as one planned in the grand manner and on a large scale.

Careful planning can keep expenses from getting out of hand, and at the same time "the big day" can be a perfect one, with no pinching of pennies afterward to pay for it.

What are the next steps?

Now that the family council has decided into which category their wedding plans will fall, here are a few hints about how to get started.

They are based on a formal church wedding. A few variations necessarily occur here and there for the semi-formal and informal ceremonies. Remember, however, that traditions remain the same for all. (Most of the following applies to weddings in the home also.)

1. Select the date, hour, and place for the ceremony.

2. Immediately contact your religious advisor, ascertaining that the day and time of the ceremony (and don't forget the rehearsal) which you have chosen will not conflict with other commitments he may have.

3. Do the same with the caterer. Wherever the reception is to be held—in the home, a hotel, or club—reservations must be made, and then the menu decided upon.

4. Tell the florist when you will need decorations and bouquets.

5. These four important details dovetailed, now buckle down to the guest list. Get those invitations ready. Remember: They must be mailed at least three weeks (preferably four weeks) before the wedding.

6. If you wish a portrait photographer for the bridal pictures, make arrangements with him well ahead of time.

7. As the fateful day draws near, notify the caterer of the approximate number of expected guests at the reception, the menu having been decided on. Remember he's got to know how many mouths he has to feed and how much liquid refreshment will be necessary. Double check with the florist on your selections for the bouquets and the church and reception decorations. (Be sure he knows the time the bouquets should be at the church—at least an hour before the ceremony.)

8. Make the decision about music to be played by the organist and pass it on to him.

9. Last-minute talk about details with the church sexton.

10. Make sure enough limousines are ordered to convey the bridal party from your home to the church and to the place where the reception will be held. Have their time schedule down pat. (Should the budget not stretch to the rather expensive hiring of limousines and their drivers, friends may be asked to fill in, using their own cars. However, it is suggested that the bride and her father and mother use a limousine.)

11. Decide whether or not to trust that the sun will shine, or be safe and order an awning for the church.

12. Designate at least two relatives or close friends (even if you have servants) to superintend the household on the great day. Remember, Mother is busy with the bride. Last-minute

gifts always arrive, telegrams, and so on, and never forget the minor emergencies that will pop up. Utter chaos can take over if someone is not designated to control the situation.

13. The same thing applies at the church itself. The unexpected sometimes, and usually does, happen. Have someone on hand about an hour ahead of time to be sure that the bouquets arrive when they should. Outfit her with a little box for emergencies, said box containing smelling salts (it's usually a bridesmaid who is overcome by excitement, seldom the bride!), safety pins, needle and thread, aspirin, and so on. You will be glad you did.

14. If there are small children in the family, make every effort to find some kind soul to pack them off for the day. The belief held by some that because they are part of the family they should be part of the wedding is the biggest mistake you can possibly make. Confusion to the child, unpleasantness to guests, and usually bedlam is the result. Small children just don't belong at a wedding.

What is the best way to plan the floral decorations?

Smilax and green plants usually form a backdrop on both sides of the altar (whether in the church or behind the improvised altar in the home). If white flowers are also used, avoid overdoing it. Too many will detract from the beauty and dignity of the altar itself. In too much profusion they also tend to take away some of the effect that rightfully belongs to the bride's gown and those of her attendants.

Whether the reception is held in a club, hotel, or in the home, the floral *décor* is usually green and white. Centerpieces at the bride's table, if there is one, the buffet tables, and the "cake table" may have ferns softly looped across the front of the tablecloths (the cloths should hang almost to the floor), and the flowers on the tables themselves, are, for example, arrangements of white roses, baby's-breath with ferns or greens of some kind forming a background.

SUGGESTION: Take the advice of a florist as to the decorations at both the church and the home, or wherever. Get his ideas (and an estimate) on what he thinks best. He's had a lot of experience. Only the most unethical will try to overload you with too much of everything, and it goes without saying that you will be able to spot the florist (and they are few and far between) who will try to take advantage of you. If there are any doubts whatsoever, get two florists and let them suggest, and bid against each other.

What is expected of the caterer?

The caterer will offer menus, depending upon your budget, and the approximate number of guests you expect. Usually, if the reception is held in the home, he will supply silver, dishes, glassware, linen, tables, chairs, and so on, free of charge, if he handles the refreshments (including the wedding cake) in their entirety. If the reception takes place in a club or hotel, all details are usually discussed with and taken over by them. Don't be shy. Be frank. It makes it easier all around. Be specific about the amount of money you can afford to spend. Based on this they will do their utmost to arrange a celebration as close to your wishes as the budget will allow.

What about photographs?

A visual remembrance of the great day will be treasured always. If the pictures are taken by an amateur, say a friend of the family, be sure he doesn't get in people's way or pop flash bulbs all over the place. The same applies to a professional who may be engaged to get candid shots from the beginning until the end of the festivities. Both should remember one thing: no pictures in the church itself without the express permission of the clergyman. If a professional portrait photographer is desired, arrangements should be made with him way ahead of time. He may take pictures of the bride in her wedding gown a week or so ahead of the ceremony. (The florist will cooperate in this case by supplying a pseudo bouquet if necessary.) If this is done, proofs may be seen, poses approved by all the bride's family, and then "glossy" prints sent to the newspapers ahead of time to be released with the wedding story. On the day of the wedding more pictures of the bride alone and with her bridesmaids may be taken before they leave for the church (or at least an hour before the service is to start if it is in the home). If the entire wedding group is to be photographed after the ceremony is over, it should be done *immediately* after their arrival wherever the reception is taking place. The photographer should be all set up and ready to go. Never allow him to take over. *Make it clear. So many minutes and no more.* In his overanxiety to get as many pictures as possible he may keep the wedding group from getting in the receiving line. This forces guests to stand in line waiting for things to get going—an inexcusable rudeness that all too often mars a wedding reception.

How should a guest list be compiled?

Never underestimate the importance of this behemoth. You

can either get fun out of the chore (and it is one) or you can make it a nightmare. A card file can assure the first—the second can be accomplished by jotting names down (as they come to mind) on slips of paper, backs of envelopes, or what have you—with the final result that Cousin Susie lands in the waste-basket and is forgotten. Well, she won't forget, ever.

The card file may seem a lot of trouble, but you can be assured you won't regret it. Get started immediately after the engagement announcement, even if the wedding is months away. The sooner the better. Get it behind you before the final rush and excitement start.

First, the bride's family should decide the approximate number of guests to be invited. Then a conference with the bridegroom's family is in order, telling them how many people they may invite. Every effort should be made by them to co-operate and stick within the number that is set. Not to do so may and probably will start everything off on the wrong foot between the two families.

Now, purchase 3 x 5 inch lined cards in two colors, say white and blue. An alphabetical index and a 3 x 5 inch file box complete the equipment. Cost, not much. Members of both families can make out cards for all those to be invited—the white for the bride, the blue for the bridegroom. To make filing easy, enter the names as follows on the cards:

Phillips, Mr. and Mrs. Warren Francis
2722 Forest Avenue

By placing the white and blue cards together, in the alphabetical file box, all duplications will be avoided.

If the ceremony is to take place in a church with a reception following, the decision must be made when the alphabetical file is complete as to just how many ought to be asked to the church only, and how many to both church and reception. Go through the file, marking those for the church only with a "C" in the upper right-hand corner of the card, those for both with an "R." This facilitates addressing of the invitations in the two categories—those who receive the reception card and those who do not. Be sure to find out how many people can be accommodated in the church.

What is the best way to keep track of acknowledgments?

This is easy. Those receiving an invitation to the church only should not reply at all. When an answer to the reception invitation is received, mark whether it is an accept or regret in the upper right-hand corner of the person's card in red pencil. When the times comes to make final plans with the caterer, an easy count of those accepting the invitation to the reception can be made from the cards.

How else can these cards be used?

They come in mighty handy when the gifts begin arriving. As they are unwrapped, mark on the card of the individual sending the gift what it is and then when the thank-you note is written, mark the date thereon.

SAMPLE OF COMPLETED CARD:

accept (or *Regret*)
"C" (*church only*)
"R" (*and reception*)

Phillips, Mr. and Mrs. (or XX*) Warren Francis
2722 Forest Avenue
Silver bowl—2/5 (meaning "thank you" written)

* It helps and saves time to use xx in place of Mr. and Mrs.

NOTE:' This may all seem complicated and unnecessary, but once you get going it will definitely make the burden a much lighter one.

FACTS OF LIFE — WEDDING INVITATIONS

To whom are invitations sent?

To all relatives, members of the bridal party (and their wives and husbands if any), close friends of both families, business associates of both fathers and the bridegroom, and if she has been a career girl, those of the bride herself.

Should invitations be sent to relatives and friends who live so far away it is a certainty they will not be able to attend?

Of course. It is a courtesy and an honor to the recipient.

Would it be better to have announcements instead of invitations sent in these cases?

Definitely not. An announcement should be sent only when no formal wedding invitation has been issued.

Who issues invitations and announcements?

Parents or relatives of the bride, even the bride herself. Never those of the bridegroom or any of his relatives.

If the mother of the bride or the father is deceased, may the surviving parent issue the invitations alone?

Certainly.

If both parents are deceased, what then?

The nearest relative, grandparents, an aunt or uncle, an older sister or brother, even a cousin or guardian may do so.

If no close relatives survive?

The bride may send out her own invitations. This should never be done, however, if there is a relative, no matter how distant, who can do so.

If the parents of the bride are separated, but not divorced, who issues the invitations?

They should send them jointly, just as if they were not separated. This is one time the hatchet should be buried.

If the parents are divorced, and neither has remarried, what then?

The parent with whom the bride makes her home should send the invitations alone.

If the parents are divorced, and either or both have remarried?

If the bride lives with her mother and stepfather, the wording would be 'Mr. and Mrs. John William Smith request the honour of your presence at the marriage of her daughter, Mary Jane Green." You will notice that her surname is given in this instance. Should the father and his new wife issue the invitations, the bride's name would appear as simply "Mary Jane," because the surname would be the same.

What if relations are strained and both divorced parents insist upon their names appearing on the invitations?

Only the most unkind parents can be so thoughtless as to blight their daughter's happiness. If they refuse to behave, the result is not only awkward, it is ludicrous. If neither has remarried, it may not be so bad. "Mrs. Ward Smith and Mr. John William Smith request the honour of your presence at the marriage of their daughter." But if the mother has remarried, "Mrs. James Robert Jones and Mr. John Chase Perkins request the honour of your presence at the marriage of their daughter." Correct, but it doesn't sound very nice, does it?

Is it correct to send engraved invitations for the second wedding of a young widow?

Yes; but the wedding itself should be informal and the bride should not wear a white wedding gown.

If the man has been married before, does it change the form of an invitation?

No. Only the status of the woman is considered.

Does a divorcee send engraved invitations to her second wedding?

Definitely not. The informal wedding should include only relatives and close friends, and the invitations should be handwritten notes from the bride herself or her mother. If it is a very small guest list, the invitations may be extended by telephone.

May a divorcee send engraved announcements of her second marriage?

In former years, no. Today, yes. Common sense dictates that in order to know who's married to whom, a formal announcement is a "must."

Who issues these announcements?

Her parents, nearest relative or, if necessary, she herself.

How are invitations for a double wedding issued?

For a double wedding where the brides are *not* sisters, separate invitations may be issued by the parents of both brides, and these two invitations may appear on the inside pages of one folded sheet. There is no "rule" as to which should appear on the left inside page; it may be the parents of the elder of the brides, or by alphabetical arrangement of the surnames of the parents of the brides.

When should formal engraved invitations or announcements be ordered?

At least two months before the date of the wedding. Engraving takes time. Get the envelopes at the time you place the order so there will be no delay in addressing them.

What paper and style of lettering are considered proper?

The proper arrangements of phrases and lines to be used in a wedding invitation are shown on illustrations appearing on succeeding pages, and have been approved by years of custom.

The wording of wedding invitations is always formal and should be engraved (never printed) in the third person. Lines should be centered as evenly as possible, capitalization should be used only where necessary, and commas used sparingly; periods are used only for the abbreviations of Mr., Mrs., Dr., and Jr.

All invitations should be engraved. However the illustrations given here only resemble engraving when parts of the invitation must be written by hand (as in the first example).

There are many choices in the styles of engraved lettering. Script, Antique Roman, and Shaded Roman are always in good taste.

White or off-white paper is always used, and the paper should be of fine quality in smoothness and texture. The engraving is always in black ink.

A double, or folded, sheet is always used for wedding invitations. Its size or shape may be selected to correspond with the choice of the engraved lettering; however, it should impart dignity.

A wedding is always a legal ceremony, and in most instances a solemn religious rite. Therefore, invitations bearing decorative designs, colors, or gilt "trimmings" are to be avoided.

Should two envelopes be used for the invitations or announcements?

Yes, always. The engraver will furnish the matching outside envelopes in advance, so they may be addressed and stamped ahead of time. It is entirely proper for the outer envelopes to have a return address blind embossed, not engraved, on the envelope flap. When the invitations have been engraved, folded, cards inserted, and placed in the "inner" envelope by the engraver, these second envelopes can be readily addressed.

What cards may be enclosed with the invitation?

Reception cards may be enclosed with a wedding invitation; they should use the same formal wording as the invitation, and be engraved in the same style of lettering. The engraver will insert these cards in the fold of tissue protecting the engraved face of the invitation in the "inner" envelope. ("At Home" cards are never sent with wedding *invitations*—only with announcements.)

How should an invitation to a married couple be addressed?

On the outer envelope (always handwritten):

> *Mr. and Mrs. John Gordon Gray*
> *1525 Pleasant Street*
> *New York, N. Y.*

On the inner envelope only:

Mr. and Mrs. Gray
(never the given names or address)

Is it proper to use the phrase "and family" when there are several members of one family to be invited?

No, never. Adults other than married couples should receive a separate invitation. For example, suppose there were three sisters in one family, all over seventeen. They should each be sent a separate invitation. The same thing applies to young men. Small children should never be invited.

Should invitations be sent to members of the wedding party?

Yes, by all means. Their wives, and/or husbands, if any, not included among the attendants, should, of course, also be included.

Should the wife and/or husband (unknown to you) of a business associate be asked also?

Of course.

Should the small tissue enclosed with the invitation be removed before inserting it in the envelope?

No. Engraving is apt to smudge, and the tissue insures the invitations being received in immaculate condition.

Are the same rules followed when announcements are sent out?

Yes.

When should invitations be placed in the mail?

Preferably four weeks, never less than three, in advance of the wedding. All should be mailed at the same time.

When should the announcements be mailed?

Not until the day the wedding takes place. They should all be placed in the mail on that day.

Is it ever proper to use a typewriter when addressing wedding invitations or announcements?

Absolutely not. To do so would be to show the worst possible taste. They should be addressed by hand by someone with legible and clear handwriting, and great care should be taken to make them look as neat as possible.

How should the invitation be worded?

If signed by the bride's father and mother:

The most formal invitations are those which leave a space for the guest's name to be written in by hand.

However, the following form is the one most generally used:

> *Mr. and Mrs. James Gardiner Johnstone*
> *request the honour of your presence*
> *at the marriage of their daughter*
> *Susanne Mary*
> *et cetera*

NOTE: An invitation to the church only, such as the above, does *not* require an acknowledgment.

If for a Nuptial Mass?

> *Mr. and Mrs. James Alfred Gardner*
> *request the honour of your presence*
> *at the Nuptial Mass at which their daughter*
> *Josephine Marie*
> *and*
> *Mr. Michael John Gillett*
> *will be united in the Sacrament of Holy Matrimony*
> *on Saturday, the eleventh of May*
> *at eleven o'clock*
> *Holy Sacrament Church*
> *Saint Louis, Missouri*

> *Mr. and Mrs. James Alfred Gardner*
> *invite you to offer with them the*
> *Nuptial Mass*
> *at which their daughter*
> *Josephine Marie*
> *will be united in marriage to*
> *Mr. Michael John Gillett*
> *et cetera*

If for a synagogue wedding?

Mr. and Mrs. Ralph Griffith Glazebrooke
request the honour of your presence
at the marriage of their daughter
Alice Carolyn
to
Harold James Howitz
Lieutenant, United States Navy
son of
Mr. and Mrs. Stephen Harold Howitz
Sunday, the fourteenth of July
at four o'clock
B'nai Israel Congregation
Battle Creek, Michigan

If issued by a widowed parent who has not married again?

Mrs. Sidney John Lawrence
requests the honour of your presence
at the marriage of her daughter

———————

Mr. Sidney John Lawrence
requests the honour of your presence
at the marriage of his daughter

Similar forms may be used by a widowed stepmother or step-father, where the relationship of the bride is a close one, and no natural parent has survived. "Stepdaughter" is, of course, used in place of "daughter." A divorced mother would use "Mrs. Smith Jones."

Where a widowed (or divorced) mother has remarried?

Mr. and Mrs. Francis Myers Griggs
request the honour of your presence
at the marriage of her daughter
Miss Frances Ida Hamilton
et cetera

Where a widower (or divorced) father has remarried?

Mr. and Mrs. Harold Ward Hamilton
request the honour of your presence
at the marriage of his daughter
Frances Ida
et cetera

It is also correct to say: "At the marriage of Mrs. Griggs' daughter" or, "At the marriage of Mr. Hamilton's daughter." Note that the bride's surname is used when her mother's surname has changed.

Where a married brother and his wife issue the invitation for his sister?

Mr. and Mrs. Willard Dale Gillett
request the honour of your presence
at the marriage of his sister
Catherine Adelaide
et cetera

Where a bride's married sister and her husband issue the invitation?

Mr. and Mrs. John Gilbert
request the honour of your presence
at the marriage of her sister
Miss Catherine Adelaide Gillett
et cetera

Where an older bachelor brother issues the invitation for his sister when both parents are deceased?

Mr. Willard Dale Gillett
requests the honour of your presence
at the marriage of his sister
Catherine Adelaide
et cetera

Where other relatives issue the invitation?

Grandparents, an uncle or aunt, or a cousin, may also issue wedding invitations when the bride's parents are deceased. The form should be similar to the others in this book with the proper changes as to relationship. Where a surname is different from the surname of the bride, her full name should appear, prefaced by "Miss." Invitations extended by a guardian or very close friends make no mention of relationship, but in such instances the bride's full name is used, preceded by "Miss."

> *Mr. and Mrs. Raymond Stewart Smith*
> *request the honour of your presence*
> *at the marriage of their granddaughter*
> *Miss Catherine Adelaide Gillett*
> *et cetera*

Where the invitation is issued by bride and bridegroom?

Either of the forms shown below may be used when a bride and bridegroom wish to extend their own invitations to the wedding ceremony. The bride's parents may be deceased; she may have no other living relatives; she may have resided for some years in a city distant from her family; or she may be of mature age.

The single woman uses her full maiden name, prefaced by "Miss."

The widow uses her first given name, her maiden surname, and her married surname, prefaced by "Mrs."

> *The honour of your presence*
> *is requested at the marriage of*
> *Mrs. Edith Brown Griffith*
> *to*
> *Mr. William Alfred Grosvenor*
> *on Tuesday, the sixteenth of April*
> *at four o'clock*
> *First Methodist Church*
> *Canton, Ohio*

> *Mrs. Edith Brown Griffith*
> *and*
> *Mr. William Alfred Grosvenor*
> *request the honour of your presence*
> *at their marriage*
> *et cetera*

If it is a double wedding ceremony?

Where the brides are sisters, a single form of invitation may be used for the two marriages. Usually the elder sister's name appears first in the invitation.

> *Mr. and Mrs. Franklin Pope Hasbrooke*
> *request the honour of your presence*
> *at the marriage of their daughters*
> *Edith Margaret*
> *to*
> *Mr. Cleveland David Jones, Junior*
> *and*
> *Eleanor Carolyn*
> *to*
> *Mr. William Ray Smith, II*
> *et cetera*

Where the grooms are brothers, but the brides are not related, the families of each bride will wish to issue separate invitations. This may be accomplished by having separate forms engraved on each of the inside pages of the customary folded wedding invitation. Each form, showing the same time and location of the ceremony, indicates the double wedding ceremony; and the surname of the grooms indicate they are related. Here it must be decided by the parties themselves whether the invitation appearing on the left inner page (the first one to be read) shall be for the elder brother, the elder of the two brides, or for the bride whose surname comes first alphabetically.

The surnames of the brides are not used in this single invitational form, because in reality it is two invitations, and the surnames of the parents indicate the surnames of the brides.

How should the reception card be worded?

Enclosed with the invitation to the church, the wording on the small card is usually as follows:

> *Reception*
> *immediately following the ceremony*
> *Hotel Ritz*
>
> *The favour of a reply is requested*
> *Twenty-five Poplar Street*

It is absolutely necessary to indicate where the reply is to be sent because only the church is mentioned on the ceremony invitation, and the hotel on that for the reception.

How should the acknowledgment read?

When acknowledging the reception invitation, it is to be remembered that the names of the bride and bridegroom are not mentioned at all; only the persons issuing the invitation, as, for example, the bride's parents. Actually the phrasing is much the same as when answering any other reception invitation.

"Wedding reception" may be used if you wish, but it is not necessary. The following should, of course, be written by hand.

> *Mr. and Mrs. Philip John Greene*
> *have the honour to accept*
> *the kind invitation of*
> *Mr. and Mrs. Jones*
> *to a reception*
> *on Monday, June the sixth*
> *Ritz Hotel*

In case of inability to attend: "Regret that because of absence from town, they will be unable to accept," et cetera.

How should a combined invitation to both wedding and reception read?

Occasionally a single invitation is extended for both the ceremony and the reception, when the latter is given at the same place as the wedding ceremony. No request for a reply

appears on such combined form; if a reply to the function is
desired, a separate card should be enclosed.

> *Mr. and Mrs. Philip David Johnstone*
> *request the honour of your presence*
> *at the marriage of their daughter*
> *Ellen Elizabeth*
> *to*
> *The Reverend Richard Gage Davis*
> *on Tuesday, the seventeenth of November*
> *at five o'clock*
> *The Second Presbyterian Church*
> *New York City*
>
> *Reception follows*
> *at the Church Parlours*

Another form concludes:

> *at five o'clock*
> *The Second Presbyterian Church*
> *and afterwards at the reception*
> *in the Church Parlours*

If a reply for the reception is desired, the enclosure card
would read:

> *The favour of a reply is requested*
> *One fifty-five Grant Avenue*
>
> or
>
> *Please send response to*
> *One fifty-five Grant Avenue*

**How should the invitations read when the ceremony is not held
in a church?**
The principal change in the wording of these invitations is
that "honor" is changed to "pleasure"; and "your company"
is substituted for "your presence." However, many persons prefer to use the phrasing which is employed for invitations
to church ceremonies, and there is no objection to this. *But*

"pleasure" and "company" should *not* be used for invitations to church weddings.

If the ceremony is held at the bride's home, the city may be included, or it may be omitted. Usually a reply is requested so that the bride's parents may make proper plans, for an informal reception, breakfast, or luncheon ordinarily follows a home wedding. No reception cards are necessary in this case.

Mr. and Mrs. Alfred Davies Gillis
request the pleasure of your company
at the marriage of their daughter
Martha Louise
to
Mr. Edward Martin Graham
Friday evening, June the eleventh
at eight o'clock
Seven hundred five Kenmore Street
Baltimore, Maryland

The favour of a reply is requested.

Where the bride's home will accommodate but a limited number of guests for the wedding ceremony, she may wish to invite others to a reception. In this instance, her parents would issue the reception invitation to all guests, and enclose a card invitation to the ceremony for those being asked to it.

Mr. and Mrs. Edward Thomas Gilman, II
request the pleasure of your company
at the marriage reception for their daughter
Louise Margaret
and
Mr. Bernard Sidney Graham
Thursday, the seventeenth of September
at half after three o'clock
One hundred fifteen Lexington Avenue
Detroit, Michigan

The favour of a reply is requested.

The ceremony card would read (this requires no answer):

> *Mr. and Mrs. Edward Thomas Gilman, II*
> *request the pleasure of your company*
> *at the marriage ceremony*
> *at three o'clock*

If the ceremony is held at the home of a relative or friend?

When the bride's parents live in an apartment or hotel, a relative or friend may wish to offer her home for the wedding ceremony and reception. The invitation is extended in the name of the bride's parents, but the names of the relatives or friends must also be included, together with their street address. A reply request should show an address, or indicate the person to whom it is to be sent.

> *Mr. and Mrs. Alfred Morgan Garner*
> *request the pleasure of your company*
> *at the marriage of their daughter*
> *Jeanne Isabel*
> *to*
> *Mr. Edward Philip Hammer*
> *Friday, the fourteenth of June*
> *at eight o'clock*
> *at the home of Mr. and Mrs. John Lane Hardin*
> *Fifty-six Montclair Avenue*
> *Milwaukee, Wisconsin*
>
> *Please reply*
> *in care of Mrs. Hardin*

If the ceremony occurs at a relative's home, the relationship is not shown.

When the bride's parents do not reside in the city where the ceremony is to be held, the invitation is still extended by her parents, even though they may not be present at the ceremony, and the foregoing form would be used. The invitation would not indicate that the home of the bride's parents is elsewhere.

If the ceremony is held at a club or a hotel?

Here, too, the invitational phrase is: "Request the pleasure of your company."

If the location of the club or hotel is well known, a street address is not necessary.

The invitation should include the request for a reply, as it is presumed that a reception will follow the ceremony, and a specific address must be shown to which the reply is to be sent.

Mr. and Mrs. Thomas Lanier Covell
request the pleasure of your company
at the marriage of their daughter
Lucille Marie
to
Mr. Edward Thomas Martin
on Friday evening, June fourteenth
at eight o'clock
The Silver Spring Club
Seattle, Washington

Please send response to
Twenty-five Dent Place

EXAMPLE OF REPLY:

Mr. and Mrs. John Philip Doe
accept with pleasure
the kind invitation of
Mr. and Mrs. Covell
for Friday, June fourteenth
at eight o'clock
The Silver Spring Club

Where it is a second marriage for a widow?

Although a widow may properly have her second wedding take place in a church, often the ceremony is held elsewhere. The old custom of the bride's name being that of her deceased husband is *never* followed today. Her given name, maiden surname, and married surname are used, and it is customary to preface these with "Mrs." Her parents may issue the invitation, or any relative other than her own child.

Mr. and Mrs. John Edward Gilman
request the pleasure of your company
at the marriage of their daughter
Mrs. Edith Gilman Cunningham

to

Doctor Alfred Thomas Davison
on Tuesday, the fourth of September
at four o'clock
Woodlawn Farm
Quincy, Massachusetts

The favour of a reply is requested.

When it is a second marriage for a divorcee?

Customarily a divorcee does not have engraved invitations to a second wedding ceremony sent to her friends; she usually invites them in person, over the telephone, or informally by note. It is important, however, for the sake of clarity, that announcements of the second marriage be engraved and mailed to relatives and friends.

The old custom of a divorcee's name being written without a given name, and combining only her maiden surname with that of her first husband's surname (assuming she has retained the first husband's name), is certainly not employed on a wedding announcement (or invitation, if she insists on this, which she shouldn't). She uses her given name, her maiden surname, and her married surname. If her parents make the announcement, her name is not prefaced by "Mrs."; if she makes the announcement herself in conjunction with the bridegroom, she does use the "Mrs."

Where it is a second marriage for a woman whose first marriage was annulled?

Where an annulment has been granted, the woman usually has her maiden name restored. While her legal status is still "Mrs." she seldom uses that prefix in the announcement of a second marriage. It is better taste for her not to issue invitations to the second marriage, but have her parents or some relative issue announcements.

FACTS OF LIFE — WEDDING ANNOUNCEMENTS

How should a wedding announcement be worded?

> *Mr. and Mrs. Andrew Hunt Davison*
> *have the honour of announcing*
> *the marriage of their daughter*
> *Elizabeth Frances*
> *to*
> *Mr. John David Mulligan*
> *on Thursday, the sixteenth of April*
> *Nineteen hundred and fifty-nine*
> *Phoenix, Arizona*

The names of relatives other than parents appear in wedding announcements in the same manner as in invitations to a wedding, and the bride's relationship is shown. Only her given names appear, except where her surname is used because it is dissimilar to the surname of the relative issuing the announcement. (See page 27.)

What happens in the case of an elopement?

A bride's parents or other relatives announce the marriage of a bride who has eloped with forms the same as those used for any wedding announcement. As with all wedding announcements, the date and the place of a marriage are shown. Even though the announcement is sent out at a considerably later date than the wedding date, no reference is made to an "elopement."

How should the announcement of a second marriage be worded?

> *Mr. and Mrs. David Edward Redmond*
> *announce the marriage of their daughter*
> *Jeanne Redmond Gillette*
> *to*
> *Mr. Alfred Goodwin Billings*
> *on Tuesday, the twenty-third of June*
> *Nineteen hundred and fifty-nine*
> *Baltimore, Maryland*

Where the announcement is issued by the bride and bride-groom?

Where there are no near relatives to issue the announce-ments, the bride and bridegroom may issue their own.

Miss Phyllis Lucile Brewer
and
Mr. Robert Allen Gibson
announce their marriage
on Tuesday, the fourteenth of July
Nineteen hundred and fifty-nine
Tulsa, Oklahoma

Where the bride is a widow or divorcee and there are no near relatives to issue the announcements?

Mrs. Hortense Hamilton Gates
and
Mr. Nelson William Le Fevre
announce their marriage
on Saturday, the eighth of August
Nineteen hundred and fifty-nine
Seattle, Washington

How should the at home card read?

It is enclosed only with the wedding announcement—never with the wedding invitation.

Mr. and Mrs. Robert Charles Ryan
at home
after the tenth of July
Sunnybrook Farms
Jefferson, Arkansas
or
Mr. and Mrs. Robert Charles Ryan
After the tenth of July   Sunnybrook Farms
Jefferson, Arkansas

How does one announce a wedding in the newspaper?

It is necessary to ascertain the procedure followed by your local newspaper, and follow its instructions.

In a small community a description of the wedding covering all details may and probably will be given. Sometimes, in large cities, just a short announcement, stating the names of the bridal couple, their parents, and where and when the ceremony took place may be all there is space for.

Who can tell you how your local paper handles wedding announcements?

Call the society editor of the paper in which you wish the announcement to appear at least three weeks before the wedding. If a detailed account is planned, the paper will, in all probability, send you a "wedding blank" to fill in. This usually covers everything pertinent to the background of both families, a complete description of the bridal gown and those of the attendants and parents, an account of the decorations at the church and the reception, and any other interesting facts concerning the wedding. After filling this in (on the typewriter if possible, so no names will be misspelled), you return it to the society editor, who then puts it into story form.

What is most important?

To be sure to indicate the release date. The same date should be placed on each writeup, if more than one newspaper is to carry the story.

EXAMPLE: if the wedding is taking place on, say Friday, May tenth, it should be indicated at the top of the wedding blank and underlined *"For Release, Saturday May Eleventh,"* or perhaps you would prefer that it be published on Sunday, the twelfth. It's up to you. The release date is always after the wedding because naturally the story cannot appear until after the ceremony has actually taken place. No newspaper will release the story ahead of time, for it is an unwritten law that a release date should never be broken. Whatever the information you are requested to send to a given newspaper, be sure that it is in their hands well in advance of the time of release—at least a week before the day it is to be published.

Should a photograph of the bride accompany the story?

This depends on the policy of each newspaper. Some welcome bridal pictures and will make every effort to use them. Others simply do not have the space, and will make it clear that if you send a picture, it cannot be used. If you yourself send the photograph, remember it must be on "glossy" paper for the best reproduction. Often the photographer himself will send the print directly to the newspaper for you.

FACTS OF LIFE — THE WEDDING ITSELF

What does the bride wear?

Most brides, whether gowned formally or informally, adhere to the age-old custom of wearing

> *Something old, something new,*
> *Something borrowed and something blue*
> *And a four-leaf clover in your shoe.*

(If no four-leaf clover is available, a piece of silver replaces it.

SUGGESTION: Make it a dime, otherwise it will hurt!)

In Biblical days both the bride and the bridegroom wore a band of blue around the bottom of their wedding costumes to symbolize love and fidelity. The other ideas came later. Following another tradition, only the first time may a bride wear white, a bridal veil, myrtle wreath, or orange blossoms, as they are all symbols of virginity.

What colors and materials are used in the wedding gown of today?

At a first wedding, whether it is to be formal or semi-formal, a white gown with a bridal veil is traditional. But some modification is permissible today. While white or cream and satin or lace are preferred, gowns of peau de soie or silk taffeta are also acceptable for year-round wear. Summer silk organdy or cotton *mousseline de soie* are also proper for warm weather. Gowns of very pale pink or blue are sometimes chosen when they are more flattering than the pure white or cream.

What is the difference between the gown of the formally dressed bride and the semi-formal?

FORMAL: The gown is always floor or ankle length with a veil that should be long and gracefully flowing into the back panels of the gown, ending near where the train begins. The train should be at least three feet long on the ground. Height comes into this. Longer trains may be worn, of course, but if the bride is short, five feet billowing out behind her can only make her look ridiculous. A tall girl could carry it. Make sure also that the train is not wider than the church aisle, as disaster is the result if it is. It's bound to catch on something.

SEMI-FORMAL: The gown is of ballerina length, and the veil should reach only to the waist or fingertips. There is no train.

What are the rules governing the wearing of the veil today?

Modern brides don't usually fear evil spirits, but most of them do wear bridal veils. The custom originated with the ancient Greeks, who thought that the veil would be a protection for the bride against evil spirits flying around during the marriage ceremony.

The face veil is seldom worn now. If, however, it is chosen, it is always about chin length, usually made of a separate piece of tulle, about a yard square, which can be easily removed by the matron and/or maid of honor when she returns the bouquet to the bride after the ceremony.

How long should the veil that flows down the back from a cap or coronet be?

For a formally gowned bride, it should be long enough to intermingle gracefully with the train. For the semi-formal, it should reach only to the waist or the fingertips.

What about make-up and accessories?

Go easy on make-up. The less the better. Also jewelry. Bangles and beads are definitely superfluous.

What does the informally gowned bride wear?

The bride wears a suit or afternoon gown of a pastel shade and her attendant (usually one—either a matron or maid of honor) is dressed in the same manner, but of course in a contrasting color. The suits or gowns should be of different styles. A hat is always worn.

Should a bride wear gloves?

In years gone by, yes. Today it's up to the individual. If gloves are worn, the seam on the wedding-ring finger is ripped so that it may be slipped off during the ceremony. HINT: If the sleeves of the gown are wrist length, gloves are superfluous and a decided nuisance.

Who can best help the bride in the selection of a gown?

Most department stores and some women's apparel shops have a special section set aside just for you. It is strongly advised that you contact the "bridal consultant" in one of these departments. She will assist you in keeping within your budget, not only as far as the wedding gown itself is concerned, but also your entire trousseau as well. Her invaluable advice will help you make it your "dream come true" wedding.

Is there any ruling with regard to the dress of a second-time bride?

Definitely, yes. Never, under any circumstances, should she wear a white wedding gown or veil, or orange blossoms, et cetera. Pastel shades are a "must." Either a suit or an afternoon gown should be worn.

What flowers may a bride carry?

This is up to her. Often a florist will design a special bouquet to complement the wedding gown, or she may carry a prayer book, usually covered with white satin, with perhaps white streamers with lily of the valley hanging from it.

May all brides carry bouquets?

No. Only those wearing the formal or semi-formal gown should do so. If attired informally, the bride always wears a corsage.

What should the mothers of the bride and bridegroom wear?

Since they stand together in the receiving line, their gowns should be similar in style and particularly length. EXAMPLE: if one wears a ballerina length, so should the other. Why? They look better standing side by side. Soft pastels are best. Even should you be in mourning, this is one time when a soft gray or blue is proper. Black is never worn.

In the *morning hours*, even if it is a very formal wedding, a street-length "dressy" dress is preferable. For the *afternoon*, the "cocktail" type of gown is appropriate. It may be any one of three lengths—street, ballerina, or ankle. (The latter for the most formal wedding.) Hat and gloves should complement the ensemble. For the *evening*, dinner dresses, never décolleté ball gowns, are correct. Elbow-length gloves should be worn and a scarf, veiling, or flowers may be used to cover the head while in the church.

What do the fathers wear?

The father of the bride is easy. He conforms with the clothes worn by the bridegroom and ushers, as he is active in the actual ceremony. The father of the bridegroom, while having no part in the ceremony itself, does stand in the receiving line, so he usually wears what the bride's father and the rest of the men in the bridal party wear. (See page 47.)

Is there a rule governing how many attendants the bride may have?

No. For the very large wedding there may be a matron of

honor, maid of honor, six or eight bridesmaids, junior bridesmaids, flower girls, pages, and ring bearer, though so many attendants tend to make a theatrical procession out of it. The
average group is usually a matron of honor, a maid of honor
(either one or both), and four to six bridesmaids.

May a bride have no attendants at all?

Yes. However, even though her wedding may be extremely
small and informal, it is always best to have at least one to
attend her, even if she only holds her hand and gives moral
support.

Can a married friend be asked to serve as a "bridesmaid"?

Yes. She is referred to as a bridesmaid, too, even though it
is ambiguous. She is not a "bride's matron." But the maid of
honor must always be unmarried.

**Do the husbands of the matron of honor or married bridesmaid
have to be included in the wedding party as ushers?**

No. The husbands, of course, are invited to the wedding,
but simply as guests. The same rule applies in the case of the
wives of married ushers.

**If an attendant lives in another city, is the family of the bride
responsible for her traveling expenses and putting her up during the wedding festivities?**

Not for the traveling expenses, but from the time of her
arrival until her departure an attendant is a guest of the bride.
If unable to have her stay at her home or at the home of relatives or friends, and a hotel bill is the result, the bride picks
up the tab.

**Is the bride expected to pay for her attendants' gowns and
hats?**

No. It is her prerogative to choose them, but the attendants
pay for them. GENTLE HINT: The thoughtful bride will take
the financial status of those serving her into consideration,
and make her choice a reasonable one for all concerned.

**What does the bride take into consideration when selecting
what her attendants are to wear?**

The dresses of the matron of honor and maid of honor never
exactly match those of the bridesmaids. EXAMPLE: If the
bridesmaids are gowned in Nile green trimmed in yellow, the
colors could be reversed for either one or both of the especially honored attendants. The bridesmaids all carry similar

bouquets, while those of the matron and/or maid of honor contain contrasting arrangements. The attendants' gowns should all be of the same pattern, no matter what color scheme the bride chooses. In all cases avoid those that are cut too "low down." This is a solemn religious ceremony, not a peep show. Aim for conservative simplicity and you can't go wrong.

Do the attendants wear gloves?

This is optional today. Lace mitts are very popular and white or pastel gloves to match the ensemble may be worn. However, it is perfectly proper to wear no gloves at all.

What type of flowers do the attendants carry?

They may be bouquets or sheaths of flowers that blend with the color scheme. Little baskets of flowers also may be carried. If bouquets or sheaths, those walking on the right hold them on the right arm, those on the left on the left arm, with the stems pointing toward the middle. Baskets are held by both hands in front.

What are the duties of the matron of honor?

It is her duty to "wait" upon the bride, assisting her in any way possible. At the altar she is responsible for straightening the train of the bride's gown before the ceremony, and again when she turns to start the recessional up the aisle. She holds the bride's bouquet during the ceremony, returning it before she starts back up the aisle.

What are the duties of the maid of honor?

If there is no matron of honor, she does the "waiting upon." If there is a matron, she is merely an especially honored attendant.

What is expected of a bridesmaid?

She pays attention at the rehearsal so as to know what is expected of her. On the day of the wedding she stays in the background as much as possible, until it's time to start down the aisle.

What is the age bracket in which junior bridesmaids belong?

Between the ages of approximately seven through fifteen. Their dresses are miniature versions of those worn by the bridesmaids. Their duties are the same.

What do flower girls or pages wear?

Usually they are dressed in white silk or satin. They have no definite duty to perform except to walk in the procession.

What about a ring bearer?

He is always dressed in white, and carries the ring (firmly anchored with a pin, by the way) on a small white satin cushion.

Is it advisable to have trainbearers?

No. As it is only the very young who are supposed to perform this service, anything can happen, and usually does. But if you insist, the little boys should be dressed in white.

Does the bride give a gift to the bridegroom?

If she wishes to have a double-ring ceremony she presents him with his ring (usually a plain gold band). Whether she gives him a personal gift, such as a watch or cuff links, is entirely up to her.

Must a gift be presented to each attendant?

Yes. It is customary. The gifts need not be expensive, but they are usually all the same. Compacts, cigarette cases, bracelets are just a few suggestions.

Should wedding gifts always be displayed?

Not necessarily. It is nice if it can be done, however. If there is space enough at home, set aside a room and obtain some long tables from a caterer. Cover them with white tableclothes and you are all set.

How does the bride keep track of who sends what?

Stationers have a book which has lines numbered from one on, with space for the name of the sender, the shop, and the gift. Accompanying this are small numbered squares with glue on the back. As each gift arrives, enter it in the book, and stick the corresponding number on the gift itself. Follow this, keep your card index file, and you can't go wrong. This is most important. It isn't very nice to thank the Smiths for a lovely silver spoon when they sent a dozen cocktail glasses.

Is it proper to leave cards on gifts when displaying them?

Never! Always remove all cards.

Should checks be displayed?

Horrors, no! Aunt Minnie might not like it known that she could afford to send only $10.00.

If the wedding reception is given in the home, may guests be invited to see the gifts?

Yes. They love to oh and ah and wonder who gave you what.

What about showing off your trousseau?

Yes, to your close feminine friends, but in private.

Must you personally write all thank-you notes?

Yes. It's the least you can do for those kind enough to present you with a gift. Handwrite them, too. No typing ever. A good white stationery (and only white) is correct. Mention what you are thanking a person for, too, not just "for the gift." It can be short and sweet. EXAMPLE:

> *Dear Mrs. Lampson,*
>
> *Thank you and Mr. Lampson so very much for the lovely silver bowl. Jack and I will certainly enjoy using it in our new home.*
>
> > *With deep appreciation,*
> >
> > > *Sincerely,*
> > >
> > > *Mary Brown Lords.*

Is it permissible ever to send printed or engraved thank-you notes?

No. It's the rudest thing you can possibly do.

What about those gifts that arrive so late that there isn't time to write the thank-you notes before you start on your honeymoon?

Tardy souls who wait until the last minute don't deserve any consideration. However, there's no point in returning rudeness with rudeness. So Mother or some member of the family should write these thoughtless people, telling them the gift has been received and that the bride herself will acknowledge it upon her return.

What about a gift acknowledgment card?

This card may be sent only when numerous gifts arrive during the last few days preceding the wedding, in order to make prompt acknowledgment of the receipt of gifts. However, a handwritten acknowledgment, referring to the particular gift, should be sent by the bride to each donor as soon as possible following her return from the honeymoon. If circumstances make the use of a card necessary (it may be engraved or printed), the wording would be as follows:

Miss Mary Ellen Spence
has received your very kind gift
and will write you later of her appreciation

Miss Hildegard Kenilworth
acknowledges, with appreciation, the receipt
of your wedding gift
and will write a personal note of thanks
at an early date

If a number of people group together and send one gift, how do you handle your note of appreciation? Or should it be notes?

If only two or three friends are involved, a note to each is preferable. But, for example, if the gift is from a group in the office in which you work, or from your bridegroom's business associates, one note is sufficient. Address it to the head of the department (or perhaps the person with whom you or he have been closest), asking him to extend your thanks to all the others.

Which is correct, "groom" or "bridegroom"?

The word "bridegroom" has an interesting origin. In medieval days it was customary for the new husband to serve his bride at table on the wedding day. A waiter was then known as a "groom," so he became his "bride's groom" for that one day. It gradually evolved into "bridegroom." Some consider it proper today to refer to him as simply "groom." In recent years, however, a "groom" has become known more as "one who attends horses." As this meaning of the word is hardly complimentary to the bridegroom, use "bridegroom," it's safer!

Also in those days a brother or best friend of the bridegroom helped carry off the bride. Strong-arm methods were the accepted procedure then. From this has evolved the custom of a bridegroom having a best man and ushers.

Is it necessary that there always be a best man?

Decidedly yes. No matter how small the wedding may be. *Not* to help carry off the bride, but to assist the bridegroom in every way possible.

Must the bridegroom always choose a friend as best man?

No. His father may serve, or a brother.

What are the bridegroom's obligations to his best man and ushers?

He presents each with gloves, tie, and boutonnière, also a gift. The best man's gift may be different from that of the ushers (who all get the same thing). The gifts may be cuff links, wallets, et cetera, depending upon what the budget will stand.

Does the bridegroom designate what is to be worn by the men in the wedding party?

Yes. This decision is based entirely on the type of wedding it is to be. Tradition decrees the following:

For the formal or semi-formal daytime wedding: Cutaway with striped trousers.

For the informal daytime wedding: the sack (or so-called business) suit. Dark blue or gray is preferred, and an attempt should be made to have all the men's suits as near the same color as possible.

For the formal evening wedding: Full evening dress (white tie and tails). Remember, a tuxedo should never be worn.

Special note regarding summer weddings: As both the cutaway and the full dress are extremely uncomfortable to wear in warm weather, it is considered proper—whether the wedding be formal, semi-formal, or informal—for dark blue flannel coats, white or cream-colored trousers, and black shoes to be worn. An all-white suit is also acceptable, except when the bride is wearing white. It's "her day," and the all-white suits detract from her gown. After six (and *only* then) a white tuxedo jacket is sometimes worn with black tuxedo trousers.

Must the bridegroom pay for his best man's and ushers' clothes?

No. He only designates what they are to wear. They either purchase, or rent (which is perfectly proper and is done all the time) their own. ONE RIGID RULE: The father of the bride, the father of the bridegroom, the best man, and the ushers should all be dressed alike, whether the wedding is formal or informal. The only difference is that the bridegroom and the best man wear a tie of a contrasting pattern to those worn by the fathers and ushers. Otherwise, all the ties should be the same.

Must the bridegroom have a bachelor dinner?

No. It is entirely a personal choice. Should he have one, however, he of course foots the bill. (NOT-SO-GENTLE HINT:

It is not considered "smart" or sensible to make this celebration a big blowout with many a sore head the next day.) With one exception, it is merely like any other stag dinner. Toward the end of the meal the bridegroom stands, holding a glass of champagne on high, saying: "To the bride." Every man stands, drinks the toast, and then breaks the stem of the glass so "it may never serve a less honorable purpose."

What are the obligations of the best man?

His shoulders must be broad, for his responsibilities are many. It is his job to make sure the bags are all packed, tickets are in a safe (and known) place for the start of the honeymoon trip. He must also be sure that the wedding ring is in his pocket for the climactic moment at the altar; that he has the clergyman's fee in a white envelope to be presented before the ceremony (in private, of course); that the bridegroom arrives intact and on time at the church. The best man should make himself useful at the reception and be certain that the getaway for the honeymoon goes smoothly. As the couple waves good-by, he can take a deep breath and relax—not before.

What is expected of the best man during the actual ceremony?

As the clergyman leads the way toward the altar, the best man follows, escorting the bridegroom. They stand to the left of the clergyman (as he faces the congregation), and when the bride and her attendants reach the altar, the bridegroom steps to the right side of his bride. When the time comes for the placing of the ring on the bride's finger, the best man hands the ring to the clergyman, who blesses it and gives it to the bridegroom. On the way back up the aisle, the best man escorts the matron of honor; if there is none, the maid of honor. Then his job is to see that the newly married couple get safely out of the church into their car and head for the reception. He himself rides with the rest of the bridal party.

How many ushers should there be?

This depends entirely upon the size of the wedding. There should be two ushers for every seventy-five people invited to the church. This may necessitate more ushers than bridesmaids, which is perfectly proper. If it is to be a very small ceremony, with only a few relatives and friends present, no usher is needed. If it is a home wedding, ushers have a purely honorary position, but they should help make things go smoothly.

How does a man choose his ushers?

From a selected group of his closest friends. It is a courtesy to ask the oldest brother of the bride to serve, or if she has a married sister, her husband.

Is a head usher appointed?

Yes, by the bridegroom. It is up to him to make sure that all the other ushers appear promptly at the church and follow their instructions to the letter. (TIP: A typewritten list should be given to each usher, telling him what is expected, including when and where he is supposed to be at certain times, the clothes he is to wear, and his duties. This will save many a headache later on.) The head usher is also given the honor of escorting the mother of the bridegroom and the mother of the bride to their pews.

What are the obligations that an usher owes the bridegroom?

To perform his duties with sincerity and dignity. Nothing can do more to mar a wedding than young men who think it is smart to be flip, maybe overindulging while they are doing it, acting as if it were a game of some kind. It isn't. It's a solemn religious ceremony. Act your age. Plenty of time for fun when it's over.

What are the duties of the ushers?

It should be planned that all ushers arrive at the church (or wherever the ceremony it to be held) at least an hour if not more before the ceremony. As guests arrive, each usher should be at his prearranged station. He must remember that the left side of the church (as you face the altar) is reserved for relatives and friends of the bride; the right side for those of the bridegroom. As each woman guest enters, the usher offers his right arm and escorts her to whichever side of the church she specifies. A gentleman by himself is never ushered to his seat. If he is with a lady, he follows her down the aisle.

SUGGESTION: In some cases it is necessary to try to even things up when seating guests. If, for example, the bridegroom's family is from a distant city and his relatives and friends who are able to attend are few in number—rather than have the "bride's side" of the church fill up and his side almost empty, the ushers should balance things. This is done by starting about fifteen minutes before the service is to begin to place all those arriving on the "bridegroom's side" of the church.

The mother of the bridegroom is seated by the head usher

and may be taken to her pew (the front pew on the right side) at any time. His father follows them. The last person to be seated is the mother of the bride. If other relatives arrive with her, and are to sit in the second pew, they are escorted down the aisle before she is. When all is ready to begin, the doors of the church are closed (latecomers are shut outside where they belong!), and the head usher escorts the mother to the front pew. As he returns up the aisle, the two ushers who have been designated to roll the white canvas go down together, each takes an edge of the canvas and they march back up pulling it behind them. While this is going on the bridal party is assembling at the head of the aisle. The two ushers step in their places and now all is ready. The signal is given to the organist, and the procession starts to the opening strains of the wedding march. After the service is over and the bridal party returns back up the aisle, the bride and her new husband leave together for the reception; the best man and ushers go to the cars designated for them.

At the reception an usher's job is personally to avoid the punch bowl and make sure all guests are served and cared for. Like the best man, the conscientious usher must not relax until the bridal couple leaves on their honeymoon.

How are the bride's parents seated in church, if they are divorced?

The mother chooses the members of her family to sit with her in the first pew. Other members of her family may be seated in the second pew. If the father is giving his daughter away, he escorts her down the aisle, stepping back into the third pew behind the one in which his former wife is sitting. He will have indicated those of his family that he wishes to be seated with him.

If either parent has remarried, should the new partner on either side attend the services and the reception following?

This is a situation wherein consideration for the daughter herself is of the first importance. If the feelings of all concerned toward each other are amicable, there should be no hesitation about all attending. If the opposite, however, and strained, unfriendly relations prevail, the new partners—in all fairness—should drop out entirely.

If both parents have remarried, and all is well, and the new partners attend, where would they be seated in the church?

The stepfather would be seated with the bride's mother,

taking his place alone before she is escorted down the aisle. The stepmother would be seated in the third pew where the father of the bride will join her after giving his daughter away.

Is a rehearsal necessary?

Whether the wedding is to be large or small, a rehearsal beforehand is always advisable.

When is it usually held?

No cut-and-dried rule governs this. Generally it is the evening before the wedding.

What is the first thing to consider?

Try to make the time it is held convenient to all concerned. Late in the afternoon or around eight in the evening are the preferred hours.

Does the bride instruct the attendants in the parts they are to play?

In a way, yes. Her wishes, of course, must not interfere with the religious ritual. It is wise to take the helpful advice of the clergyman regarding the best way to accomplish a well-balanced, dignified processional to the altar and the recessional coming back. He will, of course, give the instructions for the actual religious part of the ceremony.

May the bride play her own part at the rehearsal?

She is very foolish if she doesn't. Believing the old superstition that if she herself participates bad luck will result is just not good common sense. Who is the cynosure of all eyes on the wedding day? The bride, of course. Then doesn't it follow that she should be letter perfect and at ease in her role? Having a stand-in rehearse it for her won't accomplish this. Be sensible—not superstitious.

Who is a most important person at a rehearsal?

The organist. It is through him that the bridal party makes its way up the aisle and back in step, in time with the music and at an easy pace with no bobbing up and down or weaving from side to side. To complete the picture this is an all-important part of a wedding and it takes time to get everybody coordinated. Going to the altar, the pace should be fairly slow, but not too slow. People are bound to wobble if it is. On the return trip, the tempo is speeded up and they make their way at a brisk pace. Not too brisk, either. Aside from its being anything but dignified, guests want to get a good look at the newly married couple. The entire wedding party should be put through its paces over and over again if need be. While not so important as in the church wedding, music is still very much to be desired for the home ceremony. Things will run more smoothly even if it is just a piano.

IMPORTANT REMINDER: Someone must be designated to give the signal to the organist when he is to start the wedding march. When the usher returns from seating the mother of the bride and the two ushers have spread the aisle canvas, the processional is ready to start.

Should the father of the bride take part in the rehearsal?

Yes, by all means. He plays an important part until he actually "gives her away."

Is it necessary that the parents of the bride entertain for the bridal party either before or after the rehearsal?

Not necessary at all, but quite often done. It is also proper for the parents of the bridegroom to entertain for them instead of the bride's parents. The most popular mode of entertaining in this case is a buffet supper either following the afternoon rehearsal or preceding the one taking place in the evening. Don't forget to invite the wives and/or husbands of those who are in the wedding party.

Why is a time schedule necessary with regard to the arrival of the bridal party at the church?

Because without one there is utter chaos. The limousines should be ready well ahead of the time they will actually be needed, so that there will be no slip-up in any way.

Be sure there are enough cars to take care of all concerned.

What is a good time schedule?

MEMBERS OF BRIDAL PARTY	TIME OF ARRIVAL AT CHURCH BEFORE CEREMONY STARTS
Ushers	At least one hour ahead of time—preferably more
Bridegroom, escorted by the best man (to be sure he makes it)	Three quarters of an hour.
Bride's attendants—all gather at home of the bride one and a half hours beforehand	Not less than one-half hour.

| The bride and her father (no one else) | Fifteen minutes. |
| The mother of the bride, accompanied by close members of the family | Five minutes. |

NOTE: For the home wedding, all the attendants arrive at least an hour before the services begin. They may come under their own steam or limousines may be sent to pick them up one by one. Cars should definitely be sent for the clergyman and his wife, and for the parents of the bridegroom and other close relatives of his. Their arrival time: Fifteen minutes to a half-hour before the ceremony is to start.

Where do the bridegroom and best man go upon arrival at the church?

There is usually a side entrance near the chancel where they enter, where they are joined by the clergyman.

Where do the bride's attendants gather?

Most churches have a room near the entrance of the church where they may meet. The person designated to see that things go smoothly awaits them to assist in last-minute fixing of hair-dos and so forth. She hands out the bouquets. When the bride arrives, the attendants should stay in the background—never, but never, crowd around her—while her train and veil are double checked to make sure all is well. Meanwhile, her father waits in the back of the church.

When does the bridal procession form?

Real timing is needed here. When the bride's mother arrives, the bride and her attendants should be ready to step in line. The ushers attempt to seat late arrivals even if it is necessary for them to escort two women at the same time in order to clear the aisle. When the mother enters, the doors of the church should be closed, leaving unpardonable latecomers to stand outside. The head usher escorts the mother down to the front pew on the left facing the altar, where she sits alone. If other close members of the family are with her, they will have been seated first in the second pew. Remember, the mother is the last down the aisle. As the head usher starts his return up the aisle, the two ushers designated to put down the white runner go where it is rolled by the altar and quickly spread it up the aisle. Now we are ready to begin—the signal is given to the organist, and the bridal march starts.

PROCESSIONAL

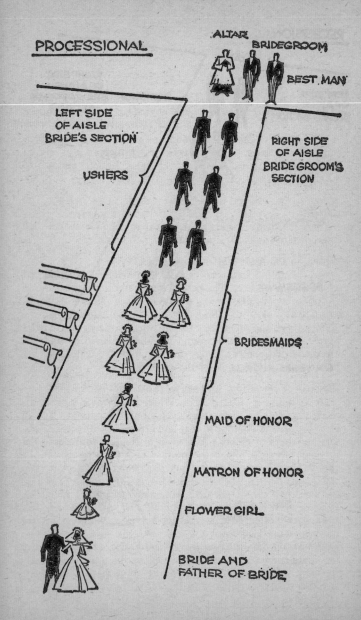

ALTAR
BRIDEGROOM
BEST MAN

LEFT SIDE
OF AISLE
BRIDE'S SECTION

RIGHT SIDE
OF AISLE
BRIDE GROOM'S
SECTION

USHERS

BRIDESMAIDS

MAID OF HONOR

MATRON OF HONOR

FLOWER GIRL

BRIDE AND
FATHER OF BRIDE

RECESSIONAL

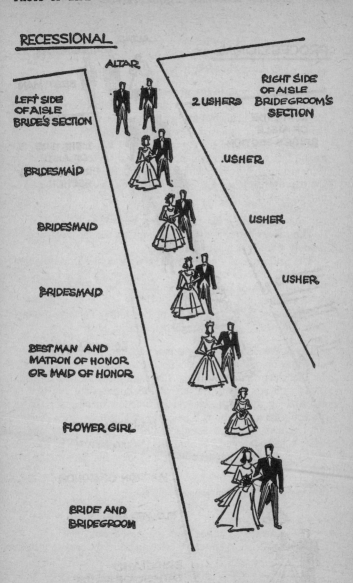

ALTAR

LEFT SIDE
OF AISLE
BRIDE'S SECTION

2 USHERS

RIGHT SIDE
OF AISLE
BRIDEGROOM'S
SECTION

BRIDESMAID

.USHER

BRIDESMAID

USHER

BRIDESMAID

USHER

BEST MAN AND
MATRON OF HONOR
OR MAID OF HONOR

FLOWER GIRL

BRIDE AND
BRIDEGROOM

NOTE: The illustrations show (pp. 54, 55) the basic procedure upon which most bridal processions are based. Deviations will naturally be made to conform with certain customs followed in different faiths. Confer with your spiritual advisor as to what these changes, if any, may be.

Who follows whom in the processional?

On the first note of the bridal march, the clergyman, followed by the bridegroom, with the ever-faithful best man behind him, take their places at the foot of the chancel steps. The clergyman faces the congregation. The bridegroom stands to the left of the clergyman, the best man to the left of the bridegroom, facing the congregation. As they take their places, the trip down the aisle is being started by the rest of the bridal party.

In what order does the bridal party come?

The ushers, two by two. (Attempt to get those of approximately the same height together.)

The bridesmaids, two by two. (Height comes into this, too.)

The maid of honor alone.

The matron of honor alone.

The flower girl alone.

The bride on the right arm of her father (always the right arm, because it is considered the arm of courtesy).

What is the procedure upon reaching the chancel?

Those on the left of the line form side by side on the left of the clergyman. Those on the right naturally to the right. The bride stands on the left of the bridegroom (so that she is on the right of the clergyman). Upon turning for the trip back up the aisle, she will be on the right of her new husband. The matron of honor stands at the left of the bride, and the bride's father directly behind her. When his part in the ceremony is finished, he steps back and joins his wife in the front pew.

What form does the recessional take?

The bride and the bridegroom.

The flower girl.

The matron of honor and the best man.

Each usher steps forward, offering his right arm to a bridesmaid.

If there are extra ushers, they wind up the procession two by two.

When the entrance of the church is reached, what then?

The best man hurries the newly married couple to their car. The other members of the bridal party make an orderly, we hope, exit to cars reserved for them. Meanwhile, in the church the close members of both families slowly make their way up the aisle (led by the mother and father of the bride). No guest should make a move to leave until this group has reached the entrance of the church.

FACTS OF LIFE — THE MILITARY WEDDING

When the bridegroom is a member of the armed services is the procedure the same as in a non-military wedding?

No. Although the basic plans are the same, the religious rituals (subject to the faith under which the ceremony is performed), and the traditions followed for both the home and church weddings are of identical pattern, the military wedding may also include such colorful customs as the arch of sabers and the cake-cutting ritual.

How is the arch of sabers performed?

Sabers may or may not be worn by the men of the bridal party who are in uniform. If they are, at the completion of the ceremony these ushers divide up facing each other outside the church doors, draw their sabers, hold them high with tips touching, forming an arch through which the bride and the bridegroom pass when leaving the church. As soon as the couple have completed their passage, the sabers are returned to their scabbards. (The bridesmaids do not pass through the arch.)

How does the cake-cutting ritual differ?

The bridegroom assists the bride in cutting the first slice, his saber being used rather than a regular knife.

If some of the men serving the bridegroom are not in the armed services, what do they wear?

This is one time when it is impossible to have all the men in the wedding party outfitted alike. What the civilians wear depends on the type of wedding, and on the decision of the bridegroom. EXAMPLE: For a formal noon wedding ceremony, say there are six ushers and the best man. Of these, four of the ushers are in the armed services. They all wear uniforms (even if in different services), as does the bridegroom. The best man and the other ushers would wear a morning coat and striped trousers (see page 47). The fathers of the couple would conform with this also.

FACTS OF LIFE — THE WEDDING RECEPTION

What happens at the reception?

The "wedding feast" of olden times has almost entirely evolved today into a "reception." Whether the celebration be large or small, the procedures followed are basically the same as those for any other reception. There are a few differences.

What is the order of the receiving line?

The mother of the bride (always first), the father of the bridegroom, then the mother of the bridegroom, the father of the bride, the bride, the bridegroom, the matron of honor, the maid of honor, and then all the bridesmaids. The best man (unless he happens to be the father of the bridegroom) and the ushers *never* stand in the receiving line. All those in the line should stay in it until every guest has been greeted.

FACTS OF LIFE — THE WEDDING BREAKFAST

Just what is a "wedding breakfast"?

This really comes under the heading of a luncheon as far as the food is concerned. Today, more often than not, it is served buffet style to the bridal party, as well as to the guests, and no one is seated. At a large formal wedding there may be a bridal table at which only members of the wedding party are seated. There may be another table nearby for members of both families. The guests are served buffet style. Also (usually at a small wedding, where only members of the family and a few friends are present) everyone may be seated at one table.

How are these tables seated?

In all cases the seating is optional. The following suggestions may prove helpful.

The Bride's Table

The bride and the bridegroom sit together (always), he being seated on her left, the best man on her right, and the matron of honor on the left of the bridegroom. The ushers and the bridesmaids are then alternated to fill out the table. NOTE: If some of the attendants are married, it is gracious to ask their spouses to sit at this table, even though they took no part in the bridal party.

The Parents' Table

The bride's mother has the place of honor at one end of the table. On her right, the bridegroom's father, on her left, the officiating clergyman. Facing them, the father of the bride, with the mother of the bridegroom on his right and the wife of the clergyman on his left. Other relatives and close friends are then seated as best fits the situation.

The Combination Table

The bride and the bridegroom together. On her right, her father, the mother of the bridegroom, the best man (or maybe an elderly male relative), the wife of the clergyman; on the bridegroom's left, the mother of the bride, his father, the matron of honor (or an elderly woman relative), and the clergyman. Go on from here, mixing the other attendants and family friends as you wish.

Who gives the first toast?

The best man always offers the first toast. Anyone else may offer a toast after he has done so. But do go easy. Don't let it get out of hand. One or two more toasts are sufficient. Also be sure that no toast is crude or suggestive. Nothing is in worse taste.

Who dances the first dance?

The bride always dances the first dance with her father and the second with her new husband. After that, others may cut in.

When does the bride cut the cake?

Two thousand years ago, in ancient Rome, the bride and the bridegroom shared a special cake symbolizing their first meal together, and it was considered a good omen for a future of plenty. Today, this simple Roman cake has become the usually elaborate white bride's cake. Cutting the cake is the high point of any wedding celebration. The bride cuts the first piece, the bridegroom's hand being placed over hers as she does so. She then gives her husband the first bite, taking the second herself. In this way they share their first meal as man and wife.

The cutting of the cake should not take place until sometime after the receiving line has broken up in order to give the newly married couple a chance to mingle with the guests. Not too long after this ritual takes place, the couple should get ready to leave for their honeymoon.

When does the bride throw the bouquet?

This custom is said to have started in the fourteenth century in France, when the bride tossed either a garter or a stocking to the waiting maidens. Today's counterpart is for the bride to toss her bouquet. The lucky girl who catches it is supposed to be the first one in the group to find romance and marriage. The bouquet is thrown by the bride as she leaves to change her clothes for the honeymoon.

How is the departure for the honeymoon handled?

Primitive man kept his bride hidden until the anger of her relatives had cooled against him for stealing her. This was not called a "honeymoon"! The early Teutons drank a honey syrup for thirty days, or until the moon had waned, and gave the honeymoon its name. While the wedding trip of today is not to escape from family wrath, it's still a period of seclusion from friends and relatives. Two courses may be followed when the couple leave the wedding reception to prepare to start on their honeymoon. They may return to their homes to change from their wedding finery; or arrangements may be made for them to make the change to traveling clothes wherever the celebration is held. They may then take their departure from there with the good wishes of the guests ringing in their ears. Of course all arrangements will have been made ahead of time with regard to transportation, packed luggage, and the change of outfits (be sure they are complete!).

FACTS OF LIFE — ELOPEMENT

What if the bride and groom have eloped?

As soon as it becomes known to the families of the couple, the parents of the bride should, as noted on page 36, immediately issue engraved announcements. No notice to the newspapers is necessary or to be desired.

What if the elopement is not made known for months after it took place?

This makes no difference. Regardless of the length of time that has elapsed, it should definitely be formally announced.

To whom should the announcement be sent?

All relatives and friends. It is thoughtful to acquaint close relatives in person, by telephone, or handwritten note, before sending them the announcement.

FACTS OF LIFE — CANCELLATION OF A WEDDING

If the couple have decided they cannot make a go of it together, and the wedding is definitely off, what then?

If wedding invitations have not gone out (even if the engagement has been formally announced in the newspapers), the less said the better. Whether or not the engagement has been formally announced in the newspapers has nothing to do with it. No retraction should be given to the newspapers either. It is only necessary to tell the family and close friends. If the wedding invitations have gone out, a card should be sent to all to whom invitations were sent. If gifts have been received, they should be returned immediately with a short note, handwritten, expressing appreciation and acquainting the givers with the fact that the wedding will not take place.

FACTS OF LIFE — POSTPONEMENT OF A WEDDING

What if the wedding must be postponed?

Illness of the bride, or a member of the bride or bridegroom's families, or an unexpected death, may cause the postponement of a wedding ceremony. If there is time to have a notice of postponement engraved or printed and mailed to the invited guests to reach them before the original ceremony date, the form below may be used. Otherwise, telegrams or telephone messages should be sent.

Bride's Illness:

> *Mr. and Mrs. Paul Hamilton Cunningham*
> *regret that the illness of their daughter*
> *Alice Leticia*
> *obliges them to recall their invitations*
> *to her marriage*
> *to Paul Marshall Harlow*
> *on Monday, the eleventh of June*

Where a Death Has Occurred:

> *Mrs. Robert Sydney Harvey*
> *regrets that the death of*
> *Mr. Harvey*
> *obliges her to recall the invitations*
> *to the wedding of their daughter*
> *on Saturday, the eleventh of May*

The names of the bride to be and the bridegroom to be may be included before the date line.

Usually these forms for postponements, or recalls, are engraved or printed on a card that fits into an envelope of the same size as one used for an engraved wedding invitation.

Where a New Date Is Known:

> *Mr. and Mrs. Sidney Albert Gillett*
> *announce that the marriage of their daughter*
> *Margaret Aline*
> *to*
> *Mr. James Angus Oliver*
> *has been postponed from*
> *Saturday, the eleventh of February*
> *until*
> *Tuesday, the twenty-first of February*
> *at three o'clock*
> *The First Lutheran Church*

Where Marriage Plans Have Been Canceled:

> *Doctor and Mrs. Charles Stanley Glenn*
> *are obliged to recall their invitations*
> *to the marriage of their daughter*
> *Margaret Jeanne*
> *to*
> *John Alexander Gilman, II*
> *as the marriage will not take place*

FACTS OF LIFE — ANNIVERSARIES

May a couple invite others to help them celebrate their anniversary?

Certainly. Usually only the family and intimate friends are asked as, except in the case of a very formal "At Home" or reception, guests are expected to bring gifts. Even though these gifts are usually of an inexpensive nature and sometimes on the amusing side, it isn't good taste to ask mere acquaintances.

What kinds of parties are held for these celebrations?

Usually on the informal side, anything from being "At Home" either in the afternoon or evening, to buffet suppers or just an evening get-together will do. It's up to you.

How are invitations issued?

By telephone, handwritten notes, or on informal cards.

May others entertain for the couple?

Yes. Usually some member of the family and often planned as a surprise to the couple.

If the function is to be a formal one, what procedure is followed?

When this form is followed it is usually when celebrating the silver (twenty-fifth) or golden (fiftieth) wedding anniversaries. Often the children of the couple will act as hosts at a tea, large afternoon or evening reception.

The eight special observances are:

1 year, paper
5 years, wood
10 years, tin
15 years, crystal
20 years, china
25 years, silver
50 years, gold
75 years, diamond

For more than a century it has been a tradition that eight different things were symbolic for certain years of married life. When presenting gifts it is usual, and fun, to have them fit in with the year that is being celebrated. It is not necessary on the silver, gold, or diamond anniversaries to present a gift of something actually made of one of these expensive items. EXAMPLE: Silver-edged china or glassware is appropriate (and inexpensive) for the twenty-fifth year.

Until comparatively recently these were the only years that were definitely recognized. Today other things have been added for each of the first fifteen years and every five years thereafter. Actually this is a purely commercial idea. It is borne out by the fact that not just one thing, but in some cases several, things have been designated to mark each anniversary. As opinions are divided and there are no definite rulings to abide by, it's up to you as to whether or not you wish to follow this trend. If you do, consult a shop in your community for the "latest" ideas.

What is the wording for the engraved, formal invitation?

In honour of
the fiftieth wedding anniversary of
Mr. and Mrs. Gordon Joseph Gray
their sons and daughters
request the pleasure of
the company of

Mr. and Mrs. Dean

at a reception
on Monday, the sixteenth of March
Nineteen hundred and fifty-nine
at eight o'clock
The Mayflower Hotel

Please reply to
Mrs. Gordon Joseph Gray, Jr.
229 Kenwood Boulevard
Milwaukee, Wisconsin

How is the handwritten acknowledgment worded?

> *Mr. and Mrs. James Richard Dean*
> *accept the kind invitation*
> *of*
> *Mr. and Mrs. Gray*
> *to a reception*
> *on Monday, the sixteenth of March*
> *at eight o'clock*
> *The Mayflower Hotel*

How does a formal anniversary invitation read when issued by the couple?

Figures representing the year of marriage and the anniversary year may appear respectively, to the left and right of the upper portion of the invitation. These may be blind embossed, or engraved in the same ink as the balance of the invitation. Gold, silver, and colors are used much less frequently than heretofore. Black is preferred.

> *1934   1959*
> *Mr. and Mrs. Sidney Perry Davis*
> *At Home*
> *Monday, the eighth of June*
> *from five until eight o'clock*
> *624 Elmwood Lane*
> *Columbus, Ohio*

. . . .

> *Mr. and Mrs. Gordon Joseph Gray*
> *request the pleasure of*
> *the company of*
>
> *Mr. and Mrs. Dean*
>
> *at a dinner to celebrate*
> *the fiftieth anniversary of their marriage*
> *on Monday, the sixteenth of March*
> *Nineteen hundred and fifty-nine*
> *at eight o'clock*
> *The Mayflower Hotel*

R.s.v.p.

Reply: (handwritten)

> *Mr. and Mrs. James Richard Dean*
> *have the honour to accept*
> *the kind invitation*
> *of Mr. and Mrs. Gray*
> *to a dinner*
> *on Monday, the sixteenth of March*
> *at eight o'clock*
> *The Mayflower Hotel*

FACTS OF LIFE — SPECIAL TO THE WEDDING GUEST

Is there a ruling governing the answering of a wedding invitation?

Yes. If invited to the church only, NO acknowledgement should be made. If to the reception also, an acceptance or regret should be sent immediately. (This also applies in the case of the home wedding because the invitation to the ceremony itself would automatically include any celebration afterward.) The wording of the acknowledgment to the reception invitation is exactly the same as to that of a regular reception (see page 30). No mention is made of the bride or her future husband. You reply to those extending the invitation. For example: her parents. Reminder: Only handwriting on white stationery will do. Never typing!

Must wedding guests send gifts?

In years gone by, if you were invited to the church only, no gift was expected—if to the reception, it was. Today the individual makes his own decision about sending a gift. TIP: It's nice to follow the old custom.

When should the gift be sent?

As soon after receiving the invitation as possible. It is inexcusable to wait until a day or two before the wedding.

How should the gift be sent?

Address *only* to the bride to be, using her maiden name, and send it to her home.

What is put on the enclosed card?

Nothing is necessary except the name of the sender. (Good

wishes may be added if you care to.) Use your full name. Not just "Mary" or "Mary and John." The bride may know several bearing such names and detective work is necessary to find out who sent what. Use a calling card if you have one. If on very familiar terms and a "Mr. and Mrs. Philip John Green" seems more formal than you would like to have it, put an ink line through the engraved name and handwrite "Mary and John" below it if you wish. However you do it, be sure clearly to identify yourself.

What initials should be placed on gifts of silver or linen?

This is controversial. Formerly, only the bride's maiden name initials were ever engraved or embroidered on a gift. For two reasons: One, if a hope chest had been started long before her "Prince Charming" came along, naturally everything therein would bear only her initials. Two: the gift is to the bride, not the man she is marrying. Today, however, it is also considered correct by some that the bride's surname initial and that of her prospective husband be placed together. Use either one you wish. It is suggested, however, that you stick to the old custom.

Is there a helpful procedure to follow when purchasing a gift?

Yes. Most brides of today are wise enough to acquaint the stores in their community with their preferences in silver patterns, china, or linens. If upon inquiry you find that this has been done, it is a simple matter to select the gift that fits your budget.

How do you send a telegram on the wedding day?

If it is to be received before the ceremony is to take place address it to the bride in her maiden name, wishing her happiness. If scheduled to arrive after the services, address it to the bride and bridegroom, offering congratulations and wishes for their happiness.

Is there any particular procedure to follow while attending the church service?

Be sure to tell the usher whether you are a friend of the bride's or the bridegroom's, so he will know which side of the church to seat you on. If you are a woman, he offers his right arm and escorts you to a pew; the man accompanying you follows behind. If a man alone, he seats himself.

Is a wedding reception any different from any other?

No. Your behavior would be the same except when going

through the receiving line (and be sure you do). Express wishes to the bride for her future happiness, never congratulate her. The congratulations are for the bridegroom only. (SUGGESTION: Never ask leading questions about "where are you going on your honeymoon," etc. It's none of your business.)

Do you have to stay at the reception until the couple depart on their honeymoon?

It is proper to leave any time after the bride has cut the wedding cake, not before.

FACTS OF LIFE — BIRTH ANNOUNCEMENTS AND CHRISTENINGS

Is a birth announcement a must?

No. It is entirely up to the parents. However, if either parent is living in a city other than his or her own home town, it is the easiest way to spread the good news.

Is it proper for an announcement to be made in the society sections of the newspapers?

Yes. Not done too often, though.

How is the informal announcement made?

Very popular today are cards that may be purchased at any stationer's, usually cunning baby faces illustrating them, with a line or two of poetry. The name of the baby, and date of birth, and the names of the parents may be printed or written in on the lines left blank for this purpose. In this case the parents' signatures should be "Catherine and John Brown," not "Mr. and Mrs. John Brown." The baby's name may either be given in full or only the Christian names used.

WARNING: Avoid the so-called "clever" birth announcements. They are apt to border on the crude and vulgar, and can only cause acid comment on your bad taste.

What is the most formal way of announcing the birth of your baby?

An engraved card (a little larger than that used for calling) containing the full name of the husband, preceded by "Mr. and Mrs." A small card with the name of the baby and the date of birth engraved upon it is attached to this by a tiny white bow.

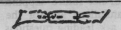

Mark Robert Samuels

June 19, 1959

Captain and Mrs. Christian Samuels

NOTE: A little less formal way of doing it: A blue ribbon for a boy, or pink for a girl, may be used in place of the white one, and a blue or pink border on the card.

Is there a semi-formal approach?

Yes. A folded-over informal card with the name of the baby and date of birth engraved or printed or written by hand on the outside, and the parents' name on the inside.

Is it proper to announce the adoption of a baby?

By all means, yes. For the sake of clarity in the future, it would seem a "must." A small card on which is engraved the following is considered the best taste in this case:

Mr. and Mrs. Robert John Spencer
have the happiness to announce
the adoption of
Charles William
aged six months

Should an announcement of the adoption be made in the newspapers?

No. This is not done, simply because there is no reason to announce an adoption to anyone but your friends.

Is the recipient of a birth announcement expected to send a gift?

Definitely not. However, there is nothing to stop you from doing so, if you want to.

What about showers for the baby?

Follow exactly the same procedure as for giving a bridal shower (see page 13). The mother to be is, of course, the honored guest and all gifts are for the expected baby.

REMINDER: No member of the mother's family should entertain for her in this manner.

Are showers given only for the first baby?

Usually, yes. There's no rule against having one for a later arrival, however.

At what age does the christening usually take place?

This is flexible. In some faiths baptism is expected to take place before the infant is a month old; in others, age does not come into it and the ceremony may occur at any time.

What is the first step in planning a christening?

The godparents should be chosen. Godmothers, usually two for a girl and one for a boy; godfathers, usually one for a girl and two for a boy. Be sure to ask only intimate friends to serve in this capacity. It places a responsibility on their shoulders that must not be taken too lightly. A chosen godparent should never refuse the honor.

May a relative, for example, an aunt, serve as a godparent?

Yes. More often, however, close friends are given the honor.

What obligations does a godparent assume?

He is held responsible for the child's religious training. Birthdays and Christmas each year should be remembered. If the child becomes an orphan, and alone in the world, the godparent should step in and oversee the plans for the youngster's future.

Does a godparent present a gift?

Yes. Usually a silver porridge bowl, silver cup, or fork and spoon. Starting a small bank account (even if only ten dollars), which may be added to on birthdays and Christmas, is an excellent idea, as is an add-a-pearl necklace for the baby girl.

If a godparent is unable to be present at the ceremony, what then?

A proxy is chosen by the parents to take his or her place at the services.

What is the next step?

Consult your religious advisor relative to the rituals to be followed. Different faiths observe different rites. Also, make sure that the day and time you have chosen fit in with his commitments.

Whom do you invite to a christening?

Only relatives and close friends.

How are the invitations issued?

Always informally, by telephone, handwritten note, or on an informal folded-over card. For example:

> *Dear Phyllis:*
>
> *The baby is to be christened next Sunday at four o'clock in St. Thomas church. Do hope you can be with us there, and afterwards at our home for a small celebration.*
>
> *Affectionately,*
> *(s) Elizabeth Graham*

Can a christening take place in the home as well as a church?

Some faiths forbid the home ceremony, but if this is not the case, a christening in the home is to be preferred. The young guest of honor won't put up such a howl if he isn't dragged hither and yon.

What is the procedure for the church service?

Guests should arrive about fifteen minutes before the time designated for the ceremony to start, and seat themselves near the baptismal font. The ceremony begins when the clergyman enters. All present should rise and gather near the font. A godmother holds the infant, and the other godparents and the parents stand close by. When the time arrives in the service, the clergyman takes the baby, baptizes it, and returns it to the godmother, who holds it until the ceremony is over.

REMINDER: When a clergyman asks what name the child is to bear, the godmother holding him says only the given name, the surname is not mentioned.

What are the differences in the procedure if the rites take place in the home?

With one exception it is about the same. The exception: A font to hold the bowl of holy water. The bowl is usually silver (if you don't own one, borrow it). It is placed in the center of a small table. NOTE: A room should be set aside for the clergyman where he may change into his vestments.

Is it obligatory that the parents entertain after the ceremony?

No. It is entirely up to them.

If you do celebrate, what type of party is given?

Always on the informal side. Usually a tea party. The only difference from a regular informal tea is that there is a christening cake (with white icing) and caudle, the traditional christening drink, which originally was a gruel, but in recent years has turned into a hot eggnog. However, caudle today is often replaced by punch or champagne. All three are correct to drink when offering a toast to the baby for his future health and prosperity.

Does the clergyman receive a fee?

As baptism is a sacrament of the church, no fee is ever charged. However, a donation (not less than $10.00) is usually presented, in private, to the clergyman to be used for charity, at his discretion.

Are those invited supposed to bring gifts?

It is not obligatory. If you wish to do so, however, go ahead.

FACTS OF LIFE — FUNERALS

Who makes arrangements for the funeral?

Those most closely related to the deceased should designate a distant relative or intimate friend to take over the sober duties that have to be performed.

What is the first step?

Consult the family's spiritual advisor as to the time and place of the services. His guiding hand is needed in this time of sorrow, for different procedures are observed by different faiths.

The second step?

After ascertaining the family's wishes with regard to funeral expenses, et cetera, the funeral director should be contacted and all details gone over with him. He employs especially trained men who can be depended upon to take care of everything in a dignified manner.

Who issues the death notice to the newspapers?

The family itself may do so, but it is usually done by the funeral director. The deceased's name and the names of his surviving relatives, the time and place where the rites are to be held, are included. Also, any specific requests of the family with regard to flowers and so forth should be included.

If the time and place of the funeral are included in the death notice, may anyone attend?

Yes. In this case anyone who knew the deceased, whether professionally or socially, should make every effort, as a mark of respect, to be present.

If flowers are permitted, how are they handled?

If the funeral is to be held in the home, the person in charge designates someone to make a careful list of all flowers received. As each floral piece arrives, a description should be written on the back of the card accompanying it. EXAMPLE: "Basket of yellow roses." This is helpful when the time comes to write the notes of thanks. If the funeral is to be held from a funeral home, the director there will make a detailed list of all floral tributes.

Should cards be left on the flowers when they are displayed?

Never. Cards should always be removed.

In what further ways may friends be of service?

If the family announces that calls may be made at the funeral home prior to the services, the person assisting the family may, with their advice, ask various friends to take turns greeting those who make condolence calls. No member of the family itself should ever be asked to perform this duty.

Are flowers or streamers placed on the front door of the home of the deceased to indicate there has been a death?

In years gone by most funerals took place in the home, and the emblem of mourning was always placed on the door. Today the deceased usually rests in a funeral parlor from which services and burial are held. Therefore, the outside indication of sorrow at the home has more or less been dropped. If it is done, however, white flowers and streamers for a child and purple for adults are correct. They are removed by the funeral director before the family returns from the services.

How are pallbearers chosen?

Six or eight men who were close friends of the deceased are chosen by the family. The person in charge notifies them by telephone or wire. Members of the family never serve in this capacity. Rarely today do the pallbearers actually carry a casket. This is usually done by assistants of the funeral director, and the pallbearers' role is purely on honorary one. When the service takes place in a church, they precede the casket, two by two, to the chancel, where they enter the front pews at the left, facing the altar. If there is no processional, they take their places in the left pews shortly before the services begin.

Are invitations ever issued for a funeral?

No. With one exception. When the funeral is to be private, it is then necessary to notify relatives and close friends by telephone or handwritten notes, or telegram, and they are expected to attend. The person assisting the family takes care of this.

What are some of the other duties of this person?

He or she should designate another close friend to be stationed near the front door of the home to greet those who pay a call of condolence, to accept telegrams, messages, flowers, et cetera.

When is a memorial service held?

This service is sometimes held in lieu of a funeral. Usually it is done when the deceased has died and been buried in a foreign country. A notice is placed in the obituary columns of the newspapers, giving the name of the deceased and the time and place of the memorial service. Persons attending follow the same procedure as when going to a funeral. If it is desired by the family of the deceased that only relatives and close friends be asked to attend, a friend may be given a list of these people and asked to telephone them the necessary information.

Is it correct to acknowledge expressions of sympathy with engraved or printed forms?

Definitely not. Only in the case of the death of prominent persons, where hundreds of messages and flowers are received, is it permitted. Even then such expressions of appreciation should not be sent to close friends.

If such a card is issued, what would the wording be?

Mrs. Gordon John Widow
wishes gratefully to acknowledge
your kind expression of sympathy

How may the family express their appreciation for flowers, letters of sympathy, et cetera?

A personal handwritten note should be sent by the closest relative. As no one expects an immediate acknowledgment the notes do not have to be written until time has softened the first shock. Only a few lines are necessary, such as, "Thank you for your beautiful sheath of pink roses, and for your kind sympathy. Your thought of us was deeply appreciated." That is all that is needed.

If, for some reason, the closest relative is unable to perform this task, who would handle it?

Another member of the family or a close friend may write the notes saying, for example: "My uncle asks me to thank you, et cetera."

What stationery should be used?

Plain white, usually the small "correspondence" size.

Is it necessary that it have a black border?

No. This custom has practically gone out in recent years. It is still correct, if you wish, but seldom done.

Is a fee presented to the clergyman who officiated?

Yes. Actually this is not considered a fee, as payment is never made for a church sacrament. It is a donation, usually used for a charity chosen by the clergyman. Send it to the clergyman after the funeral with a letter of appreciation for his comfort and assistance. The amount depends upon the financial position of the family, and may be anywhere from $10.00 to $100. After a church funeral (in same instances) a bill is presented by the sexton for the use of the church. If this is not done, he should be paid about $25.00.

What is the custom regarding the wearing of mourning today?

It is the usual procedure that close relatives attire themselves in black when attending the funeral. The all-enveloping black crepe or long veils of former years are seldom worn by women today. A simple black gown or suit and black hat, gloves, hose, and shoes, are all that is generally considered necessary. If a man has a black suit, he should wear it. If not, a dark blue or gray is acceptable. Black tie, socks, and shoes should be worn. He may also wear a black sleeve band, if he wishes. This is a piece of dull black cloth measuring approximately four inches wide and is worn above the elbow on the left arm. (How long this is worn after the bereavement is a matter of personal choice.)

Early in the century the wearing of deep mourning after the funeral was expected of all close relatives of the deceased, usually for a year at least. Today mourning has assumed a more sensible aspect. Many feel that draping themselves in deep black is casting the shadow of their sorrow upon others. By wearing soft pastels they are not depressing others and are aiding their own readjustment. However, this is definitely a decision that only the individual can make.

REMINDER: Children, under no circumstances, should be attired in black.

What social activities may be attended by those suffering a bereavement?

Shutting oneself away from the world for months, or even years, as in the past, is a practice sensibly outmoded. Naturallly (usually for a period of six months) one does not attend conspicuously gay and formal parties, such as balls, or big receptions. However, quiet evenings with friends, small informal parties, or attendance at the theater, certainly are not to be frowned upon, in general, today. But this again is a case where it is up to the individual to make his own decision.

What should friends and acquaintances do when death strikes the home of someone they know?

In your eagerness to be of assistance and consolation to the bereaved, guard against adding to their burdens. Intrusion upon grief, no matter how well intended, is inconsiderate and thoughtless. If possible, go to the home of the deceased, and leave your card, writing the words, "with sympathy" thereon. You may also offer your assistance. Never ask to be admitted. Only relatives and very close friends should do this. You may prefer to make the call of condolence at the funeral home, where you will be asked to sign the visitors' book, which will later be given to the family of the deceased.

If the funeral announcement states "funeral private," what does it mean?

Just that. Relatives and close friends are notified by telephone or handwritten note by the person helping out as to the time of the rites. Only they attend.

If asked to "please omit flowers"?

Do so. All too often people disregard this request. Besides being the wishes of the family, it is to be remembered that some faiths do not permit them, the Jewish particularly. So do not send them if asked not to.

If, in lieu of flowers, it is suggested that a donation be sent to a specified charity, how do you go about it?

Send your check to the charity indicated, mentioning that it is in memory of the deceased. The charity, in turn, will notify the family that you have done so, and of course will not mention the amount you have given.

If flowers are sent, how are they addressed?

Never to the deceased. Address them "To the funeral of John Doe," or to the nearest relative. The former should be used by those who knew the deceased but not the family, and the latter by those who know the relatives.

Should anything be written on the card accompanying the flowers?

As the flowers themselves are an expression of sympathy, a card containing only the names of the senders is all that is necessary. Always the full name, by the way, "Mr. and Mrs. James Monroe," never "Mary and Jim." It is not wrong to include "with deep sympathy" on the card, if you prefer to do so.

When attending a funeral, should black be worn by either sex?

Only if you are sitting with the family, or if you are a pallbearer, is it considered necessary to wear black. However, women should wear clothes of somber colors (a red hat, for example, would certainly be out of place) and men should attire themselves in dark, conservative suits.

Do ushers advise you where to sit when you attend a church funeral service?

No. There are never any ushers. You must seat yourself.

What are the rules governing a church funeral service?

In most cases a processional up the aisle does not take place today. Just before the services start, relatives who are gathered in the vestry file in and take their places in the front pews on the right of the altar (as you face it). Only family and very intimate friends of the deceased seat themselves near the altar.

Close friends, while not entering with the family through the vestry, unless specifically asked to do so, seat themselves up near the front, in the pews back of the family itself.

Acquaintances never seat themselves far up near the family. This is an imposition. They choose a place on the right-hand side facing the altar, preferably toward the back from the center of the church.

When do you leave the church?

At the conclusion of the service the casket will be wheeled out and placed in the hearse, followed by members of the family and friends. Leave then, and not before, after the family have all left the church.

If the burial is to be private, you of course do not go on to the cemetery. If not, do as you wish.

What is the procedure if the funeral services are held in the home?

Relatives either take their place near the casket, or, if space allows, stay in seclusion in a room nearby. If they do stand by the casket, the women wear hats as they would in church.

Close friends, who have not been asked to join the family, and acquaintances, stand during the services. The women wear hats and coats, the men their coats, with hats in hand. No one leaves until the casket has been carried out.

What if the services are held in a funeral home?

In these days of small apartments and homes, services often take place in a non-sectarian chapel within the funeral home itself. Your actions would be the same here as in the private home.

What is expected if you wish to join the procession of cars that go to the cemetery for the burial, after the church services are over?

If the deceased was a relative, or close friend, you have probably been instructed by the funeral director which limousine you are to occupy. If you are driving your own car, you get in line behind the hearse and the limousines, turn on your dim lights, and follow the procession to the cemetery. In this case, you never make a move to go, after the rites are over, until the relatives have left.

THE SOCIAL AMENITIES

THE SOCIAL AMENITIES — INTRODUCTIONS

What terms are used when making an introduction?

In general use today, and by far the best form, is to mention the names only. "Mrs. Ward, Mr. Brown." The phrase, "May I present," while perfectly proper, is not really necessary. It is best to use this phrase only when presenting a man to a woman, not when introducing one woman to another. A woman sometimes resents being "presented" to one of her own sex. Stick to the use of the names only, and you can't go wrong.

When making an introduction, which name is mentioned first?

Always the name of the person to whom the presentation is being made.

Are other introductory phrases permissible?

Yes. "I would like to have you meet," and "May I introduce?" are considered acceptable, but advised against. Why? Because they are awkward and unnecessary.

Are there phrases that should never be used?

Yes. Never say, "Make you acquainted with"; "Mr. Smith, this is Mr. Watts"; or "Mr. Smith, shake hands with Mr. Wyatt"; or "Meet the wife!"

What about introducing one woman to another?

The younger is presented to the older, "Mrs. Matron, Miss Younger." The unmarried woman is introduced to the married, "Mrs. Green, Miss James." Only if the unmarried woman is obviously much older would this be reversed.

What if two women are about the same age?

Use tact here. Either name may be said first, but don't stress it.

Is a woman ever introduced to a man?

Never, with three exceptions: When he is an official of high rank, an ecclesiastical dignitary, or an extremely elderly man.

Is there any special rule to follow when introducing two men?

Only that the younger be introduced to the older. Approximately the same age, it makes no difference, unless one of them is one of the three abovementioned exceptions.

How do husbands and wives introduce each other?

In both cases the surname is never used.

The wife: "Mrs. or Mr. Jones, my husband."

The husband: "Mrs. Brown, my wife."

If presenting her to a man, he would say: "My wife," pause, looking at her during this comment, and then "Mr. Brown." (Remember she is mentioned before the name of the man who is being introduced to her.)

What is a simple way to introduce other relatives?

If the name is the same as yours, "Mrs. Green, I would like to present (or have you meet) my mother." If not, "Mrs. Green, I would like to have you meet my mother, Mrs. Hill." When introducing someone to a relative, mention the relationship for the sake of clarity. The terms such as: "My husband's sister," "My husband's mother," "My brother's wife," all sound much better than the use of "mother-in-law," and so forth.

How do young people introduce their parents to their own age group?

"Mother and Dad, I would like to have you meet Mary Green and Bobby Smith."

How do you introduce one person to a group?

Mention his or her name, first (saying it only once), "Mr. Green, I would like to have you meet Mr. and Mrs. Brown, Mrs. Gray, Miss Phillips," and so forth. Ladies first, or age, do not come into the group introduction.

Is it proper to personalize an introduction by mentioning a topic of interest to both of those being introduced?

Yes. If time allows, it is a thoughtful way of opening the doors of friendship. "Mrs. Brown, Miss Hays. As you are both so active in the Red Cross, I am sure you will enjoy meeting."

When you think two people already know each other, is it all

right to say, "Mrs. Smith, you have met Mrs. Jones, haven't you?"

Definitely not. This is unfair to both parties. Maybe they have met, and one has forgotten. Safer to introduce them in the usual way. If they have met before, let them say so.

If someone comes up to you saying, "You don't remember me, do you?" and you haven't the vaguest idea who it is, what line of action do you take?

Return honesty for rudeness. Your answer, "I am very sorry, but I don't." Let the offender take it from there. There should be a special punishment for those guilty of this thoughtless, inconsiderate habit.

How should you greet an acquaintance whom you haven't seen for some time?

Be kind. Assume your name has been forgotten. Say, "How do you do. I am Mary Smith," or "Mrs. Smith," whichever you prefer. She will bless you for it if she has forgotten your name.

When faced with the problem of introducing someone whose name you have forgotten, what do you do?

You wish fervently you were somewhere else! But face it honestly. Mumbling something incomprehensible is more of an affront to the person whose name you have forgotten than it is frankly to blurt, "I am sorry, but I have forgotten your name." Remember, we all experience this at one time or another.

If you are attending a party, knowing only your hosts, and they neglect to introduce you to anyone, what then?

All guests under one roof are automatically considered introduced. So just go ahead and present yourself, saying, "How do you do. I am Mrs. Lane" (or Mrs. John Lane).

How do you acknowledge an introduction?

Only one phrase is correct. "How do you do." Depending upon the circumstances, one may add, "It is so nice to meet you," or words to that effect. Never resort to the use of "A pleasure, I am sure," or "Pleased, I am sure." The expression, "Pleased to meet you" or any of its derivatives may boomerang back with an "I'm pleased you are pleased." So forget these, by all means.

Do you stand upon being introduced?

Men—always. Women—never except for a very prominent person, man or woman, or one of extreme age.

Is it always considered proper to accompany an introduction with a handshake?

Generally, yes. A good, firm handclasp, too. Avoid a flabby, cold-fish grip, and above all don't be a bone-crusher. Strike a happy medium.

THE SOCIAL AMENITIES — CONVERSATION

What is the best guide to being a good conversationalist?

The poor conversationalists are those who talk too much, never those who talk too little. As George Eliot once put it, "Blessed is the man who has nothing to say and abstains from giving in words evidence of the fact." This obviously means don't chatter just to hear yourself talk. A nervous desire to make a good impression sometimes is behind this fault, particularly when you meet someone for the first time. Always have some current subject to start the ball rolling. Between the radio, television, and newspapers, this presents no problem. So if you piece your conversation together with banalities, it's nobody's fault but your own.

What is the definition of a bore?

One who likes to talk about himself when you want to talk about you. Enough said.

REMINDER: When conversation is boring—remember you have played a part in making it that way.

What is a sure way to up your popularity rating?

Listen. It takes perseverance to learn how, especially if you want to express your own views. Don't fidget, sneak glimpses at your watch, or stare into space, even if you are bored. Look the speaker in the face and give him your undivided interest. It's a nice feeling when somebody does the same for you, isn't it?

Do you have these conversation faults?

Answer these questions honestly, and you are on the road to correcting conversational faults you don't even know you have.

1. Do you interrupt an expression of another's opinions by butting in and stating your own before he has finished?

2. Do you monopolize the conversation by a recital of your personal affairs, and/or cute antics of your baby or the hectic day at the office?

3. Are you an operation or illness fanatic? Believe it, no one is interested in your aches and pains—only their own.

4. Do you avoid malicious criticizing of others? The old adage, "If you can't boost, don't knock," is well worth remembering.

5. Do you pass on that juicy piece of gossip without caring whether it's true or false?

6. Do you avoid controversial subjects, such as politics or religion?

7. Do you make tactless remarks? Remember, and never forget, you can't regret saying something when you haven't said it.

8. Do you a braggart be? No matter how wonderful your exploits, they can become extremely tiresome to others. Avoid the use of the word "I" as much as possible.

9. Do you try to govern your tone of voice, avoiding the loud and boisterous?

10. Do you tell off-color stories in mixed company? Usually this is not funny, but embarrassing to everyone.

11. Do you intersperse your conversation with slang and profanity? This is a giveaway that your vocabulary is limited. Make a point of learning a new word every day. You'll be surprised at the results.

12. If you are proficient in a foreign language, do you carry on a conversation in that tongue when others are present who do not understand? It's unpardonably rude.

THE SOCIAL AMENITIES — VISITING CARDS AND CALLING

Why are visiting cards used?

Centuries ago the Chinese started the custom of leaving a card as evidence of a person's formal visit to the home of another. The Germans were the first in the Western world to adopt the practice. During the reigns of Louis XIV and Louis XV the calling card became the rage in France. Not the little pasteboard so familiar today, but large-size cards ornately decorated. It was not until the eighteenth century that England took up the custom, and it gradually spread during that time to our country.

Unfortunately, because of the fast pace of our present-day life, people just seem too busy to observe the age-old expression of courtesy shown by one person (or family) to another by paying the formal visit. Only in the so-called "high society" groups, official, diplomatic, and military circles, do you find this an expected custom today.

However, the use of "visiting cards" has been broadened so much now that, whether you make formal calls or not, they are extremely useful to have. If you do have them, every effort should be made to observe traditional forms that have come down through the years (naturally with changes here and there, to conform with our modern way of life).

Is it all right to have a calling card printed?

Never. Cards for social purposes must always be engraved. Only those for business use may be printed.

May colored inks be used?

No. Only black is considered correct.

Are all cards the same size?

The size varies in accordance with the circumstances.

EXAMPLE: A woman's card measures 2¼ x 3¼ inches, a man's 1¾ x 3¼ inches.

Are they made of special paper?

Yes, usually white or cream-white Bristol board. They may be either glazed or unglazed. It is not incorrect to use a fine, thin parchment paper if you wish.

What type of lettering is preferable?

Script is always correct. However, several styles are considered proper today. Have your stationer show you samples and choose the one you prefer. SUGGESTION: Always avoid ornate or overlarge lettering.

In placing your name on a card, may initials be used?

No. The full name should be given. Only if the name is so

long that it would be awkward or well-nigh impossible to place on one line should initials be resorted to.

What else goes on the cards, and why?

Remember, their purpose is to identify. Therefore, your status in life should be made clear by the prefix before your name, "Mr.," "Mrs.," "Miss," "Doctor," et cetera, whatever the case may be. Also the address should be placed in the lower right-hand corner. Seldom included in the past, today it is a necessity that this be done, owing to the spreading out and growth of our cities and towns. If your address is a temporary one, it is correct to handwrite it in ink in the lower right-hand corner of the card.

What is the correct form for the card of a married woman?

Mrs. Alan Philip Proper

1331 Logan Street
Chevy Chase, Maryland

A widow's card would be exactly the same (never Mrs. Mary Black Doe).

NOTE: If the husband uses "junior," II, or III after his name, his wife also does.

For some unknown reason it has been considered bad form through the years to place "senior" after the name of a widow, in order to distinguish her from her son's wife, if he is named for the father. For the sake of clarity, and from the common-sense angle, it is now no longer frowned upon.

EXAMPLE: "Mrs. John Richard Brown, senior," with a small "s" (or the abbreviation "Sr." with a capital "S").

What is the proper card for the divorcee?

Mrs. Weaver Brown

2431 Rosemont Street

Her maiden surname and that of her former husband are used. The use of her Christian name, "Mrs. Mary Weaver Brown," is also considered correct, but the example given above is in more general use today.

What about the cards of the married woman who uses her maiden name in business?

Her social card must be the same as any other married woman's—"Mrs. Robert James Moore." When calling upon those who know only the name she uses in business, it is correct to handwrite that name, in parenthesis, across the bottom of the card.

~~Mrs. Robert James Moore~~

Mary Philips   1032 Grove Street
Chevy Chase, Maryland

Does an unmarried woman use "Miss" before her name at all times?

No. Until she reaches the age of seventeen her full name without the prefix is given; after that the "Miss" is used. Don't forget the address.

What is used on a man's card?

Mr. Alan Philip Proper

Only the unmarried man places the address on his card. The married man does not. REASON: Almost invariably it accompanies that of his wife, which bears the address.

Does a young man use "Mr." on his card regardless of his age?

No. Only his full name (with no prefix) is used until he graduates from high school or attains the age of eighteen. The address should be given.

What is the proper use of the suffix "junior" and Roman numerals to indicate a man's place in the family line?

The suffix may be given in one of two ways: "Mr. Harrison Gray Doe, junior," or "Mr. Harrison Gray Doe, Jr." If spelled out, no capital, if abbreviated, the capital is used. Numeral suffixes using II and III are used only when a young man bears the identical name of his uncle or an older cousin, or when he has the same name as his living father and grandfather, and the father is using the suffix "junior."

"Mr. Henry Paul Phillips II" (nephew or cousin);

"Mr. Henry Paul Phillips III" (grandson where father uses "junior" or grandnephew, where father uses II).

When the elder men die, suffixes are altered by the surviving members of the family. Sometimes they are not changed, because of legal complications that might arise if it were done.

Your personal preference is the guiding factor. To do either is correct.

How is a title indicated on a man's card?

Clergyman: It is always preceded by the word "The" (and is never abbreviated) "The Reverend John Bell Coe."

Physician, Surgeon, Dentist: On cards in social use, initials indicating professional degrees are always omitted. Only "Doctor" spelled out with a capital "D" or the abbreviation "Dr." may precede the full name.

Does a married couple find the joint "Mr. and Mrs." card necessary?

Mr. and Mrs. Alan Philip Proper

1331 Logan Street
Chevy Chase, Maryland

Not necessary, but mighty handy to have to enclose when sending gifts or flowers. It may be used, of course, when paying a formal call.

What is the folded or folded-over card?

Sometimes referred to as an "informal," the engraving that appears on the front of this card is the same as a joint Mr. and Mrs. (or it may be just one or the other). Never, under any circumstances, used for calling, these cards are ideal for informal invitations, writing short notes, or to accompany a gift or flowers.

Is there another card that serves the same purpose?

Yes. This is a large single card, measuring 4½ inches by 3½ inches.

As you can see, there is plenty of space for a note, informal

> 221 North Place
>
> # Mr. & Mrs. Edward Coe Brown

invitation, or greeting to be placed thereon. (Never use this card for calling purposes.)

If you have no social calling card, how do you manage?

Having the engraved card is a definite social convenience, and it has many uses, as already explained, other than calling. However, if you have little use for engraved cards, and do not wish to go to the expense of having them engraved, it is possible to get along without them very graciously. Never fall back on a printed card, however. These are really tabu. When calling, if you have no card to leave, don't tell a fib and say you left the cards at home. Be honest. If the person you are visiting does not answer the door, tell whoever does, "Please tell Mrs. Brown that Mrs. Miller is calling." If sending flowers or a gift, most shops have plain white cards and matching envelopes that you may use on which to sign your name, or write a message if you wish.

Must calling cards always be left when paying a visit?

The ways of paying a visit to the home of another vary according to the customs followed in a given community. For example, in a small town where practically everyone knows everyone else, the so-called "leaving of cards" would be superfluous, to say the least. The following questions and answers relative to calling are based on general procedures where formal or informal calls are made. These forms may be altered to suit the circumstances under which your community pattern is conducted.

What visits should be made that do not come under the heading of social calling?

Calls to express condolence to friends when death occurs in their family. These should be made at once.

When the engagement of a man in your family, or family in law, is announced, his fiancée and her family should be called up as soon as possible.

A visit should be paid to the mother of a new baby, and a gift, if you wish (this is up to you), may accompany your personal congratulations.

A call to inquire about the health of a friend who has been seriously ill is always in order. It is so much more personal than a telephoned message. A gift of a book, flowers, or fruit is good. No fancy foods. The patient is probably on a special diet. If invited to see the ill person for a moment, do so (remember, only for a moment!). If not asked, don't make the suggestion that you see him. Leave your message of good wishes, your gift, if any, and go your way. You have done your part.

What other occasions are there which demand social calls?

In years past it was considered extremely rude not to pay a call of appreciation after having "broken bread" at the table of another. Luncheon or dinner calls were always paid within three days, a week at the most. Today this gracious custom has almost died out in the rush of our modern way of life. However, if you do not call, it is unforgivable to take this hospitality for granted. The way you express thanks depends to a degree upon your relationship with the hostess. If not well known to you, a short handwritten note of appreciation is in order, written the day after the event. A note scribbled on a calling card won't do. Use white stationery. Also, the sending of flowers is a nice gesture. Even if you know her well, however, at least a telephone call should be made to express your pleasure. By all means do something.

The custom of immediately calling upon a new neighbor has also faded into the past. In cities this is particularly true. Only in suburban communities, small towns, and in the country does it still prevail. It's easy to understand why. In the city apartment living is not conducive to friendly overtures.

A "how do you do" in the elevator is about the beginning and end of the social amenities.

If the paying of calls is a custom in your community, is it permissible for the wife to assume this duty alone, leaving her husband's card as a courteous gesture?

Yes. She shoulders the family's social obligations. Of course her husband may accompany her if he wishes.

Is there a rule governing how many cards should be left at each residence?

Very definitely. Remember, first, a woman *never* calls upon a man. Therefore, she leaves one card of her own for each lady of the household and one of her husband's for each adult member of the family, man or woman. The joint "Mr. and Mrs." card may be used, but be careful that when doing so the woman doesn't accidentally leave a card for a man.

EXAMPLE: Let's say that Mr. and Mrs. Inexperienced are calling upon Mr. and Mrs. Weaver. The Weavers have an adult son. Mrs. Inexperienced should leave one of her cards (for Mrs. Weaver) and three of her husband's (one each for Mr. and Mrs. Weaver and one for the son).

REMINDER: More than three cards from each person calling should not be left at any one residence regardless of the number of adults living therein.

What are the accepted hours for paying formal calls?

Between the hours of three and six in the afternoon.

Just how do you go about making such calls?

Have the correct number of cards to be left ready in your hand (do not place them in an envelope). If the door is opened by a servant, ask "Is Mrs. Weaver receiving this afternoon?" If the answer is a polite "No, she isn't," or "I'm sorry, but Mrs. Weaver is not at home," simply leave your cards and go on your way. Should the person upon whom you are calling answer the door herself (which often happens in these days of small homes and apartment living and virtually servantless households), you would, of course, be invited to enter. Never stay longer than twenty minutes, even if urged to do so.

If the person whom you are visiting does answer the door, do you give her your card?

No. Usually a card tray is placed on the table by the door, and you drop your cards therein as you pass by. If there is no tray, just leave your cards on the table.

Suppose no one answers your ring. What then?

If there is a mailbox, or slot in the door, put your cards within these receptacles.

If calling on someone who lives in an apartment, must you announce yourself?

If there is a reception desk in the lobby, it is extremely rude not to do so. If no desk, you can only go to the door of the apartment in which the person lives and ring the bell, just as you would if it were a house.

Suppose the receptionist in the lobby tells you that "Mrs. Weaver is not at home" or "receiving," what do you do with your cards?

This is one time when it is advisable to enclose them in an envelope (being small, they are apt to get lost) with the name of the person upon whom you are calling written thereon. Leave them with the receptionist. This same rule applies when leaving cards at a hotel.

Is the recipient of the call expected to return it?

Circumstances come into this. If it is a first call, by all means, yes. Only a very serious reason can excuse the rudeness of not returning the first visit of an acquaintance. It should be made in person, if possible. If unable to do so for some good reason, such as illness, or a heavy work schedule, send your card by mail to those who have been courteous enough to call on you. You would send the same number of cards as you would if leaving them personally, and nothing is written on them. Years ago this would have been considered the height of rudeness, but today it is accepted because it fits in with our modern way of living.

If someone calls on you and you are not presentable, or for some reason you do not wish to receive them, is it out of order to have a servant say, "Mrs. Weaver is out"?

This is one time a white fib is permissible. But be careful how you do it. Being told "Mrs. Jones said to say she is out" is certainly no compliment to the caller. The phrase to be used is "Mrs. Jones is not at home." It is also correct to say that "Mrs. Jones is not receiving this afternoon." Never send back either of these messages if the servant has taken the card, told the visitor to wait, and come to you. To say you are out, or not receiving, after a card has obviously been seen by you is an inexcusable rudeness.

Is it ever proper to telephone somebody upon whom you are planning to make a call?

It all depends. It is advisable not to do so in the case of a formal call upon someone you do not know very well. Upon casual friends, it's up to you. Telephoning first is becoming more and more the general rule to follow, however, these days. It's nice, too. So many of us live in a small abode that it's good to have fair warning so as not to get caught with the ironing board in the middle of the living room floor and perhaps one's hair in curlers.

What about turning down the corner of a card?

In the old days it was quite the thing to turn down the corners of cards to signify different reasons for the call. For example, one corner was turned down if it was one of sympathy, another corner was turned down if it was one of congratulations. You practically needed a guidebook! Today this custom has been done away with, and it is now considered proper that a card be turned down in the upper right-hand corner—just the edge turned in—if you make the call in person. If someone leaves the cards for you, which is often done in Washington, the nation's capital, the card is not bent in any way.

It is correct to place handwritten initials in the lower left-hand corner of your card to indicate a certain circumstance behind your call. Most of these initials are taken from French or Latin phrases that have come down to us through the years. Those generally in use are:

N.B. (*Nota Bene*)—Note Well—calls special attention to any words which they precede. For example, when placed before the address on a card they indicate the fact that the address is a new one.

P.P.C. (*Pour Prendre Congé*)—To Take Leave—indicates that one is leaving town for an extended absence.

While it is correct to use the following abbreviations, they are not in general use today, as the courteous person usually prefers to write a short note in these instances.

P.F. (*Pour Feliciter*)—To Felicitate.

P.C. (*Pour Condoler*)—To Condole.

P.R. (*Pour Remercier*)—To Thank.

It is correct to use P.R. when acknowledging receipt of cards marked P.F. or P.C.

THE SOCIAL AMENITIES — SOCIAL CORRESPONDENCE

What stationery is considered in the best taste?

You can never go wrong if you stick to plain white. It is correct for any kind of correspondence. Colored paper should never be used for formal letters. This includes letters of condolence, appreciation, and the answer to formal invitations.

What is the most useful type of stationery for a woman to buy?

The double note paper, folded on the left; it takes only one folding to place it in the envelope. This is preferred when answering invitations or writing other formal letters. You may use a single sheet that folds twice to place it in the envelope. An assortment of sizes is correct for this.

Is it incorrect to use colored stationery?

Any conservative color is permissible, except for formal correspondence—gray, blue, or light green, for example, will not cause criticism, if used properly. Avoid violent colors. It is advisable to stay away from paper on which colored flowers or birds are depicted. For the young girl, yes—for the matron, no.

What is proper for a man?

A large white single sheet measuring approximately 8 x 10 inches, folded twice to place it in the envelope, is considered the most correct stationery for all social correspondence including the most formal.

Is it all right to have your name, address, or initials, on your stationery?

Certainly. But for formal letter writing the paper should be engraved, not printed. In this case the address or initials are used. The engraving should be at the top of the paper, in the center, either in black or blue-black ink. For routine, everyday correspondence, your full name and address, or your initials, may be printed. The use of bright-colored inks, except for the very young, is not in good taste. Black or blue-black ink is preferred.

When writing a social note, do you put the date at the top of the page, and your address if it is not on the stationery?

The date should appear in the upper right-hand corner. If you wish to include the address, place it above the date. Also permissible: place the date or address, or both, opposite and a little below your signature on the left-hand side of the page at the end of the letter. The first form is preferred.

When writing a letter or sending a gift to a child, how is it addressed?

In years gone by a little girl was "Mistress" until she reached the age of twelve. This form has almost disappeared and today the "Miss" is used from the time she is tiny. The custom of using "Master" for a little boy until he is twelve has remained in force, although he may be correctly addressed by using only his name, with no prefix. This name-only form, "James Roe," is followed until he reaches his senior year in high school and then he assumes the grown-up title of "Mr."

When is the designation "Messrs." used?

When addressing brothers. Never a father and son. It is an abbreviation for the French word for "Misters." It may be correctly written in two ways: "The Messrs. Roe" or "The Messrs. Paul and James Roe." The latter is preferably used when there are more than two brothers in a family and only two are to be invited, for example, to a wedding.

What about "The Misses"?

This follows the same form for the daughters as for the sons. "The Misses Roe" or "The Misses Elizabeth and Grace Roe."

NOTE: In both cases, if the given names are used, the name of the oldest son or daughter is placed first.

What about "thank-you" notes?

To receive a gift and not immediately express your appreciation is an inexcusable affront to the person who has been kind enough to try to give you pleasure. The note need not be long, but it should be thankful and kind. Even if you don't like the book Aunt Minnie sent you, it pleases her, and doesn't hurt you, to say you did. Whatever the case, write that note. It is a *must*.

Should an acknowledgment be sent if the giver has been thanked in person?

Not necessarily. Verbal thanks are enough, but it never hurts to follow up with a note if you care to.

May a printed "thank-you" card take the place of a note?

Never. To use a printed card shows an utter lack of the fitness of things. It's a poor return to the person presenting the gift to find out that you can't take the time to express your thanks personally. Better no thanks at all!

What about stationery?

This depends upon your relationship with the donor. If the gift is from an acquaintance, plain white note paper is preferable. If from a relative or friend, you're on your own. It makes no difference to whom you are writing, a "thank-you" note should be handwritten—never typed.

Example:

> Dear Paula:
>
> You were a dear to remember my birthday! The scarf is so lovely, and just by chance blends perfectly with my new green suit. You couldn't have pleased me more.
>
> I certainly hope that we can get together soon and have a real gab fest.
>
> Again many thanks for your thought of me.
>
> > With love,
> > Molly

When should a bread-and-butter letter be written?

If you stay overnight (or longer) at the home of another, a letter should be written immediately upon your return home thanking your hostess for the hospitality that was shown you. Verbal thanks are not enough. A note should always be written. Not to do so is extremely rude.

What stationery should be used?

As bread-and-butter letters are invariably on the informal side, any kind of stationery is appropriate. It is preferable that the letter be handwritten but if the person you have been visiting is a very close friend, and you want to use a typewriter, go ahead.

Example:

> Dear Ruth:
>
> Jim and I had such a wonderful weekend with you and Bill! We enjoyed every minute of it and that buffet supper that you had for us Saturday night was

*perfect. It was such fun meeting all those nice friends
of yours.*

*Do let us know the next time you plan to come up
from the country because we certainly want to be
sure to see you.*

*Again many many thanks for giving us so much
pleasure.*

> *Affectionately,*
> *Anne*

What about the letter of condolence?

All too often this is a letter that is put off and finally never
written simply because you can't think of what to say. It is
extremely thoughtless to let this happen, for in time of great
sorrow the fact that one's friends are standing by can mean
so very much.

To whom should a letter of condolence be written?

When a friend dies, a letter should be written to the closest
relative, whether you know him or not. If a close relative of a
friend dies, a letter should be written to the friend expressing
your sympathy, even if you did not know the relative.

What stationery should be used?

Always plain white. Preferably on the double-fold note
paper.

Always handwritten, too. To type such a letter is unpardonable.

The following examples of letters of condolence are merely
suggested wordings that may be changed to fit particular circumstances.

To a friend who has suffered bereavement:

Dearest Mary:

*Words are hopeless things sometimes when it
comes to expressing oneself. I can only tell you that
you are in our hearts and thoughts and if there is
anything we can do for you, we hope that you will
let us know immediately.*

With warmest sympathy and love,

> *Edith*

It sometimes helps to ease the burden to comment upon some happy remembrance in connection with the deceased. For example: "Sam was such a wonderful person. His unfailing kindness to us all and his delightful sense of humor will long be remembered."

A more formal letter might be written by an acquaintance:

> *Dear Mrs. Andrews:*
>
> *We were so sorry to hear of the deep sorrow that has come to you.*
>
> *Should there be anything that my husband or I could do, we hope you will not hesitate to call upon us.*
>
> *With deepest sympathy,*
>
> > *Ruth North Adams*
>
> *(Mrs. Richard Adams)*

REMINDER: Always avoid using the words "bereavement," "death," "died" or "deceased," "killed," or the phrases "passed on," "passed to his reward," or "the dear departed."

Should letters of condolence be acknowledged?

Yes. No one expects an immediate reply, as all realize that time has to soften the shock a little. When written, the note may be a very short, simple expression of appreciation:

Letter to a friend:

> *Dearest Edith:*
>
> *Your comforting note meant a great deal to me. I will be calling you as soon as I feel a little better able to face things.*
>
> > *My love,*
> >
> > *Mary*

To an acquaintance:

> *Dear Mrs. Adams:*
>
> *I was very touched at your kind expression of*

sympathy and do want you to know I appreciated it
so much.

> *Very sincerely,*
> *Mary Andrews*

NOTE: If the note is expressing appreciation for flowers, it may be added to either of the above. Mention what kind of flowers were received.

Is there something special to guard against when selecting any kind of greeting cards?

Yes. Regardless of the reason for selecting the card, avoid those that border on the vulgar. Unfortunately there are far too many of these on the stationers' shelves today. For some occasions, such as the birthday of a close friend, for example, a comic card may fit amusingly in with a certain shared experience. Just make sure the card isn't too comic. During recent years, for instance, some have thought it clever to send out smart-aleck Christmas cards that range from the irreverent to the obscene. Criticism, certainly not amusement, will be the only result of your bad taste.

Is it all right to send a personal "family" card (one containing pictures or drawings of the children, the family pets, or what have you) to mere acquaintances?

While fine for friends, it is wise to purchase a less personal card for business associates and acquaintances.

May a greeting card be sent to one who has suffered a recent bereavement?

Most certainly. This is a time when the thoughts of friends are needed. Select a simple card whatever the occasion may be. If for Christmas, one with a religious theme is best, for it is obvious their Christmas will be neither "Merry" nor "Happy."

What signature is placed on a greeting card?

To a friend, merely one's first name is considered correct. It is advisable, however, to include the last name, too, just in case the recipient may know more than one "Mary" or "John."

If signed by a married couple, which name comes first?

This is a case of "ladies first" always. For example: "Mary and John Brown."

When sending out a large number of cards, as at Christmas-time, may the names be printed or engraved?

If printed, the informal "Mary and John Brown" may be used. If engraved, the formal "Mr. and Mrs. John Henry Brown" should always appear. This form can also be used on the informal printed card, but it is preferred for the formal engraved one.

How do you send a card to your employer if he is married?

If for a birthday, it would, of course, be addressed to him alone. If for Christmas, Easter, or some other special observance, it should be addressed to both him and his wife, whether you know her or not.

What about a married woman who uses her maiden name in business and has engraved or printed cards which carry her husband's name?

Either get other cards to send to business associates or write under the "Mr. and Mrs." signature on the card the name by which the recipients will know you.

How do you address an envelope which contains a card for a whole family?

"Mr. and Mrs. Homer K. Lane." Never place "and family" on the envelope. On the card itself write "best wishes to all" or words to that effect. This clearly states your message.

What is the proper way to sign a letter?

It goes without saying that when writing relatives and close friends you sign your first name, or nickname, the one by which they know you. That's up to you. It's when writing to mere acquaintances or signing a business letter that the confusion occurs. In these cases every effort should be made to identify yourself clearly. For example, in former years placing a prefix, Miss or Mrs., in parenthesis before your signature was considered very bad taste. Today to clarify the category a woman belongs in, and to let the person receiving the letter know how to address her when replying, it is not only proper, but good common sense. This is particularly true for business correspondence.

The following are the correct forms for the signing of your name that are in general use today:

The unmarried woman:

The name, "Mary Jane Miller," with (Miss) in parenthesis

placed before the signature. When signing a hotel register the parenthesis is left off.

The married woman:
"Elizabeth Brown Popper" is the signature directly under the closing. No "Mrs." is placed before this. Instead, to the left, and a little lower down, write in parenthesis (Mrs. Richard W. Popper). Or it may correctly be just (Mrs. Richard W.). It is not good form ever to sign a letter in any other way, with one exception. If ordering something from a store, you may forego the maiden name and use the full married name, "Mrs. Richard W. Popper." The only other time this form is proper is when signing a hotel register. Never use the maiden name in this case.

The widow:
Follow exactly the same procedure as that of a married woman whose husband is alive.

The woman who is separated but not divorced:
You are still married. Sign accordingly.

The divorced woman:
"Ann Moore Patrick" with (Mrs.) before it. In signing a hotel register either "Mrs. Ann Moore Patrick" or "Mrs. Moore Patrick" is correct. If the maiden name is reassumed after the divorce, the married name being dropped entirely, it is the same as an unmarried woman with one exception: "Mrs." should always precede the name, never "Miss."

The married woman who uses her maiden name in business or profession:
For business correspondence, "Katherine Hill." Either (Miss) or (Mrs.), whichever she uses, should be placed before the signature in this case. For her personal letters, her signature would be the same as any married woman's.

The man:
He always signs his full name on a letter, never placing "Mr." before it.
REMINDER: When registering at a hotel the "Mr." does precede the name. If accompanied by his wife, "Mr. and Mrs. John Samuel Green." *Never* "Mr. John Samuel Green and wife."

THE SOCIAL AMENITIES — TRAVEL

How can a travel agent help?

Travel can be broadening to those sure of themselves—to those unsure it can be a series of nervous, embarrassing experiences. For a trip of any length, such as one to Europe, a cruise, or a trip across the country, it is strongly advised that you contact a reputable travel bureau. Without charge (other than the regular price of your ticket) they will prepare a complete itinerary for you based on your budget and where you want to go. Reservations will be made straight through to your destination. They will even advise you on the clothes you will need wherever you are going. If traveling to a foreign land, help will be given in obtaining your passport and you will be briefed on the customs of the country you expect to visit.

How necessary are traveler's checks?

Play safe, and use them. They can be cashed anywhere. Hotel bills can be paid with them. Carry only enough cash with you to cover your miscellaneous daily needs. This is particularly advisable on a long trip.

What are special things to watch when packing for a trip?

Be sure your luggage is presentable. It need not be expensive, but do avoid carrying broken-down bags. Plan your packing so as not to be loaded down with cumbersome and unsightly bundles and odds and ends in paper sacks.

What is the best way to insure a pleasant trip?

Show consideration to your fellow traveler. Pushing, shoving, and loud berating will not get you there any quicker, and will certainly not endear you to anyone. Never force yourself upon other people. Of course conversation comes naturally with the stranger across the aisle, but make it brief. On shipboard you can unbend much more than when traveling by plane or train, but don't bend over too far.

What about the bon voyage present?

Don't forget to write thank-you notes to those who have been kind enough to give you a parting gift.

Use common sense when you are the one presenting the gift. Make it something easy for the recipient to handle. Huge baskets of fruit take up a lot of room in a small ship's cabin. And what do you do with flowers on a train? Never give something to a person who is traveling by air that will add weight to the luggage.

Gifts that are always good: Books, magazines, cosmetics, cigarettes, hose, scarfs, leather passport folder, and small kits to hold necessities.

What about restaurant meals?

Always remember the difference between à la carte meals and table d'hôte, when ordering in a hotel or restaurant. À la carte (also known as the European plan) means you select any item you wish on the menu, and each is separately priced. Table d'hôte (American plan) means you order your complete meal from soup to dessert at one price.

What is important to remember when traveling by train in a coach?

Upon entering the car, select your own seat. If you have not engaged a porter, place your bags, coat, et cetera, on the wall racks over the seat. Be sure to anchor them safely so they will not tumble down. If on an overnight trip, you will find a lever, or button, on the arm of the chair which, when pressed, will incline the back so you may relax for the night. When you leave the car at the end of your trip, it's up to you to get your luggage onto the station platform.

On a Pullman car?

You may reserve a parlor-car seat for a daytime trip. Having paid extra fare, you get special privileges. There is a porter on each car who takes your luggage as you enter. If you want anything, push the bell by your seat. He will answer it. Upon leaving the car, he will see to it that your luggage is placed on the railway platform.

For an overnight trip?

You may reserve an upper berth or a lower berth, each for one person; a roomette for one person (in this little room you can let the bed down yourself and there is no need to call the porter; however, on your first trip in a roomette it is well to have the porter show you how it works); bedroom for one or two people; compartment, one to three people; drawing room, one to four people. Small courtesies should be followed by those holding lower or upper berths. Two seats face each other (later being turned into the beds). The purchaser of the lower has the right to sit in the seat facing forward. This means that the upper berth companion must ride backward. While not obligatory, it is a courteous gesture to suggest that he sit with you. Some folks are very unhappy about facing the wrong way. Around ten or ten-thirty, if you wish to retire, ask if you may ring for the porter to make up the berth. As the seats cannot be used after this is done, it is thoughtful, if one wishes to stay up later, to go to the observation or smoking car. It is suggested that you disrobe in the dressing room. You may do so in the berth, but only if you are a contortionist. If you have the upper berth, do not attempt to get up and down by yourself. Ring for the porter. He will bring a stair ladder for you in the evening, and also in the morning, or if you wish to visit the dressing room during the night. If you want a drink of water it is in order to ring for the porter and ask him to bring it to you.

What do you do in the dining car?

The steward will seat you. It is not considered rude if you do not speak to your table companion. If you do, take it easy.

What is the first consideration when you travel by air?

Be sure to check the amount of weight you will be allowed to carry in your luggage. You are permitted only a certain number of pounds. On arrival at the airport take your baggage to the proper airline desk to be weighed and your ticket checked. Make your reservation well in advance—space is limited. Verify this before take-off, according to the information given you with your ticket.

What do you do upon boarding a plane?

You will be greeted at the entrance by a steward or stewardess. Choose any seat available that is to your liking, unless the seats are reserved, in which case you will be notified. When a sign in the front of the plane flashes, "Fasten seat belts," do so immediately, and leave the belt fastened until the sign goes off. Another flashed admonition, "No smoking," must be observed.

Are meals served on planes?

Yes. They are included in the price of your ticket (except on tourist flights), and are served on lap trays by the steward.

How do you prepare for bed on an overnight flight?

In the dressing room. There is definitely not enough space in your berth.

What do you do when alighting upon arrival?

Go to the baggage room in the airport and wait until your luggage is brought in from the plane.

If traveling by ship, what do you do on the day you sail?

Arrive at the ship in plenty of time. Make sure your luggage is on board. After checking on your cabin, go to the dining room and reserve a table, specifying whether you wish a first or second sitting for the voyage. Then go to the main deck and see the head deck steward about reserving a steamer chair. The early bird gets the best location in both cases.

What should your attitude be toward your fellow passengers?

Congenial people usually introduce themselves to one another. You naturally speak to those at your table, and the people next to you in deck chairs. Go easy, though, and don't intrude. Be gracious in responding to friendship that is offered, but don't overdo it. On cruise trips there is usually a hostess or director who will introduce you to others who like the same things you do, such as deck games, bridge, or dancing.

THE SOCIAL AMENITIES — TIPPING

What about tipping?

"Every time I turn around, somebody has his hand out." Is this the way you feel about tipping? If it is, you're wrong. Actually you are only paying for services rendered. The person receiving the tip makes part of his living that way. You should offer tips in a gracious "Thank you very much" manner—not grudgingly. But you don't have to go overboard. If the service is sullen and indifferent, no tip.

How much does one tip in a hotel, restaurant, night club?

DOORMAN—nothing unless he procures a cab for you, then 15 cents to 25 cents.

BELLBOYS—Depends upon services performed. Upon arrival at a hotel, usually 50 cents for carrying one bag (and 25 cents for additional ones) and getting you settled in your room.

For ice water, newspapers, and other small services, 25 cents each, minimum.

CHAMBERMAIDS—(day and night) Nothing if staying for only one night. A dollar or more, depending upon the length of your stay thereafter. Leave it on the dresser if the chambermaid is not about when you leave.

PORTERS—If making reservations for you, 50 cents, for additional special services, up to $2.00.

VALETS—Nothing unless you wish to because of special service.

ELEVATOR OPERATORS—Nothing.

STAFF PERSONNEL—such as managers, room clerks, et cetera —nothing.

NOTE: These figures are based on stays of short duration. If spending several weeks, your tipping must be increased accordingly.

HEADWAITER—No tip if he merely seats you and gives you a menu. If he has made arrangements in advance, or performed any special service, a tip is in order. For example, reserving a table, or arranging for guests, it should be $2.00 and up.

WAITERS—This varies. Fifteen per cent to 20 per cent of the total amount of the check is usual, except if the check is of a very low amount, or very high. For example, 10 cents for a 50 cent check—never a nickel. For checks over $20.00 the percentage may come down to 10 per cent.

BUSBOY—Nothing.

WINE STEWARD—If he takes the order and serves, 10 per cent of wine bill. If the waiter serves it, no tip necessary.

BARTENDER—Fifteen per cent or 20 per cent of each bill in restaurant or bar. If each round is paid for when received, tip each time. If only one check for several rounds, one tip.

REST-ROOM ATTENDANTS—Ten cents or 25 cents if handed a towel. More if other services are rendered.

HAT-CHECK GIRL—At least 15 cents. More in expensive places.

CIGARETTE GIRL—Ten cents for one pack.

In a resort hotel or motel?

This depends on how long you stay. Usually, if your visit is for a week or more, tips are given at the end of each week. Only in the case of waiters would this procedure vary. If the same waiter serves each meal during your stay, he would be tipped weekly. If a different one at every meal, he would be tipped each time.

Use the foregoing scale of tipping as your guide. The amounts may go up or down, being governed by the type of hotel or motel at which you may be staying and the approximate amount you are spending per week.

TAXI DRIVERS?

They are the most unfairly treated among those who serve you.

The following tips are average:

A 50 cent fare: 10 cents.

From 50 cents to a dollar: 15 cents to 25 cents

$1.00 to $2.00: 30 cents to 35 cents

$2.00 to $3.00: 40 cents to 50 cents

$3.00 to $5.00: 75 cents

Thereafter: At least $1.00.

AT A BEAUTY SHOP?

This depends on your total bill. For example, about 20 per cent for a shampoo and wave. If only a manicure, with a smaller total charge, 15 cents to 25 cents. If for a permanent, a minimum of $1.00. No tip whatever if the proprietor of the shop serves you. Masseur: Usually 50 cents for one-hour massage.

BARBERSHOP?—Twenty-five cents for haircut or shave; 40 cents to 50 cents for both. If he is the owner, don't tip.

MANICURIST?—Twenty-five cents.

SHOESHINE?—Ten cents.

How much do you tip those who serve you at home?

POSTMAN—Nothing expected. However, at Christmas $1.00 or $2.00 is a thoughtful gesture.

TRASH AND GARBAGE COLLECTORS—Nothing expected. One dollar or $2.00 each at Christmas is thoughtful, if the same men collect throughout the year.

GENERAL REPAIR SERVICES—The television man, the plumber, electrician, telephone man, et cetera do not expect tips.

How much do you tip at a club?

Very few clubs allow tipping of any kind. If they do, follow the usual routine of each club—they all differ.

How much does one tip when traveling on a train?

In most parts of the country there is a set fee of 25 cents a bag for the redcap or skycap, none of which he receives. He should be tipped at least 15 cents and preferably 25 cents per bag over and above this. Porters on a day trip get 25 cents or 50 cents. Overnight 50 cents to $1.00, or more, if special services are rendered. The dining-car steward is not tipped, unless he gives unusual assistance, but the waiter gets the usual 15 per cent to 20 per cent of the bill.

On a plane?

No tips of any kind are permitted aboard a plane. This includes all those wearing the airline uniform, such as stewards, pilots, reservation clerks, or drivers of the airport limousine.

On a transatlantic voyage?

FIRST CLASS:
>   Cabin Steward .... $10.00 per person
>   Table Steward .... 10.00 " "
>   Deck Steward .... 4.00 " "

SUITES:
>   There is no set rate, but if you occupy two rooms, the rate is usually from $15.00 to $20.00 per person at the end of the voyage, to *Cabin Steward*. Others are tipped following regular first-class rates.

CABIN CLASS:
>   Cabin Steward .... $5.00 to $7.00 per person
>   Table Steward .... $3.00 to $5.00 " "
>   Deck Steward .... $2.00 " "
>   SUITES: Cabin Steward, $10.00 rather than $5.00 to $7.00

Tourist Class:
>   Cabin Steward .... $3.00 to $5.00 per person
>   Table Steward .... $3.00 to $5.00 " "
>   Deck Steward .... $1.00 to $2.00 " "

BATH STEWARD—If you don't have a bath in your cabin, he should receive from $2.00 to $3.00 per person. (All classes.)

WINE STEWARD—Tip about 15 per cent every time service is used.

BOOTMAN—Or the man who picks up your boots outside your cabin, $1.00—or whatever you would give for any extra service rendered.

LIBRARY STEWARD—$2.00 to $3.00—First Class
> $1.00 to $2.00—Cabin Class

HAIRDRESSER—10 per cent to 15 per cent of your check.

Tips on ocean liners are given at the end of the trip, except for Wine Steward and Hairdresser, who are tipped each time services are rendered.

NOTE: Never tip any ship's officer or the doctor. They would consider it an insult.

How much does one tip on a cruise?

On long cruises tip about as follows:
>   Cabin Steward and Dining Steward—One dollar a day per person or about $7.00 a week.
>   Bath Steward—From $2.00 to $3.00 per week.
>   Bootman—About $2.00 at end of trip.

NOTE: On cruises you should tip periodically (probably weekly) and not wait till the end of the voyage.

COURTESY IN DAILY HABITS

COURTESY IN DAILY HABITS

Why is courtesy important?

Perhaps the most important "manners" of all are those for which there are few set rules. Our habits and mannerisms in daily living—the almost automatic things we do—stamp us as refined individuals, sensitive to the rights of others, or as thoughtless and rude persons. In every human contact and in every action we expose the degree of consideration that we have for others. An awareness of some of the most common offenses in such matters as table manners, answering the telephone, smoking, driving a car, et cetera, can be gained from the following.

COURTESY IN DAILY HABITS — TABLE SETTINGS

Why is it important to set a table properly?

Because the placement of plates, glasses, and cutlery according to an established pattern makes it easier for everyone concerned to enjoy the meal.

What does the usual "place setting" consist of?

Until fairly recently two separate sizes of silver implements were considered a necessity. One, the large or dinner-sized knives and forks, et cetera, the other, a smaller version formerly referred to as the luncheon size. Today, with the exception of those who entertain very formally, the dinner size has been taken over completely by the luncheon or medium-size implements which are used for all occasions, from the semi-formal dinner to the most informal family meal. The standard pieces that comprise a place setting today are: the medium-sized fork, knife, salad fork (salad knife is optional), soup spoon, teaspoon, and butter spreader.

Are other implements necessary?

Yes. Serving spoons and forks and a carving knife and fork are really needed even when it's "just family." If you entertain frequently, the dessert spoon (which is a little larger than a teaspoon) is very handy to have. The oyster or sea-food fork, if you serve shelled sea food very often, is a helpful addition to your "place setting." As teaspoons are used for so many things, an extra half-dozen or so is almost a must.

What about tablecloths?

In years gone by a tablecloth was traditionally used on the dining table at all times. Today, because it is so practical, the table mat has taken its place for everyday and general use. Only for the formal dinner, when a damask cloth and napkins are obligatory, is it considered a must that a tablecloth be used.

A tablecloth, particularly the formal damask one, should overhang a table for about fourteen inches and have a "silence pad" of flannel or felt beneath. White linen or lace covers are laid on the table itself. For informal dining, colored cloths are perfectly proper at any meal.

Can the table ever be bare?

Acceptable today but only for the very informal occasion. Attractive when colorful pottery dishes, silver, or stainless-steel implements and bright paper napkins are used.

When are table mats used?

In general use today even the semi-formal luncheon or dinner. In these cases they are usually of sheer appliquèd linen or lace, with matching napkins. For daily use and informal entertaining they may be of gaily-colored cloth, with or without matching runners and napkins.

What napkins are proper for what occasions?

For the formal dinner only large white damask napkins will do. Otherwise, plain white linen ones are acceptable at all times. Colored napkins to match tablecloths or mats are fine, too. Use your own judgment as to when to bring out the ever-faithful and useful paper napkin. It is not frowned upon today for any informal entertainment, such as, for example, a cocktail buffet or supper. Of course, when it's "just family," it is invaluable.

What is the right way to set a table?

Each implement should be lined up with the pieces about

an inch from the edge of the table. Naturally, the amount of silver placed on the table depends upon the food to be eaten.

FORKS: Tines up, on left of plate (except for the oyster or sea-food fork, which is placed on the right, outside of the knives, and on the outside of the spoons, if any).

KNIVES: Cutting edge pointing toward the plate, on the right (with exception of butter knife, which is on the butter plate).

SPOONS: Bowl up, to the right of the knives. In years past, except at breakfast, the only spoon to appear on the table was that for the soup. The dessert fork and spoon were and still are placed on the dessert plate itself for a formal dinner or lunch, and the coffee spoon on the saucer with the cup. Today, for convenience sake, it is not considered improper to put these implements on the table when it is set for the informal meal.

NOTE: There is a rule of three which dictates that it is not proper to place more than three forks, knives, or spoons on the table at one time.

China and glassware

The old custom that required that there always be a plate on the table between place settings is fast disappearing. Called a "service plate," no food is ever placed upon it. A plate for the first course is substituted when it is removed. This is seldom followed today, except at the most formal dinners. Instead, if there is no first course, such as oysters, for example, the dinner plate is substituted. This is not removed before putting the meat course thereon.

SOUP: The bowl is always placed in the center on a plate, never on the table itself.

BUTTER PLATE: Above the forks on the left.

MAIN COURSE: On the dinner plate in the center.

SALAD PLATE: When served after the meat course, the plate is in the center. If an accompaniment to the meat course, it is placed on the left of the forks. A salad fork is not necessary in this case, as it is simpler to use the dinner fork.

DESSERT: If in a bowl, it must always rest on a plate. The dessert fork and spoon may be on the plate, or placed beforehand on the table. The fork is to the left and the spoon to the right, whether on the plate or the table. If a finger bowl and doily are upon the dessert plate, their position would be the same. As soon as the dessert plate is placed before you, remove the silver to each side of the plate. The finger bowl and doily go on the table at the top of the forks on the left.

GLASSWARE: The water glass is placed directly above the knives. Other glasses, such as wine, or iced tea, to the right of that and a little toward the front.

SALT AND PEPPERS: Individual shakers or pepper shaker and salt dish are placed in the top center of each place, or between every two. (These are placed slightly toward the middle of the table.)

JAM, RELISHES, GRAVY BOWLS, et cetera: These bowls should be on a saucer and each should have its own serving implement, spotted about the table wherever there is a convenient space.

NAPKIN: To the left of the forks. Also may be put in the center of the service plate or the dinner plate when there is no first course. Avoid ornate folding. A square triangle or rectangle is preferred.

COFFEE: If there is coffee after dessert, it is usually in a "demi-tasse" or small-sized cup, and may be served either at the table or in the living room. However, if the regular sized cup is preferred, that's up to you, except for the formal dinner, when only the small one is used.

LIQUEURS: Always presented after the meal is over, and usually with the coffee. A tray containing a decanter and the tiny liqueur glasses (or brandy snifters) may be passed, or the host may do the pouring.

SMOKING: It is considerate to accommodate your guests who smoke by making it easy for them. An individual ash tray placed in the center of each place, or between every two places, if your guests are many, solves the problem. Two cigarettes and a folder of matches may be put on each one, or there may be boxes of cigarettes at each end of the table. These, of course, are passed between courses if you wish, or at the end of the meal if you prefer.

COURTESY IN DAILY HABITS — MANNERS AT TABLE

What were George Washington's ideas on table manners?

It is not generally known that George Washington, the father of our country, was a great stickler with regard to the observance of good manners. So much so that he even wrote rules about them. It is said that he did this when he was only sixteen years of age. It is interesting that the following observations made by him with regard to table manners, nearly two hundred years ago, are as appropriate today as they were then. This certainly goes to prove that no matter how our mode of life may change, the basic rules governing our habits of manners do not.

His admonitions were:

"Make no show of taking great delight in your victuals."

"Eat not with greediness."

"Lean not on the table, neither find fault with what you eat."

"Drink nor talk with your mouth full."

"Cleanse not your teeth at table with napkin or fork, but if others do it let it be done with a picktooth."

"Be not angry at table whatever happens. If you have reason to be so, show it not, but put on a cheerful countenance, especially if there be strangers present, for good humor makes a dish of meat a feast."

What is the basic reason behind the rules for table manners?

The purpose behind all "how to eat" rules is to keep us from making unsightly spectacles of ourselves to others. Eating is not a particularly pretty performance at best, but eat we must, so every effort should be made to do so in as polite and unobtrusive a way as possible.

May chicken drumsticks or chop bones be eaten with the fingers?

The pleasure we derive from gnawing on a bone comes to us from our caveman ancestors. But it's not an attractive sight. Therefore, when dining at the home of another or in a restaurant use your knife and fork. At home you are on your own.

What other foods raise the question of fingers or forks?

French-fried potatoes, asparagus, and bacon are three that cause trouble. A limp and greasy potato slice or a dripping piece of asparagus is not an attractive finger food. The same applies to bacon. Only if it is very crisp should it be eaten with the fingers, to avoid having bits fly around the table. At home it's up to you. With sandwiches use your own judgment. If dripping with mayonnaise or very soft filling, a sandwich should be eaten with a knife and fork. Firmer ones may, of course, be broken into smaller pieces and eaten with the fingers. The same applies to cake. If the icing is thick and gooey, a fork is needed. If not, break off small pieces, and eat a bite at a time.

What are some of the foods that may be eaten with the fingers?

Corn on the cob, olives, radishes, potato chips, celery,

steamed clams, shoestring potatoes, artichokes (the fork is used to eat the center or heart of this vegetable); all forms of bread except spoon bread may be picked up—it is almost impossible to eat them in any other way.

May a knife be used to cut head lettuce?

Custom used to frown upon this, chiefly because before steel knives were invented, vinegar would turn a silver knife black. Today it is common sense to cut your lettuce regardless of the knife. Attempting to separate it with the edge of a fork usually lands lettuce in your lap or the middle of the table. Use your knife, and play it safe.

What is the correct way to eat bread, biscuits, or rolls?

Bread is the most mishandled of all foods. It should be broken, a small piece at a time, buttered, then placed in the mouth. Never take a whole piece of bread on the palm of the hand and plaster it with butter. The same small-piece-at-a-time rule applies to biscuits and rolls. Crackers, too. REMINDER: None of these should be crumbled up and dunked in your soup. A spoonful of soup, followed by a small piece of buttered bread, or cracker, is a sightlier idea.

What do you do when faced with cocktails of large jumbo shrimps or huge oysters?

These are two of the hardest foods to manage. Usually served in glass bowls, precariously balanced on cracked ice, eating them without mishap is difficult under any circumstances. The sensible way is to fork the shrimps onto the serving plate, cut them in half with your oyster fork, then dip each piece in the sauce. Not very attractive, but this is one time when it is better to do so than to run the risk of choking to death. As to oysters, they are too slippery to handle in this manner, so don't cut them.

SOLUTION: Get small oysters.

What about those tempting slices of pineapple, bananas, oranges, et cetera, in a cup of fruit punch?

Forego them. Fishing around with one's fingers and then popping a dripping bit into one's mouth is messy looking, to say the least. This also applies to cherries and onions in the bottom of a cocktail glass. Sad, but true.

What do you do when you place too-hot food in the mouth?

Never spit it out! Take a swallow of water.

Suppose you choke on a fishbone?

Leave the table quickly, covering your mouth with your napkin. If in a restaurant, and this is impossible, place the napkin in front of your mouth and remove the piece of bone with your fingers. This is only an emergency measure.

What if you put a piece of bad food in your mouth, say a spoiled clam?

Place the napkin before your mouth with one hand, as cover, and with the other hand remove the offensive mouthful, placing it on the edge of your plate.

What do you do with watermelon seeds, grape seeds, olive pits, et cetera?

Never spit them onto the plate. The same method of placing the napkin before the mouth with one hand and quietly removing the seeds or whatever they may be with the other is followed in this case. It is also to be remembered in all of these situations that it is not considered proper to remove seeds or whatever it may be from the mouth, place them on the fork and then on the plate.

What is the best way to squeeze a piece of lemon?

Cup your left hand around the lemon as you squeeze it with your right. In this way you will avoid not only squirting yourself but your neighbor.

Does the same rule apply when eating grapefruit?

Yes. Cupping the hand will avoid any chance of unpleasantness.

What rules are there concerning the use of the knife?

Food should never be eaten from it. It should never be used as a "push piece" to load food on a fork or shove food around on your plate. It is for cutting and cutting only, and this should be resorted to as little as possible. This custom evolves from the Chinese, who for centuries have believed that to cut food at the table is crude and barbaric. They carve everything in the kitchen in pieces small enough to be picked up with chop sticks. Some of our unsightly ways of handling the knife might be corrected if we did just that!

What about the fork?

This, of course, is used more than any other eating implement. Remember not to place more food on it at one time than can be consumed easily in one mouthful. Never wave a forkful of food in the air or hold it suspended while you talk.

How do you use a knife and a fork together?

There are two forms that are considered correct today. The first is known as the American, or zigzag. Hold the fork in your left hand, cut the food with the knife in your right, put the knife across the edge of the plate, switch the fork, tine up, to the right hand, and place the food in your mouth. A little involved, but neat when well done. Second, the continental or European mode of eating. The fork stays in the left hand after the food is cut, tines down, as the food is conveyed to the mouth. The main thing to avoid is using the knife to push layers of food onto the back of the fork, say a piece of meat, with a dab of potatoes on top of it and a dab of vegetable on top of that. It is not only unsightly but impossible to get into the mouth without making more or less of a spectacle of yourself.

What do you do with a knife and a fork when not eating with them, or when you have finished eating?

If you have not finished eating, you put them side by side on the plate (toward the right side), the fork toward the center with the cutting edge of the knife toward you. Don't place them on the edge of the plate, and certainly never balance the handles on the table. The entire implement should be on the plate. When the meal is finished, they should be placed together in the center of the plate, the fork on the left with the knife on the right with the cutting edge facing you.

How do you use a soup spoon?

Remember that the cup or soup bowl is tipped away from you. The spoon is also filled by dipping it away from you. The soup is then sipped from the side of the spoon, as noiselessly as possible, it might be added. The whole spoon is never placed in the mouth.

How is a teaspoon used when served with coffee or tea?

It is for the purpose of stirring either coffee or tea, not to convey the liquid to one's mouth. It should never be used to sip the beverage spoonful by spoonful. After stirring, the teaspoon should be placed on one side of the saucer. Never leave it in the cup.

What do you do with an iced-tea spoon, if the glass is not on a plate?

Your hostess has goofed. Iced-tea glasses should be on a saucer, with room for a spoon. However, if there is a coaster, never place the spoon on the table. Put it across the edge of your plate. Above all, do not leave it in the glass when drinking. Decidedly awkward, it may also result in a poke in the eye.

How do you use serving spoons and forks?

Using the left hand, place the spoon under the food being served, and with the right hand use the fork (placed on top of the food) to guide a portion of it to your plate. Be sure not to lift too much food at one time.

When dining out in a style more formal than you are used to, with more eating implements on the table, how do you know which fork or knife, et cetera, to use and when?

If the table is set correctly, you will have no trouble. Work from the outside in. EXAMPLE: The fork farthest away from your plate is the one you use for the first course. Oysters are an exception. A two- or three-tine oyster fork is always placed on the right of the knives and soup spoon, on the right of the plate.

EXPLANATION:
> On the *left* of the center plate:
> > salad plate, fork, salad fork
>
> On the *right*:
> > salad knife, knife, soup spoon, seafood fork

Upper left—butter plate and knife
Upper right—water glass

NOTE: The napkin can be placed to the left of the
salad plate.

How do you handle a dessert plate that arrives in front of you with a small doily under a finger bowl? A fork on left of the bowl, and a spoon on the right?

You remove the bowl and doily together and place them to
the left of your plate. Do not forget the doily—it is not edible.
The dessert fork and spoon go to the left and right of your
plate. After eating, you dip your fingertips only into the finger
bowl, never your whole hand. You dry your fingertips on your
napkin.

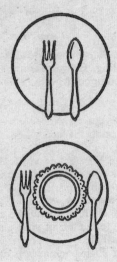

EXPLANATION:

Top: dessert plate, without finger bowl and doily.
Bottom: dessert plate, with finger bowl and doily.

What must you never do while eating?

Never use a spoon that you have been eating from to dip into
the sugar bowl. Not only is this bad manners, it is unsanitary.

Never blow on food or liquids to cool them. It is much
more dignified to wait a moment or two, and certainly more
pleasant for the observer if you do.

Never use the "boardinghouse reach" technique when you want something across the table. It is nicer for all concerned to ask to have what you want passed to you.

Never talk with your mouth full, or chew your food with your mouth open. Not only is it hard to understand you—it's certainly not pretty to watch.

Never put your face down toward your plate instead of sitting up straight and raising the fork to your mouth. Looking like a turtle when you eat is far from attractive. Keep that head erect and use the fork to convey the food to the mouth.

Never put a little dab of salt on the table to dip celery in. Place the salt on your butter plate. If there is no butter plate, then put the salt on your dinner plate, but never on the table.

Never make an untidy eater of yourself. The secret of not doing this is to eat slowly. Spilling food on the table and bread crumbs hither and yon is a sure sign you just don't care what impression you make on others.

Never use the double-elbow spread, or place the elbows on the table while eating. Between courses, one elbow, but not both, may be leaned upon, with the elbow leaning on the table and the arm up, not spread out.

Never use a piece of bread as a "push piece." This is only for the very, very young.

Never dunk in public. When alone at home, have fun.

Never use toothpicks. If you do so in front of others, you are definitely out of line. If you must, do so in private.

Never use your fingers when helping yourself to lump sugar and there are no tongs. Use a spoon.

Never throw your napkin any old place when the meal is finished. If it is of cloth, it should be folded over once and placed on the table to the left of your plate. If made of paper, don't wad it into a ball.

Never push your chair back as you rise from the table and then just leave it there. It should be pushed back to the table.

COURTESY IN DAILY HABITS — THE TELEPHONE

How should the telephone be answered?

In the home: The accepted procedure is simply to say "hello," if answering yourself. If by a servant, she should say "Mrs." (not Mr.) "Roberts' residence." After ascertaining who it is, she should say, "Just a moment and I will call Mrs.

Roberts." Or, "I'm sorry, Mrs. Roberts is out. May I take a message?"

In an office: See page 155.

Do you bellow into the mouthpiece or speak in too low a voice?

Remember, your voice expresses your personality, particularly when people can't see you. Use a pleasantly modulated tone if you wish to have people enjoy talking to you.

When making a call, do you give your name as soon as the phone is answered? Or do you take for granted that your voice identifies you?

It's so easy to say "Mrs. Dow, this is Mary Green" (or Mrs. Green) "calling." It's certainly much more polite. When the phone is answered by someone other than the person you want to speak with, give your own name as you ask for the person you are calling.

Do you think it is amusing to start your conversation with "Guess who this is," or to change your voice and try to mimic someone else?

In both cases the recipient of the call has every right to return rudeness with rudeness. The receiver should be hung up —but promptly.

When you ask "Are you busy?" and the answer is "Yes," do you continue to talk?

This is inexcusable. Why ask the question in the first place, if you are not going to abide by the answer? Request that your call be returned when the party is not tied up, and say good-by at once.

Do you think it is cute to let Junior, age three, answer the telephone?

It's anything but cute to the caller as she struggles to get him to call Mama. Also, only the most doting relatives care to have Junior brought to the phone to show off his vocabulary.

Do you phone your friends for no particular reason and chat on and on just to kill time?

This is decidedly annoying when the person whom you are calling is at work or busy at some household task. Short of being downright rude, there is little the listener can do but listen. You'll be blessed if you make your calls short and to the point—always.

When you're on the phone and the doorbell rings, do you make the person at the other end wait endlessly while you argue with the laundryman or handle other household matters?

Excuse yourself, hang up, and then call back, but don't leave someone dangling on the wire.

Do you carry on a two-way conversation, one with the person on the phone, the other with someone near you?

This is thoroughly irritating to both listeners.

Do you hold someone on the line while you search for pencil and paper to take a message?

Why can't you keep a pad and pencil by the phone? Anchor them if it is necessary.

Do you slam down the receiver when someone gets your number by mistake?

You undoubtedly make this same error yourself upon occasion.

Do you ever answer the query, "Is Mrs. Jones there?" with the answer, "Yes, do you wish to speak with her?"

Why would anyone ask for Mrs. Jones if she doesn't want to speak with her?

Do you always allow some time to elapse between your calls if you are on a party line?

This is true consideration of the rights of others. Also, never interrupt when someone else is using the line, unless your call is one of extreme urgency. If it's unimportant, don't keep picking up the receiver every two seconds to let the other person know that *you* want to make a call. And never give in to the temptation to listen in, thereby invading the privacy of others.

COURTESY IN DAILY HABITS — SMOKING

May a woman smoke on the street?

She won't if she has a sense of propriety. Smoking by women was generally accepted about forty years ago (before that no lady ever did). A woman might smoke in her own home, or the homes of friends, but never in public. Today a woman may smoke in public places, such as restaurants, without fear of criticism. But on the street the answer is still no. Ask any man his opinion on the subject, and he will agree.

Does a man always throw a lighted cigarette away when he meets a woman acquaintance on the street?

Yes, he does, if he stops to chat. If he merely bows a greeting and tips his hat, continuing on, it is not necessary.

Does a man (or a woman either, today, for that matter) ask permission to smoke when in a group?

Under certain conditions, yes. If no one in the group is smoking, ask permission. Obviously, if some of those present are doing so, it is not necessary.

If you are a guest in someone's home and there are no ash trays around, what do you do?

Your host either doesn't approve of smoking or prefers not to have it done in the home. Take the hint. Don't even ask if you may. Just don't.

If you are dining at the home of friends, and ash trays are placed on the table, is it permissible to smoke between courses?

No. Wait until the meal is over. Even if some do, they shouldn't. Some folks just don't like smoke blowing around when dining, and are too polite to say so.

Do you smoke your own cigarette if offered others in the home of friends?

You will be rude if you do. Even if it is a brand you particularly dislike, accept the hospitality offered. Keep your own in your pocket.

May a man smoke when escorting a woman on the street?

No. This just isn't done.

Do the same rules hold true for the cigar or pipe smoker as for the cigarette smoker?

Even more so. A cigar should never be smoked during a meal. And never chewed, or clamped between the teeth, while talking. Pipe smokers should ask permission before lighting up in the home of friends. Your ambrosial briar may smell like burning rubber to others.

What are the bad habits smokers must guard against?

Showing a disregard for the non-smoker—this is unforgivable. He may even be allergic to it. Try not to blow smoke in his direction (or anybody's for that matter).

Talking with a cigarette drooping from the mouth is unsightly and rude. It should never be between the lips except when actually taking a puff.

Tamping out a cigarette on anything other than an ash tray is unforgivable. Used tumblers, coffee cups, or plates, decorated with stubs and ashes, are nauseating to say the least.

Don't scatter your ashes over yourself, your chair, the carpet.

Not chaperoning your cigarette—just letting it go out on its own—is dangerous. Charred furniture is but a minor result of leaving lighted cigarettes behind you. It can bring fire and death.

To balance a cigarette on the side of an ash tray, or place it on the edge of a table, is inexcusable—and dangerous.

To smoke while dancing is the worst possible exhibition of "no" manners. It can also be disastrous should the cigarette brush against a filmy gown.

Of course one never smokes when visiting the sick, even if asked to do so. Only if the patient is smoking is it permissible for the visitor to do so.

Borrowing a cigarette if you have run out is all right, within reason. The habitual borrower is a nuisance. Make it a point to keep yourself well supplied.

COURTESY IN DAILY HABITS — DRIVING

Why is courtesy while driving important?

Once he is behind the wheel of a car, even the most courteous person will sometimes lose all consideration for others, became belligerent and ornery, and take unnecessary risks to outdo other drivers. The mechanical side of driving and the courtesy with which one does it are so closely interwoven that they are practically one and the same. Therefore, it would seem obvious, based on the harrowing death toll on our streets and highways, that a road test on courtesy should be an obligatory part of the examination for a driver's license. As this, unfortunately, is not the case, try yourself out on the following basic rules of road courtesy:

Do you make a left-hand turn from a right-hand lane, or vice versa?

Aside from being an outright violation of traffic rules, this shows an utter lack of consideration for the other fellow.

Are you the driver who assumes that everyone else is a mind reader?

Failing to signal your intentions, turning right or left or

stopping as the spirit moves you, may land you—and unfortunately others—in the hospital.

Is it your habit to save that extra half second by beating a red light or going through on a yellow one?

This is one way of meeting people—those coming the other way who have the same idea.

Are you the road hog who saunters along at twenty miles an hour, refusing to allow others to pass?

If so, when finally persuaded to move over, you probably speed up as the other car attempts to go by. This may force the passing car to be trapped in face of traffic coming in the opposite direction.

Are you, worse yet, the most dangerous driver on the road, passing another car on an upgrade when it is impossible to know what's coming from the opposite direction?

This is a sure prelude to sudden death. Unfortunately, not just yours.

If you see someone backing into a precious parking space, do you drive in nose first, blocking the other car?

This is despicable.

Have you ever, when parking, blocked the car in front or back of you so that it cannot possibly get out?

There should be a huge fine for those guilty of this selfish act.

Most important, do you ignore the rights of pedestrians?

To leave one stranded in the middle of the street by starting up immediately when the light changes is inexcusable. To make a fast turn, just missing someone stepping off the curb, is another serious offense. You won't miss someday. Speeding through a mud puddle, splashing all those on the curb, is not thoughtless, it's mean. Oddly enough, you are probably the person who, when a pedestrian yourself, curses at the drivers.

And finally, do you glare, mutter epithets that do not have to be heard to be understood, even bellow at other drivers— sounding your horn when the car ahead does not leap forward on the very instant the light changes—or blast your horn as you pass another car?

This is most unnerving to its driver. As for you—you're impossible!

COURTESY IN DAILY HABITS — AT CHURCH

Are there special rules of courtesy one must observe in church?

An attitude of decorum and reverence is so implicitly a part of church attendance that it needs no elaboration. But there are small actions that one sees, occasionally, that could stand correction.

EXAMPLE:

When we arrive early for church services or for a wedding and find desirable seats on the aisle, are we required to move over and relinquish these seats when latecomers enter the pew?

Either move over or stand up and give them room to get by. Remaining seated and turning your knees to one side won't do it.

Must one follow the usher regardless of where one chooses to sit?

At regular church services you can indicate to the usher where you prefer to sit. But follow him by all means. Don't let him lead the way to a seat and then find you have chosen a place several rows back.

What do you do with your wraps?

Fold them and lay them on the seat beside you if there's room; if not, hold them. Don't throw them over the back of the pew into the faces of those sitting, or kneeling, behind.

What about taking children to church?

Until they've reached the age when they can behave themselves they should be left at home. Wiggling, whining, crying, running about are unwelcome distractions to those who are absorbed in the service. (You might help to organize a church nursery, where mothers could alternate in caring for the children during services.)

Any special notes on clothes?

Simple and dignified attire should be the rule. If gloves are worn by women they should be kept on, except when taking Communion. A man removes his gloves upon entering the church. Whether a woman wears a hat or not would seem to depend upon the custom followed by your faith. It seems fitting, however, that a hat should be worn if merely to add to the dignity of your appearance.

If unavoidably late for services, what is the best thing to do?

Make every effort to enter as quietly and inconspicuously as possible. If you arrive in the middle of a prayer, wait until it is over, and then seat yourself near the back of the church.

If going into a church that is new to you?

In some churches certain pews may be reserved. If attending a church for the first time, do not seat yourself without asking an usher to guide you to a pew not reserved for a church member.

If you know you will have to leave before the services are over?

Sit near the back of the church, and preferably make your departure during the singing of a hymn.

If you see someone you know?

Obvious greetings to friends while in church is definitely in bad taste. A nod and a smile are sufficient recognition.

COURTESY IN DAILY HABITS — OTHER MANNERS

What is the main thing to watch with regard to the radio and television?

Never inflict either upon those whom you invite to be guests in your home. Nothing is more irritating to a guest than to try to make conversation by yelling over and above the blaring sound that may go on and on with the hosts completely oblivious to the annoyance being caused. Unless you especially invite people for the purpose of listening to a particular radio or television program, have the instruments turned off as the guests arrive—and leave them off until they take their departure. If the guests themselves suggest one or the other be turned on, go ahead. Otherwise, off. If you miss something you wanted to see or hear, it's just too bad.

If an uninvited visitor drops in while you are listening to a program in which you are particularly interested, what then?

Explain that it is something you want to hear or see and ask that they join you. "Come in and listen if you care to, it will be over in half an hour." The visitor can either do so or go on his way.

REMINDER: All of the above applies to your hi-fi record player, too—not everyone shares your interest in opera, or rock and roll.

COURTESY IN DAILY HABITS — PETS

Is there anything special to guard against when you have pets in your home?

Never forget that a newcomer to your home may be downright afraid of that dog you love so much—he also may be allergic to him. There are many people who cannot stand being around a cat, call it allergy or what have you. (In both cases—you don't understand why—but maybe it's the same as your aversion to high places.) To guard against offending the newcomer, always ask immediately upon his entrance whether or not he minds animals. If he is honest, he will say so—yes or no. If it's "yes," shut them up until he leaves, and don't make a to-do about doing it either!

Never allow Fido to jump on people, lick their faces, or otherwise get in their way. While folks may like animals, they do object to having dog (or cat) hair festooned on their clothes or runs put in their stockings. It takes a little time and patience to teach Fido his manners, but it can—and should—be done. If not, enjoy him by yourself.

Should you take a dog or cat along when you visit friends?

Only if invited to do so, or if you are on very familiar terms with them. If you do take him, make sure he stays on the floor —not on the furniture.

JUST US HUMANS

JUST US HUMANS — CHILDREN

How does one teach a child courtesy?

When a child hands you a toy, never forget your "thank you." When you ask him to do something, always say "please." Sooner or later he will be doing the same thing automatically.

"I'm sorry" and "excuse me" are more or less interchangeable. They can be taught only by example. If you trip over a child's foot, or by accident knock down the block house he has built, your "I'm sorry," or "excuse me," must be quick and sincere. Eventually it will become natural for him to do as you do, even if at the time he doesn't understand why.

He must be taught that a flat "no" or "yes" should never be the answer to a question. A "no, Mother," or "yes, Mrs. Green," is the proper way.

Not to interrupt when others are talking is another important lesson. If it is necessary, for a very good reason, permission should be asked first: "Excuse me, Mother, but the furnace man says he must see you."

Also point out that one person does not flatly contradict another.

Another bad habit to correct is a failure to reply to a question or a remark.

Begin as soon as possible to insist that a child address ladies as "Mrs. Green" and men as "Sir." It is up to you to decide whether or not he may call close friends of the family by their first names.

When guests arrive in your home, you stand to greet them. A gentle aside to Junior and Betsy that they should do the same will soon make it a habit. Also to say, "Excuse me," when passing in front of someone, and to remember that grownups should go through a door first.

How does one teach a child the important rituals of greeting and farewell?

Start early with just the word "hello" when he meets a stranger. Gradually, as his vocabulary increases, steer him into "How do you do?" By practice, he can learn to say, with a smile, "How do you do?" while shaking hands, with a slight bow of the head. This will help to put him on the road to social poise later on. If outdoors, the same procedure is followed, except that a boy must lift his hat in greeting. Little girls do the same without the hat, of course. In place of the small bow, some parents prefer that a little girl make a curtsey. Teach only a slight dip, with the right foot placed behind the left. If the right foot goes too far to the side, the child is thrown off balance, and a spill is the usual result, causing embarrassment. Invariably people laugh. A child doesn't like to be made ridiculous any more than you do.

When outdoors, a farewell is a simple "Good-by, Mrs. Jones"; in your own home, the same; when leaving the home of another, "Good-by, Mrs. Jones, I had a nice time."

As soon as Junior is old enough to bring his little friends to the house, make it understood that each one must be brought to Mother to be introduced—"Mother, this is Jimmy." It will pave the way to an easy manner when presenting one person to another. Also, now is the time to make it clear to him that toys or cookies should be shared and that his guest has first choice of games to be played.

A child at five, or even four, is not too young to begin learning how to be a host. EXAMPLE: At his birthday party he should be made to understand that he is to greet his guests, thank them for their presents, and say good-by.

Also teach him how to behave when the situation is reversed and he visits the home of others. This can best be arrived at by a game of "make-believe." Re-enact what is expected of him by making a game of it at first.

What other rules of social behavior should a child learn?

It is no longer fair to insist that a child be seen and not heard. He should be allowed to express his opinions and tell of his adventures during the day. Not, however, at the table, except in a minor way. He must not be allowed to take over the conversation, especially when guests are present, whether at table or otherwise.

Always be fair and tell a child what to expect beforehand. If it is a new experience, such as guests for dinner, a birthday party, or maybe a trip to a restaurant, explain what is going to happen so he will not be bewildered and frightened. A tantrum is often the result if he is unprepared.

Make it very clear that noisy behavior in public places is out—definitely. But don't blow up in the super-market when he lets go. Wait until you are home. Then explain, quietly, why he shouldn't.

Teach him to respect others' privacy. He must learn not to enter a room when the door is closed without knocking first.

Also he should learn to respect another's belongings. This can be taught if you show him the courtesy of respecting his possessions such as the dog-eared Teddy bear and his other toys. The principle of "don't touch" is one of the hardest things to get across. Those shiny things on the cocktail table are irresistible. The minute he can toddle, start to impress him (as kindly as possible) that those are your possessions and "don't touch" means just that. Once accomplished, understanding will prove invaluable when visiting the homes of friends.

If he pops out with a naughty word, don't be upset. It's normal. He's bound to pick up one or two. (Make sure you are not his model!) Making a to-do will only implant it in his mind. Explain that it would be better if he didn't use the word. After a few quiet reminders he'll forget it.

If you take Junior along when visiting friends, make your stay short. He won't, he can't, sit still while you enjoy yourself. He's not made that way. This also applies to church. He simply cannot sit quietly through a long service. If you can't get someone to baby-sit, stay home. It's better all around.

Never allow a small child to sit at table when you have company for meals. It's an imposition on your guests and unfair to the child. Feed him and put him to bed early.

If you have company and want to show him off, go ahead. But make it brief. Above all, never force him to recite pieces, sing, or perform in any way. Also, don't ask the child to bid everyone good night. Leave it up to him. If the guests are middle-aged, be unusually careful. They are not used to the chatter, the bids for attention, the running and, inevitably, the wailing. They appreciate very quickly that he's as cute as a button, but a little goes a long way.

Remember, if you are rude or snippy to the milkman or to the day worker, little Junior will see no reason why he cannot act the same. Being polite to those who serve him is one of the first things that should be taught any child.

What should a child learn to say when answering the doorbell or the telephone?

Let him begin by going to the door with you when you answer it. Teach him how to greet people he knows and doesn't know. For example, if he answers the door when you are otherwise occupied and it is someone he knows, he should learn to show the person into the living room, then tell you. If it's a stranger, he must know how to be courteous, but still leave the person on the doorstep until he calls you.

As for the telephone—be kind to your friends. *Never* let him answer the telephone until he knows how to do it properly. Keep the real article away until that time arrives. Play games. Teach him by talking to him on a toy phone. He will learn, but until he does, put the real telephone on the mantlepiece, if necessary.

How does one teach a child good table manners?

Patience is indeed a virtue here. Don't expect too much at first. It's all a matter of time. At about a year and a half let him make efforts to feed himself with a spoon. The results will, of course, be messy. Don't worry if he puts his hand into his food. He's experimenting with self-feeding. Eventually, by gentle prompting and assistance, he will understand what the spoon and other eating implements are for. However, you can expect the fingers to do most of the job for a while.

Never force him to eat. Put a little at a time on his plate, adding more if he wants it. Don't make mealtime a battle time. He enjoys this. He is attracting attention. If he won't eat, take the food from him without comment. He probably wants it and will stop acting up when he finds that it is going to be taken away. If this doesn't work, see a doctor. Make mealtime a happy time. Until Junior is old enough to handle his food fairly well, feed him before dinner. When he is at table, bring him into the conversation once in a while. But don't let him take over and don't spend the whole meal correcting him. Do all the teaching when he is with you alone. He must be taught by repetition that his hands and face have to be washed and his hair brushed before he comes to the table; that he must not chew with his mouth open, put too much into his mouth at one time, or tilt his chair back from the table. Take it easy in teaching him the other niceties to be observed when eating. Don't try to do it all at once or expect too much in the beginning.

If punishment is necessary, never "let the sun go down on

thy wrath." Make peace before bedtime—hear prayers and tuck him in. You are his world, and unless all is right with you all is wrong with him.

JUST US HUMANS — TEEN-AGERS

TO THE TEEN-AGER

Why is it important for teen-agers to be well mannered?

There is an old belief that we change every seven years of our lives. You are now entering the third seven—the most important of them all. Why? Because the pattern you set for yourself as you enter grown-up living is probably the one you will follow for the rest of your life.

Good manners are the open door to popularity—not only with those of your own age but with those of all ages. If you put this established truth at the head of the list in your "pattern for living," you can't go wrong, now or later. The simple, everyday courtesies and customs that the well-mannered person observes are so easy to learn, you have no one to blame but *you* if you don't. Start now and they will all become habits. Never forget, habits are hard to break! Might as well make them good ones while you're at it.

What rules should girls follow on dating?

Never be guilty of asking a boy to date you. He may accept, but he won't like it. Always wait for him to do the asking. Two exceptions: If you are giving a party, or are asked to bring an escort along to one to which you have been invited.

If you accept a bid for a date, and something better turns up later, stick to your first decision. If you don't, word has a way of getting around, and soon you won't have any bids at all.

If you refuse an invitation because you have other plans, do it graciously, and let the boy call again, if he wishes. Should you say no because you do not like the young man, be polite, don't snub him. If he calls two or three times and you refuse, he should take the hint.

If you accept a "blind date" in a group, be nice, even if you don't find the boy particularly appealing. You don't have to see him again.

If your date says, "Where shall we go?" never suggest an expensive spot. Maybe he can't afford it. Actually he should do the planning. He knows how far his pocketbook will expand. (If he ever asks for a loan—don't. And scratch him off your list.)

If asked to do specific things, such as dinner and the movies, dress for it. A sloppy sweater and skirt won't enhance you in his eyes, you may be sure. When he phones for a date, if he doesn't say what he has planned for the evening, ask him what he has in mind, just to be safe.

If you load your escort down with purse or gloves, compacts and odds and ends, he will be unhappy. Bulging pockets do not add to his comfort or appearance.

If, in your desire to be gay company, you talk and laugh loudly, act overly cute or silly, or are in any way conspicuous, you will definitely not go over. You will only embarrass your escort. As Horace said, "It's pleasant to act foolishly in the right place, but be sure of your place before you do."

If you are wise, you will always make every effort to allow your escort to perform the little courtesies which are his right. For example, don't barge through a door ahead of him. Let him open it for you.

If you can't learn to say a quiet "No, thank you," when offered an alcoholic drink, you are very foolish. Anyone who chides you for being a poor sport is one himself. Stick to your decision and know there is no reason for embarrassment on your part.

If attending a dance or a prom, remember that you always dance the first and last dance with your escort. Always introduce yourselves to the chaperones upon arrival, and say good night and thanks when you leave. Give your escort your special attention during the evening. Dance with dignity, and don't ask him to rhumba when he doesn't know how. Never wander off with other young men, and, above all, don't flirt with his best friend. No further date will be forthcoming if you do.

If you have been told to be home by midnight, it's up to you, not the young man, to suggest starting for home.

Can you avoid dissension with your parents about dating?

Tolerance, like charity, begins at home. For you to take the attitude that Mom and Dad are old fuddy-duddies only makes it difficult for all concerned. Remember, they were your age once, and are hoping only to make the road a little less bumpy for you. Try to listen and reason with them. You just might learn something. Two things particularly cause dissension. One, dating; the other, chaperones.

It's up to your parents to decide at what age you can start

dating in single couples. This is governed largely by local custom. However, if Mary's parents allow it at fourteen, and yours say you must wait until fifteen or sixteen, accept their ruling gracefully, not belligerently. They have their reasons. Try to respect them. The same rule applies to the curfew hour. If no dating on school nights, and eleven or twelve Friday or Saturday is their wish, abide by it. Your escort may protest, but he actually admires you for accepting your present edict in a gracious manner.

How important is the chaperone?

Do you resent the presence of a chaperone, feel she "puts a damper on a party and keeps you from doing the things you want to do"? If this is your attitude, the things you want to do are out of line. Granted that in days gone by chaperonage was overdone. Today chaperones are merely there to make sure things run smoothly, and to protect the reputations of you young ladies. Unfortunately, there are always "Mrs. Grundys" who see the worst in everything. It isn't a matter of lack of faith, or trust in you. It is to avoid adverse criticism, with the resultant damage to your reputation. Unfortunately, a reputation once earned pursues you through the rest of your life. Never forget this.

What's the best way to invite people to a party?

Invite your friends by phone, calling the girls first to ascertain which boys they would like to bring. Or you may ask a boy to bring a certain girl. Either way. Mother or some older person should be standing by when your guests arrive. After greeting them with you, she quietly disappears, to reappear once or twice during the evening. She is not there to police you and your guests, but is on hand because it looks better, and certainly she'll be handy in case somebody gets out of line.

How can you be a successful hostess?

Never confine your attention to one group. Mingle. If the party begins to lag, have contests or games on hand to start things rolling again. Never try to outshine your feminine guests, or to make yourself irresistible to their boy friends.

What clothes are correct for teen-agers?

The right clothes at the right time are important to your poise and self-assurance. An oversophisticated gown, too-high heels, and a fancy hair-do will make you conspicuous and uncomfortable. If your budget is limited, plan your wardrobe with simplicity as the keynote. The following will help:

FOR SCHOOL: Sweaters and skirts, suits or tailored dresses. Leave the dressy ones and high heels at home where they belong.

FOR DATES: If going bowling or to the movies, a sweater and skirt, or the clothes you would wear to school are perfectly acceptable. If going to dinner and then the movies, dress up a little, but not too much. Wear a conservative after-noon dress, high-heeled shoes (not too high), and you will be appreciated and admired. For informal evening parties at someone's home, the same outfit is tops.

FOR FORMALS: Such as proms and dances. An evening dress, naturally, but go slow. It mustn't be too naked looking. A strapless dress is permissible if not so low and so snug that you bulge over the top. The young man taking you out wants to be proud of you, not embarrassed.

SLACKS AND SHORTS: There's a time and place for these. For sports, yes. In your own back yard or your friends' back yards, yes. On the street, no, that is, if you have any sense of the fitness of things. Particularly the shorts.

What make-up is correct for teen-agers?

Go easy. Avoid stagey make-up. As you are blessed with young, pretty skin, forget the eye shadow, make the powder light, and skip dark-tone lipstick and dramatically drawn lips and eyebrows. It is much better to correct a poor complexion than to slap make-up on over it.

Nothing is more disillusioning to a man or boy than to see you fix your make-up in public. Do your freshening up in the powder room. Try not to fiddle with your hair. Looking in your mirror every few minutes makes you seem unsure of yourself.

What rules should boys follow on dating?

It is your prerogative to call a girl and ask for a date. Never ask one whom you have not met by claiming to be "a friend of a friend of hers." This is really putting it on a pickup basis, and is actually insulting to the girl you are calling. If your offer of a date is refused and it sounds sincere, wait a week or so before calling again. After the third refusal, give up. It is obvious that she does not want to date you and is being embarrassed by your persistence.

If asked to join a friend and his date, and to escort a girl whom you have not met, what are your obligations? To be gracious and attentive even if you don't like her! You are being extremely rude and unfair if you do not.

When you extend an invitation, be specific. Don't say "what are you doing Friday night"? "Could you have dinner with me and then go to a movie on Friday night?" is much better manners. Make it clear that you are planning bowling, skating, or what have you, so that she will know what to wear. High heels and dressy dresses do not lend themselves to bowling, for example. Base your plans on the state of your finances. Never borrow from the girl you are escorting. If a coke and a movie are the limit, so be it. If even these are too much, it is all right to ask if you may spend the evening with her at her home.

If you call for her in a car, do not use the "honk and holler" technique when you arrive at her home. Go to the door. Greet her parents, if they are present, and chat with them for a few minutes before leaving. TIP: If her parents ask that you bring her back by midnight, or any specific time, see that you do just that.

If escorting a young lady to a special occasion, such as a dance or a prom, wait for her at a prearranged spot when she goes to the ladies' room; never leave her stranded for one second during the entire evening. Introduce her around—if you wanted her alone you shouldn't have brought her; dance the first and the last dance with her; if cutting in is allowed, let her get around the floor at least twice before you cut back. Never make her conspicuous in any way—such as by erratic dancing, or by spending too much time at the punch bowl, or flirting with her best girl friend. When she wishes to leave (it's up to her to say when), be sure to go with her to say good night to the chaperones before you get your coats.

If corsages are in order, ask her the color of the gown she is going to wear. Red roses on an orange dress are far from attractive, and it would be ungracious of her not to wear them. If in doubt, make it gardenias. They are always safe.

What are the other rules of courtesy a boy should remember?

Many of you are guilty of not observing one irrevocable rule—to stand immediately when a woman, young or old, enters a room. You brand yourself as definitely no gentleman if you do not do so. Stay standing, too, until she sits, and rise again when she does. This does not apply, of course, at a big party where many people are coming and going.

You also rise when an older man enters the room. Allow him to precede you through a door, just as you would a woman, unless he asks you to go first. Never call an older man by his first name, unless he specifically asks you to do so. Always address him as "Sir" or "Mr. Brown."

It is to be fervently hoped that you never boast about your conquests or discuss women of any age at any time with your friends. You may think it's smart. It isn't. No man who thinks of himself as a gentleman ever does, in any circumstances.

For the general courtesies you follow, see the Index and observe the rules given for "A Man and His Manners." You are one now, remember?

How can teen-age boys and girls build up their popularity?

If you consider it beneath your notice to acquire the little courtesies and social forms that represent good manners in everyday life, you are just plain stupid. Self-assurance and poise can never be attained unless you are thoroughly familiar with the niceties to be observed in daily contacts with people, all people, not just those your own age.

Are you making an effort to overcome a feeling of shyness? Learn what to do when, and then you can forget yourself. Once you gain an easy, natural manner, through being sure of yourself, you will forget all about being shy.

Show interest in other people. Avoid the use of "I" as much as possible. It's nice when someone is modest, and considerate of you, isn't it? Return the compliment.

Make your conversation interesting. With newspapers, radio, and television there is no excuse today not to have plenty to talk about. Keep up on world affairs and daily happenings. Never let your conversation revolve around Mary said this and John did that. Interesting, of course, but it has its saturation point.

Do you avoid too personal questions?

When you are in the wrong do you apologize, or do you try to alibi?

In your gossiping with friends about friends do you try to be kind? Unjust criticism and untrue tales can cause deep hurt to others.

Are you always agreeable about joining in the fun? Never try to be the life of the party—but, on the other hand, don't always come up with a different idea than that suggested by the gang.

Are you a good sport and a good loser? To accept your honors without being a braggart and your losses without excusing them is a worthy achievement.

Try not to be guilty of any of the following, all of which show an utter lack of consideration for the other fellow:

Walking four abreast along the sidewalk, forcing others into the gutter.

Ganging up in drugstore doorways so people have to fight their way in.

Loud comments and laughter when attending a movie or eating in your favorite hamburger hangout.

Indulging in petting when attending a movie—revolting all those near you, in addition to obstructing their view.

JUST US HUMANS — PROMS, SUBSCRIPTION DANCES, AND SCHOOL DANCES

What are tips to remember when attending proms, subscription dances, and school dances?

There are no set rules covering what is expected when attending any of these functions. The reason being that schools may differ, one from the other, in the procedures to be followed. It is therefore advisable to ascertain what is expected of you before attending. This is accomplished by frankly asking the person who has invited you. In this way it is easy, among other things, to find out what is expected to be worn for a given function. EXAMPLE: Some school dances may call for a dressy afternoon gown for the young ladies and a dark suit for the young men. On the other hand, a prom usually calls for an evening dress and a tuxedo.

If a dance is given by a girls' school or a sorority, who pays for the tickets?

The girl pays for her own and her escort's ticket.

What is expected of the young man in this case?

He is responsible for transporting her to and from the party. If corsages are expected, he must not forget this important item. Should a stop be made on the way home to have hamburgers and cokes, that's his responsibility, too.

What should the young man do when escorting a girl to a fraternity dance or one at his school?

Much the same, only in this case he of course purchases the tickets as well.

If the college or school is situated far enough away from the girl's home to necessitate travel and living accommodations during her stay, who pays for what?

The girl pays her transportation and living accommodation expenses. It is perfectly proper for the young man to arrange reservations for her and he will undoubtedly choose one in a private home acceptable to the school, or, if in a hotel, he will make sure that she is placed with other girls attending the party. Chaperonage should also be arranged.

If the situation is reversed and the young man is attending a prom at a girls' school, what then?

It all depends. He may either go to a hotel or perhaps the school has selected homes in which he may stay. The girl may make a reservation for him. He is responsible for all expenses except in a case where tickets for definite functions are necessary, then the young lady would supply these.

JUST US HUMANS — YOUNG LADIES VISITING ANNAPOLIS AND WEST POINT

Who pays for what when it comes to transportation to and from and living accommodations while weekending at Annapolis or West Point?

The girl pays travel and hotel expenses. It would be completely wrong to expect an escort to assume responsibility for either one.

Is it proper for the man to make a reservation for you?

Yes. At Annapolis he may (and usually does) select one of the approved guesthouses that are run in many cases by widows of naval officers. In a given weekend such a woman may have ten or twelve young ladies as her guests. The price is nominal. Not only does she give them comfortable lodgings, she also performs the important duty of acting as chaperone while they are under her roof. There is also the famous old hotel Carvel Hall where several girls may take rooms together. At West Point a Cadet usually endeavors to make dormitory reservations at the United States Hotel Thayer, which is on the Reservation. If unable to accomplish this, he will do so at approved quarters in nearby Highland Falls. It is the wise girl who prefers the group arrangements rather than going to a hotel by herself. The young men may kid about chaperonage but you go up in their estimation when you have it and down when you don't.

Is there a special thing to remember when with your drag (escort)?

Very definitely—yes. The way you behave is all-important. To do anything that will bring censure on him is unpardonable. If you cause him to break any of the rules by which he must abide, it means demerits for him. EXAMPLE: He has to report at quarters at certain times. Don't let any action on your part delay his making it on time. You must follow the strict etiquette rules laid down or it will mean no future weekends for you. Ask your drag what is expected of you— and do just that.

What are some of the things to guard against?

Never ask, or expect him to spend money on you. Both Midshipmen and Cadets receive an extremely small amount of spending money each month. The personal financial background of each man has nothing to do wih it. While in the Academies he is allowed spending money of a certain amount and no more. It is an accepted practice that the girl herself may "treat" upon occasion. The only rule to follow if this is done is to do it without being too obvious.

Taking a drink by any member of either Academy is strictly forbidden. To do so means extreme penalties and demerits. Even beer is taboo. As this is the case, the girl who does imbibe during her stay is making a bad mistake.

Watch the clothes you wear. Put the accent on simplicity of line and avoid overdressing. An extremely low-cut evening gown can fail dismally to give that glamorous look you are praying for and instead cause intense embarrassment to your escort. Also go easy on too much make-up or jangling jewelry.

If engaged to your drag, be sure there is no public display of affection. Handholding or arms about waists is strictly out.

Never ask for "souvenirs." Insignia or buttons, if given to you, have to be replaced and paid for by the man himself. It might mean a whole month's spending money. Above all, never suggest that he give you a "miniature" of his ring. You are actually proposing marriage if you do!

JUST US HUMANS — LADIES

Why is it important for a woman to have good manners?

It was a wise person who said, "Manners, not gold, are woman's best adornment." If you go your way with dignity and follow simple, gracious rules of behavior, you can't go wrong. You will be a lady in the full sense of the original meaning of that most misused word.

When does a woman bow?

If you do not wish to stop when passing someone you know (man or woman) on the street, a slight inclination of the head (don't duck!), accompanied by a smile of recognition, is all that is necessary. You bow when recognizing friends across the room, in a restaurant, at the theater, in church, or any other public place. If you meet a male acquaintance on the street, or in a public place, it's up to you to indicate whether you wish to stop and speak. If you do so wish—take no chances. Bow, walk toward him, with hand outstretched. He will probably keep right on going if you don't follow this procedure.

When does a woman rise?

Stand to greet your hostess when she first enters the room upon your arrival, if she did not greet you at the door. A young woman should stand immediately upon being introduced to a woman, obviously much older than herself. Watch this. Women are touchy about their years, you know. If your age bracket is comparable to the person to whom you are speaking, you may offend rather than honor when, by standing up, you imply that you are younger than she. Safer to sit tight if you are not sure. You may forget age, however, if the woman is a distinguished personage. In that case, rise immediately. Never rise for a man unless he is of high rank in the government, or the clergy, or is very, very elderly.

On the street?

When walking with an escort, always take the inside track, letting him walk on the side near the curbstone. He belongs there. Even if there is another woman with you, and only one man, you both take the inside. You take a man's arm lightly when he offers assistance over the rough spots, such as curbstones. Let go when the need is over. Don't cling and continue holding his arm while walking.

Should you get into an automobile first when escorted by a man?

Yes. He should assist you by holding your elbow as you get in. If another woman is present and you are sitting on the back seat, one woman sits on the left side of the car, the other sits on the right, the man in the middle. He gets out first, assisting you both to alight.

What about getting on or off streetcars or busses?

You enter first, getting off last, to allow your escort to step down and assist you to alight. However, rather than push people around, get off first if necessary.

What about elevators?

You follow somewhat the same procedure as on busses and streetcars. Go first when entering, but if it is crowded it is only common sense that the man exit first. Otherwise, you would be forced to shove people around trying to get past him.

Who goes first on a stairway?

You lead the way up, the man following behind. However, if the stairs are very steep, he may correctly walk with you, holding your arm and assisting you, that is, if the stairs are wide enough. Coming down, follow the same procedure unless the stairs are steep, in which case he goes ahead of you (so if you fall he will act as a cushion). If the stairway is wide enough, he may walk beside you, holding your arm.

Should the woman lead the way down or up a theater aisle?

Going down, if your seats are reserved, you follow the usher, your escort bringing up the rear. If the seats are not reserved, it is up to you to choose where you want to sit, and you again go first. On the return trip up the aisle, you lead the way, your escort following.

What is the procedure on entering a restaurant or night club with an escort?

It is your prerogative to choose the table at which you sit. You indicate this to your escort, who in turn tells the headwaiter, who leads the way to the table. The waiter holds your chair and seats you. If there is no waiter, you go to the table of your choice, and your escort performs this service.

How do you give your order?

To your escort, who in turn gives it to the waiter.

If you go to the powder room?

Place your unfolded napkin on the table at the left of your plate, saying in effect, "I would like to freshen up a bit." Your escort should rise, go behind you, and pull out your chair. He does not go to the door with you. He should be waiting to help you be seated when you return. (SUGGESTION: Make your stay as short as possible. Taking forever to primp won't make you popular.)

Who makes the move to leave?

It is up to you to suggest that it is time to go—and always take it into consideration if the next day is a working day, if not for you, perhaps for your escort. A reasonably early departure may lead to future invitations.

What other points of good manners should a lady remember?

Do you conduct yourself with dignity and decorum at all times? Genteel, modest behavior is a most valuable attribute. Avoid making yourself conspicuous.

Loud talking and boisterous laughter are out of place *any* place. So is a display of gushing affection, with embraces and kissing.

How do you sit in a chair? Gracefully—in a relaxed and dignified manner—or do you sprawl?

When in a restaurant, do you make a dressing table of the dinner table? Redoing make-up or combing hair at the table is unpardonable. And aside from the bad taste, it demonstrates your unsureness of manner and appearance. It is all right to apply a little lipstick when the meal is over—if it can be done in an inconspicuous manner.

Do you deprive your escort of the privilege of performing the small courtesies—for example, do you go through a door before he can open it for you, or light your cigarette while he is fishing for his matches? A woman's show of independence in such situations is not endearing.

What about clothes?

First query yourself on these matters:

Are you possibly guilty of overdressing—too many buttons and bows, veils, curls, frills, jewelry? Simplicity and chic are very good friends. You never see one without the other.

Do you follow a fashion trend, even though it may not be becoming? Nothing can be more melancholy. Your skirt length, heel height, dress line, and color may reflect high fashion, but still may make you look ridiculous. *Know your style*—stick to it regardless of fashion fads.

HATS: Whether to wear a hat or go without is largely a matter of personal preference and local custom. On certain occasions a hat is indispensable to grooming and etiquette. AMONG THESE: Daytime weddings, luncheons, teas, receptions, cocktail parties. When entertaining in your own home, you never wear a hat. In a hotel or restaurant (except when evening clothes are worn) the hostess and women guests wear hats.

Always remove your hat in the theater, unless it is tiny. People behind you came to see the show—not your hat.

THE GLOVE QUESTION: On the street wear gloves. Not only do they enhance your outfit, they keep your hands clean. It is never necessary to remove them when you shake hands on the street. In a receiving line, it is up to you. But taking off the right-hand glove, at least, makes sense. It's friendlier to shake an ungloved hand, for one thing, and easier on your hostess, for another. She is wise to be gloveless, too. If there are many hands to shake, gloves may result in badly blistered fingers. Never, under any circumstances, keep either glove on when eating or drinking. Remove both of them. Not to do so is in extremely bad taste.

If invited before four o'clock?

For brunches, luncheons, and dessert bridges, a street-length tailored dress or suit, always worn with hat and gloves.

Four to eight?

An afternoon gown (dressy but not too much so) of street or ballerina—never ankle—length. Always hat and gloves. A "dressmaker" type suit may be worn. Teas, receptions, cocktails, and cocktail buffets are the usual entertainment during these hours.

From six on (informal)?

It depends. For most informal dinners, buffet suppers, evening get-togethers, an "afternoon" outfit is perfect. The hat may be left at home.

From six on (semi-formal and formal)?

Any evening party where "black tie" is indicated on the invitation means that you wear a dinner dress, not an evening dress. The actual difference is that the first covers you up more than the second. The dinner dress may be ballerina or ankle length, should have a modest neckline, and a suggestion, at least, of sleeves. For formal evenings, strapless and off-the-shoulder neckline may be in order. A gown that is cut too low is never in good taste. The floor-length gown is preferred for very formal functions. However, today the ballerina length is not frowned upon, particularly when worn by a young woman.

What about gloves for evening wear?

With a dinner dress, you may or may not wear them. It's up to you. If you do, they should be elbow length. With the formal evening gown, it is a must that gloves be worn. They should be very long, coming midway between the elbow and the shoulder. In years gone by only those of white kid were considered proper. Today pastel gloves of fabric to match the gown are not frowned upon.

Must these gloves be removed when eating or drinking?

Yes, even though it is a tough job getting them on and off. While severely criticized years ago, today it is considered permissible to bunch the hand part of the button glove at the wrist. Although rather unsightly, it does do away with taking off the arm part of the glove. Whatever you do, or how you do it, be sure to have bare hands when eating or drinking.

What should be worn at weddings?

DAYTIME WEDDING: Even for the morning wedding, the "afternoon" gown that you would wear for any after-four party is perfect. Pastel-colored gowns are preferred. Black used to be tabu, but today, with the exception of any close relative or members of the bridal party, it's all right. But don't overdo it. Wear a gaily-colored hat to pick things up. Hat and gloves a must, by the way.

EVENING WEDDING: For the informal evening ceremony and reception the afternoon apparel is still correct. Don't forget—hat and gloves.

FORMAL EVENING WEDDING: Usually at eight, followed by a reception—an evening dress, not too décolleté, over which a jacket or coat should be worn while attending the ceremony. A scarf should be taken along to cover your head while in the church. Both jacket and scarf may be taken off at the reception.

JUST US HUMANS — GENTLEMEN

What are the basic rules of courtesy for a gentleman?

The word "gentleman" is overworked, misused, and, all too often, misunderstood. During the years of the gay nineties the term "perfect gentleman" implied that to deserve the name a man had to be expert in the art of doffing his hat, clicking his heels, and bowing from the waist. Today the meaning of the word has been modified and a man who abides by the basic rules that govern social behavior, conducting himself with consideration and courtesy toward his fellow man, or woman, has earned the title of "gentleman." "Gentle, courteous, irrespective of conditions" is the literal meaning of the word, and it is extremely significant.

Many of the little courtesies that are expected of a gentleman have come down to us through the centuries. Take, for example, the hat. The traditions a man follows today have evolved from the age of chivalry, when it was customary for a knight in full armor to remove his helmet when entering an assembly of friends. The purpose was to signify that he felt safe in their presence. Today, lifting a hat is considered an act of courtesy and respect. The following rules should be adhered to:

1. If greeting a woman on the street, and assuming she has bowed first, lift your hat. Smile, say "How do you do?" and keep going, unless she stops. If she does stop, keep your hat off until the visit is over, that is, if the weather is fine. If it's stormy or a cold day, be sensible and put it back on.
2. If meeting another man, touching the brim of the hat is traditional. It's sort of a salute; never remove it.
3. In corridors of public buildings, keep your hat on. In crowded elevators, too. Actually, it's more considerate that way. If in an elevator in a hotel, apartment, or club, the hat should be removed, even if the elevator is crowded. This applies, of course, only if women are present.

Must a gentleman remove his gloves when greeting a lady on the street?

In years gone by it was considered rude if the right glove was not removed when shaking hands with a lady on the street. Today this has been modified. No longer must you struggle to get out of the glove while the lady waits. It is perfectly proper to keep the glove on. Make the handshake brief. If you wish to apologize—all right. It isn't necessary, though. If you do, say, "Excuse my glove," not "Pardon my glove."

May a gentleman ever appear on the street without a suit coat?

How you handle this problem is rather important. Dignity seems to depart from a man who appears minus a coat (and tie). Of course at home or among friends, it is up to you. It is to be hoped, however, that you never escort a woman in public without your coat, no matter how hot the weather.

When do you bow?

This custom has also come down through the ages. It is a

gesture of respect to the person whom you are greeting. The bow is almost second nature to most men. A very slight inclination of the body from the waist up is enough. Keep the head still. Bow when shaking hands, when greeting someone across a room, or when passing an acquaintance on the street. (Remember, if it is a woman, also raise your hat.)

When to stand or not to stand?

WHEN INDOORS: You should always stand when a woman comes into a room, and stay on your feet until she is seated. When she gets up, so do you. If a guest in someone's home, however, and the hostess urges you to stay put, do so.

REMINDER: To remain seated when ladies are standing is an indication that you either don't know any better or you don't care.

ON PUBLIC VEHICLES: Let your conscience guide you. However, if you can remain comfortably planted when an elderly or infirm woman, or one carrying a baby in her arms is standing, your conscience needs overhauling.

Where do you walk when escorting women on the street?

Always nearer the curbstone. This custom stems from the horse-and-buggy days, when my lady might be splashed by the horses going by. If accompanied by two women, stay there, not in the middle. Move to the center position only when escorting them across the street. Then resume your post by the curbstone.

How do you assist a lady along the street?

In the daytime do not offer your arm, except to an elderly woman, or unless the weather is bad. Of course you offer your arm or take her elbow when you are helping her up and down curbstones, but do not take her arm otherwise. In the evening you offer your arm, or lightly grasp her elbow. This ostensibly is to keep her from stumbling in the dark. Never grab her elbow and propel her along. You are simply offering assistance.

How else can you assist a lady when escorting her?

INTO A CAR: Always assist her in first. When driving, seat her, then go around to the driver's seat. When getting out, reverse the procedure. Go around and open the door for her. In a taxi, the lady goes first when entering, you first when leaving.

OPENING DOORS: You open doors, stepping back to allow her to enter ahead of you.

IN ELEVATORS: Lady first in and out. If crowded when getting out, you go first, as you will be nearer the door. Be sensible.

ON PUBLIC CONVEYANCES: Help the lady on ahead of you when entering. When leaving, go ahead if possible, to assist her down the step. Again, if crowded, be sensible. Let her go first if need be. Act in a manner that will bring discomfort to no one.

ON STAIRWAYS: Going up, you bring up the rear. Coming down, the same, unless the steps are very steep, then walk side by side, holding the lady's arm. If the stairway is too narrow to allow this, go first in order to catch her if she should stumble.

IN A RESTAURANT: You may indicate to the headwaiter the lady's preference regarding the table. He leads the way, the lady following, then you. The headwaiter holds her chair. If there is no headwaiter, you follow the lady to the table she indicates, and seat her, of course. When the menu arrives, ascertain her wishes and give both orders to the waiter. Later, should she go to the ladies' room, you do not escort her. Assist her to rise, and just be sure to be waiting when she returns. When departing, if the waiter does not pull her chair out, you do, and she leads the way out of the restaurant.

IN THEATERS: The lady goes ahead, following the usher down the aisle. If no usher, the same procedure is followed. Coming back up it is also the same.

What obligations do you incur with regard to returning hospitality after attending a party, if you are a bachelor?

A hostess seldom expects a bachelor to return in kind. If you make every effort to be a pleasant and helpful guest, that's all she expects or hopes for. But never forget the next day—the telephone call, a note, or flowers.

How should you entertain, if budget permits?

Circumstances, of course, come into this. A small dinner in your home, a restaurant, or night club, or a cocktail party are very fitting. None of these need a hostess.

What is expected of you if your hostess asks you to call for a woman guest?

Call for her, of course. Whether you know this person or not, telephone her and verify the time that you are to pick her up. It is also your obligation to take her home when the party is over. You are not expected to act as her escort for the entire evening. However, a little special attention on your part would never be frowned upon.

Are you financially liable in any way if a guest at a party in a restaurant or night club?

No. It is an extremely thoughtless host who puts you on the spot for any expenditure, other than a taxi, if necessary, to escort someone to and from the party.

When is full evening dress worn, and what does it consist of?

Full evening dress (white tie and tails)

WHEN WORN:

1. At a formal evening wedding, by both guests and members of the wedding party.
2. At a ball.
3. At the opera if seated in a box.
4. At a dinner or formal evening function, such as a reception, to which the invitations have been worded in the third person, and upon which appears in the lower left-hand corner "white tie."

Suit and accessories:

Tail coat of dull-faced worsted, either black or midnight blue. Silk facing on the lapels. The trousers have 2¼ inch stripes of fancy silk or mohair braid.

SHIRT: Stiff bosomed, made for one or two studs (either is correct).

COLLAR: Stiff winged.

TIE: White lawn or piqué bow. Lawn rarely used—material of tie should match as nearly as possible the material of the shirt front which in turn matches the single-breasted vest.

WAISTCOAT: White piqué *with revers*. May be single or double-breasted. Usually single-breasted.

HANDKERCHIEF: Fine white linen. If monogrammed, must be in white.

BOUTONNIÈRE: Usually white carnation.

SOCKS: Black silk.

SHOES: Patent-leather pumps.

JEWELRY: Pearl studs always correct. Plain white gold or silver cuff links. Avoid anything large and ornate.

HAT: Collapsible opera hat. Never a silk top hat.

GLOVES: White buckskin, if wearing overcoat. White kid for a ball or evening wedding.

MUFFLER: Always white, usually silk.

OVERCOAT: Black or midnight blue. (Latter preferred as it can also be worn for afternoon and semi-formal evening wear.)

What is correct for semi-formal evening wear?

TUXEDO: (dinner coat) Known as semi-formal evening attire. When worn? Never before six o'clock in the evening for any occasion whatsoever. Never for a white-tie formal function. It is worn for any evening party when the invitation contains the words "black tie" in the lower left-hand corner.

It is proper for opening nights and the theater, and dining in a first-class restaurant.

NOTE: It should not be worn by the men in a bridal party at any time—ever.

Suit and accessories:

COAT: Dull-faced worsted in either black or midnight blue. It is cut like a sack suit (no tails) and has one button at the waistline. (A double-breasted coat is also correct, but as no waistcoat is worn, it must be kept buttoned at all times.) The lapels may be either silk or satin-faced, and the collar is made of the suiting. (Except when it is a shawl collar.)

TROUSERS: Have a narrow ¾-inch-wide braid stripe on the sides.

SHIRT: Pleated. (Stiff is unusual today.)

COLLAR: Turndown.

WAISTCOAT: Very rarely worn—usually a cummerbund.

TIE: Black silk or satin bow (avoid large butterfly effects or string bean. Stick to the regulation size).

Handkerchief, socks, shoes, and boutonnière same as those for full dress.

GLOVES: none.

JEWELRY: Studs, cuff links, and waistcoat buttons may all match, but do be very conservative.

HAT: Black or midnight-blue Homberg. (It is proper to go hatless if you prefer.)

COAT AND MUFFLER: Same as full dress. Also any tailored dark coat may be worn.

White dinner coat:

Only for hot weather. It is double-breasted so a waistcoat is unnecessary. Trousers and accessories same as those worn with tuxedo.

White mess jacket:

Also for hot weather. White waistcoat or black cummer-

bund must be worn. Otherwise trousers and accessories same
as those worn with tuxedo.

When is a cutaway worn?

Even though worn in the afternoon, this is ambiguously
referred to as a "morning coat."

Worn at a morning, noon, or afternoon formal wedding
by members of the bridal party. May also be worn by the
guests if they so desire.

At church (still proper today, this old custom has practically died out except for Christmas and Easter).

Formal afternoon receptions. (Seldom seen today either.)

All daytime official functions or ceremonial occasions.

Suit and accessories:

COAT: Black, one button at the waistline, and with tails in
the back. Much in favor today, and equally correct, though
not considered quite so formal, is the black sack coat, which
has no tails. The accessories are the same.

TROUSERS: Gray and black stripe, or black with white pin
stripes.

SHIRT: White, soft-bosomed.

COLLAR: Stiff winged; very formal—for a cravat only. Stiff
turndown white collar is more usual.

TIE: An ascot of either gray or gray and white is correct
for weddings. Either a black-and-white or gray four-in-hand
may be worn otherwise.

WAISTCOAT: Gray double-breasted. Pearl gray for weddings. Same material ascot for funerals.

Handkerchief, socks, and boutonnière same as those for
full dress or tuxedo. (Always white for a wedding, of course.)

SHOES: Black calfskin, Oxford ties.

GLOVES: White buckskin preferred, but light gray also acceptable. Gray more usual.

HAT: Silk top hat, or gray top hat for summer wear.

COAT AND MUFFLER: Same as for tuxedo.

For what social occasions is it correct to wear a business suit?

For business but also for pleasure is the ever-useful dark
blue suit. Dark gray is also correct, but the blue is preferred.
Aside from business they may be worn:

When a guest at a wedding held at any hour of the day.

By the members of the bridal party for the informal ceremony, both daytime and evening.

For luncheons, afternoon receptions, teas, tea dances, cocktail parties, and all types of informal evening entertainment.

Accessories:

Always a white shirt with turndown collar.

Conservative four-in-hand tie.

Black (well-shined) shoes and socks.

Vest, of course, of the same material as the suit. This should be worn at all times. EXCEPTION: It may be discarded on a very hot day, but if so, keep that coat buttoned.

NOTE: For business, let your conscience be your guide. You can't go wrong if you are conservative, foregoing loud plaids or violent colors.

JUST US HUMANS — OFFICE MANNERS

Are good manners important in an office?

Manners are just as important in the office as in the drawing room. Even top-notch efficiency will not compensate for boorish habits and lack of consideration for others. To behave with courtesy, kindness, and tact in your business life is not subserviency or apple polishing—it is one of your best forms of job insurance.

What rules of behavior should the boss follow?

You do not rise when your secretary (or any other woman employee) comes into the room, nor do you hold a chair for her.

You do rise when a client or outside caller enters your office, be it man or woman. If a woman, you help seat her. If a man, he seats himself. You stand up and escort them to the door when they leave.

It is not considered impolite if you go through a door ahead of a woman employee.

It is not necessary to introduce your secretary to a visitor whom she may escort into your office. It's a gracious gesture, if you care to, however. If the caller is a man: "Miss Secretary —Mr. Client." If a woman, "Mrs. Client—Miss Secretary."

Do you try to instill a "happy family" atmosphere? Too much paternalism in office relationships is not good practice. Nor, of course, can you be cold and impersonal, as if your employees were office equipment. Hit a happy medium for a happy office force. A cheery "good morning" from the boss— "please" and "thank you," where in order, will do wonders for office morale. And try not to carry into the office the temperamental aftermath of last night's hangover or this morning's tiff with your wife. If you wait till near closing time to begin your dictation, and if you dictate through puffs of cigar smoke, you can depend on Susie Secretary to be on the lookout for a new job.

Check your telephone manners to see if they need polishing. When you ask your secretary to place a call for you, stick around till it's put through and resist that impulse to make another call in the meantime.

When you leave the office, say where you're going—or at least when you'll be back.

Whatever you may call your secretary in private, make sure it's Miss Jones or the proper equivalent when there's a possibility of being overheard.

While there is no positive rule about first names being used between office personnel, a business concern where "Miss Jones"—"Mr. Murray"—is the rule presents a more dignified front than the "Mary" and "Johnnie" approach. It's up to you, Mr. Boss, to set the example and make sure it's followed.

Of course, make an effort to see that your wife and other members of your family do not request favors of your secretary and, in fact, do not even come to your office except when strictly necessary.

What rules should employees follow?

Two thirds of your waking hours are spent with the same group of people, day in and day out. How do you rate with your co-workers? Maybe your courtesy is slipping. Let's do a little checking.

ARRIVAL: Always on time? Habitual lateness may not only get you in Dutch with the boss, but it is unfair to those with whom you work.

GREETINGS: Are they cheerful? If you have a headache, a hangover, or had a fight with your boy friend, take an aspirin, and smile, if it kills you.

YOUR SUPERIORS: Do you reply to them with a flat "No" or "Yes?" A "No, Mr. Smith," or "Sir," if you prefer, is more gracious. When Mr. Boss comes to your desk, it is not necessary to rise. Stop what you are doing and listen to what he has to say. Look at him while he does so. And indicate your understanding.

A habit of saying "please," "thank you," and "excuse me" can go a long way. Also such consideration as, "Do you mind if I open the window?" (If he does mind, don't.)

What are bad "office manners"?

Do you whistle while you work? Drumming on the table with your fingers, humming, singing, or whistling can drive your co-workers to distraction when they're trying to concentrate. Don't slam around and shout—be quiet.

If smoking is permitted in your office, do you overdo it? Don't smoke continuously. Keep your ash tray emptied and clean. Memo to the men: If some of your co-workers are women, this is one time when you let them light their own.

Overstaying in the rest room, at the coffee break; allowing members of your family or friends to visit you in the office; writing personal letters; making and receiving too many personal telephone calls are all bad "office manners." If Mr. Boss hasn't put his foot down, he will! So better reform first!

Don't be noisy! Be extremely careful not to intrude upon the privacy of others. EXAMPLE: "How much money do you make?" "Wasn't your husband married once before?" Such personal questions are out of order, as would be similar revelations about yourself.

Don't borrow. Habitual borrowing of lunch money, cigarettes, umbrellas, tissues, galoshes—whatever—is bad office behavior.

For the sake of appearance. To the ladies: Be scrupulously clean and well groomed. Try for the wholesome look rather than a night-club effect.

Stick to tailored suits or dresses. Spruce them up with scarves, crisp blouses, and a little simple jewelry. Avoid tight skirts and low necks. Go easy on perfume, heavy make-up, and too-fancy hair-dos.

And for goodness' sake go to the rest room to comb your hair and put on a new face. It's not desk work. Don't chew gum at the office. And always clear off your desk top before you leave.

What special points should the receptionist remember?

If a caller arrives to keep an appointment, he is greeted graciously and asked to be seated while you inform Mr. Boss of his presence. If you ask him abruptly for his name, and leave him standing while you meander to announce his arrival, you should be fired.

If someone calls who does not have an appointment, a salesman, or perhaps a person whom you know Mr. Boss does not wish to see, you should ease him out in a tactful manner, without letting him know he's getting a brush off. Mr. Boss must, of course, be shielded from unnecessary intrusion, but it can be done graciously. A courteous inquiry as to the nature of the visitor's business and a polite "I'm sorry, but Mr. Boss cannot see you at this time," "If you will telephone later for an appointment," are much better approaches than "He is tied up now. Good-by."

It might be mentioned here that it is wise to avoid the hackneyed "in conference." This covers a multitude of sins, but is overdone and an overfamiliar excuse. Better a simple "Is unable to see you now," "Is busy at this time," or just plain "Out."

If the procedure followed at your office is that either the receptionist or the secretary escorts a client to the boss's door, she should then open it, let the client pass in front of her, say his name, and then, when Mr. Boss rises to greet him, back out and close the door.

The telephone operator?

Your role is an important one. The cheerful, well-modulated voice, coupled with an effort to make each caller feel that he is important, can go a long way toward helping business relationships. Failure to handle business calls expeditiously and courteously can reflect most adversely on any business organization.

If a call came in as follows, would you handle it in this way? You are right if you do.

OPERATOR Good morning. Robert Gray and Company.
CALLER   May I speak to Mr. Gray? This is Mr. Roy.
OPERATOR (If he doesn't give his name and he should) May I ask who is calling, please? (Never, Who is this?) Thank you, just a moment, please.

When asked to place an outgoing call for someone in your office, try to have him on the line when the person he is calling is reached. For example, Mr. Boss asks you to put a call in to Mr. Green, then hangs up while you place the call. When you get Mr. Green's secretary on the line, and she, in turn, is connecting him, signal Mr. Boss to go ahead. Avoid, if possible, getting Mr. Green on the line and having to say, "Just a moment, please. Mr. Boss would like to speak to you." If Mr. Green isn't irritated at this approach, he should be.

If someone is calling in, and is willing to hold the line if told that the person he is trying to reach is talking on another wire, be sure to follow through. Don't forget he's there. When able to make the connection, before doing so say, "Thank you for waiting."

What are good telephone manners for a secretary?

There are two correct ways to answer the phone: "Mr. Boss's office." Or "Mr. Boss's office, Miss Gray speaking." The person calling should, of course, then give his name. "Just a moment, please," is your answer. Acquaint Mr. Boss with the caller. If he wishes, he then takes the call. If he does not, handle the caller graciously. "I'm sorry, he is not available just now. This is his secretary. May I help you?" You can also ask if he would care to speak with anyone else. If not, delve further, and ascertain whether he wishes to leave a message. Never inquire as to what he wants to speak to Mr. Boss about. If the caller wants to tell you, he will.

JUST US HUMANS — BUSINESS CARDS

Can one use a social card for business calling?

Never. To do so is really going overboard in the bad-taste department.

What are the differences between business and social cards?

Those for business use are a little larger and may be either engraved or printed. Conservative black type should be used, such as block lettering. No script. That's for the formal social card. The paper is usually good white pasteboard or it may be thin parchment.

Are there any definite rules regarding what is placed on a business card?

No. It is more or less up to you, based on the circumstances surrounding the card you are planning to have either printed or engraved. You may use your own judgment, but remember to avoid flamboyant oversize lettering. This will tend only to cheapen your firm. Stick to a dignified presentation of the person's name, and whom he represents, and you can't go wrong.

What is usually placed on a business card for an official of a firm?

The full name, without the prefix "Mr.," is placed in the center of the card. The position that he holds is placed in the lower left-hand corner, and in the right-hand corner the firm, address, and telephone number, on three separate lines.

What appears on the card of one who represents a firm but has no official title, as for example, a salesman?

The card is the same as for the official with the obvious exception that there is no title in the left-hand corner.

JUST US HUMANS — CLUBS

What should you remember when desiring to join a club?

Clubs, both business and social organizations, have become such an important part of our lives that no book on manners would be complete without touching on some of the customs observed in connection with membership in such groups. Perhaps the manner of admission is of greatest importance, outside of purely professional organizations where the only requirement for membership is to engage in a certain type of business or to have achieved certain professional standing.

Where membership is invitational, that is, where you must be invited to join, be extremely careful about two things: One, don't allow your name to be put up for membership in a group that you don't know about. Find out who the officers are, learn something of the history of the club's activities, ascertain its dedicated purpose. Two, if there is an organization you are eager to join don't use pressure on mere acquaintances to sponsor you. It is all right to indicate an interest in a group, even to tell a close friend who belongs to it that you are interested and would enjoy being a member. But that's enough—if your friend doesn't take it from there, drop the matter. To pursue it might cause extreme embarrassment to either or both of you.

When asked to be listed as a "patron" of a charitable organization's fund-raising affair, what obligation is implied?

Not necessarily any, other than to lend the use of your name. However, if you think well enough of the project to give it your endorsement, it might be assumed that you would want to make a contribution, buy tickets, or offer to assist in some other way. Just be sure you know exactly what the organization is and what is expected of you before you grant permission for your name to be used.

How can one who doesn't want to seem "pushy" become active —and important—in an organization?

By observing the rules, by regular attendance at meetings, by volunteering for any job that no one else wants to do, and doing it well; by making only constructive suggestions, not criticisms, and by being invariably pleasant.

What traits invariably add to your chances of club leadership?

A knowledge of parliamentary rules—such as may be obtained from studying a handbook on the subject, or taking a course in it—is very valuable. Poise and the ability to speak in public, briefly and to the point, are most important. Try to remember names, and acquire a complimentary manner (without gushing, make people feel important); and smile, smile, smile!

What traits label one as "most unlikely to succeed" in club life?

Talking too much; carrying on chitchat with a neighbor when a meeting or entertainment is in progress; a whiny, unpleasant voice.

At a large affair may all of the club officers and their husbands or wives make up the receiving line?

It is better to have no more than six persons in the receiving line; others deserving of recognition may be asked to "assist about the rooms," which means making introductions and generally dispensing hospitality; they may wear some identifying symbol, such as a host or hostess badge, to give them "rank."

Other than mixing and generally being pleasant at a club social function, what are the routine duties of a member?

Never be tempted to by-pass the receiving line even if there's a wait. This is particularly rude at a party given "in honor of" a particular person or persons. Be assured they *do* notice when arrivals make a beeline for waiting pals or refreshment table without the formality of a how-do-you-do to those who are the reason for the get-together.

What are you responsible for if you bring guests who are not members?

Do not wander off, leaving them to fend for themselves. Make sure they are introduced to others and then escorted to the refreshment table.

Are there ways in which you can be helpful to make the gathering a success?

Yes. Remember that the loneliest guest at the party can be the one behind the coffee urn or teapot. It's an honor to be asked to "pour," but when there is a spell of no demand for her services the distinguished lady may find herself unhappily isolated at the table end. Be on hand for a few remarks and a second cup when you see this happen. Also you will be blessed if you will take on the job of "un-buttonholer" and go to the rescue of prominent guests who begin to look nervous after too-long sessions with the same people.

Do these rules also apply to men?

Some of the above applies to ladies only, but the rest of the pattern is basically the same. One particular suggestion: if a group of men is present at a stag function, it is always advisable to appoint an entertainment committee to see that all runs smoothly and that the guests, particularly those "of honor," receive the attentions that are due them.

What are the "musts" of club membership?

Pay your bills. Initiation fees and dues are paid immediately upon being accepted. Follow through by never allowing a club debt to become overdue. Next, obtain a copy of the club's bylaws. Learn the customs and rules and abide by them faithfully. Abusing club privileges can result only in general unpopularity and eventual expulsion.

What are some of the "don'ts" of club membership?

Avoid an overbearing or boisterous manner to cover up your nervous anxiety to "fit in." Never barge in on a group without being invited, or ask to "join in" a card, golf, or tennis game without a specific request from the players that you do so; if active in sports remember that whatever it may be "it's a good sport only if you are." Make sure that children, particularly small ones, are never allowed to annoy anyone. If the child is old enough to understand, it must be impressed on his mind what he can or cannot do when in the club. Permitting him to run loose through the main rooms or behave boisterously in the swimming pool is extremely unfair to the child and is about as thoughtless as you can get when it comes to your relationship with the other members.

How can you be sure that the clothes you wear are appropriate?

Shorts or slacks on the golf course, or in the main dining room—unless specifically permitted by the club—can be extremely out of place. Sloppy or too casual sports clothes for a fairly "dress-up" afternoon or evening party at the club also come under this category.

Take the time and the trouble to find out what should be worn when. You'll be a lot more at ease and happier if you do.

What is expected of you when attending a club for the first time as a guest of a member?

If your host is not kind enough to tip you off, ask him. Usually there is nothing much to worry about, as he will assume most of the responsibilities. The main thing to remember is never to overstep or abuse any guest privileges. You won't be invited again if you do.

If a visitors' book is to be signed upon arrival, how is it done?

Examples: "Mrs. John E. Sampson" (never use your given name) or "Mr. and Mrs. John E. Sampson."

If you arrive at the club ahead of your host, may you order refreshments while waiting for him?

Definitely not, unless the host has arranged ahead of time for you to do so.

Are there any financial obligations that you may have to assume?

Usually none. However, if tipping is allowed (in most clubs it is not), it is proper to tip the attendants in the checkroom and rest rooms. Also, if playing golf, always offer to pay your greens fee. If your host refuses to allow you to do so, let it go at that. He should not be permitted to assume the paying and tipping of your caddy. Those are up to you.

What about borrowing club privileges from a member?

It is a definite imposition on the member even to ask if you may do so. In most clubs members are billed for services and food and the member is expected to sign all chits. He has to ask special permission for a non-member to do this (in many cases this is forbidden). There is also the fact that the member, if he does get you in, is held responsible for any infractions of rules of which you might be guilty. Play safe and don't impose. The whole situation is one to avoid.

ENTERTAINING

ENTERTAINING — FORMAL INVITATIONS

What distinguishes the formal invitation from the informal?
The formal invitation is always engraved, never printed. It may also be handwritten, although this is seldom done today. The formal invitation is always issued in the third person. For nearly a century tradition has decreed that special wording be adhered to and the way in which the words are spaced also conforms to a set pattern.

For what type of entertaining is the formal invitation used?
For the formal luncheon, dinner, afternoon or evening reception (including those for weddings) and balls (usually referred to on the invitation as "a small dance").

What paper is used?
This varies with personal preference. A white, suède-finished card, measuring approximately three inches wide by four inches high is preferred.

May the address be engraved at the top?
Never. If handwritten, only a small monogram may appear at the top center. A monogram is not used if the invitation is engraved.

What lettering is used?
This is up to you. Avoid any that is large or ornate. Script or block is invariably in good taste. Always black ink, too, by the way.

Must every word be spelled out?
Yes. No abbreviations in names or words should be used. Even the date is given in full, as are street numbers.

How is the time of the function indicated?
If on the hour, "four o'clock." If on the half-hour, "half

after four o'clock," or "half-past four o'clock." (Never "four-thirty.") When a time limit is to be set for a party, such as a reception, it is indicated by "five to seven o'clock."

Example: formal invitation

Mr. and Mrs. Philip John Proper

request the pleasure

of the company of

Mr. and Mrs. Smith

at a reception

Monday, October tenth

Five to seven o'clock

The Ritz Hotel

The favour of a reply is requested
2850 Long Drive

What is a slightly less formal approach?

The phrase "requests the pleasure of your company" replaces that of "requests the pleasure of the company of." In this case, of course, it is unnecessary for the names of those invited to be written in. This form is used for semi-formal functions.

When requesting an acknowledgment, may any other phrase be used than that of "the favour of a reply is requested"?

Yes, the initials R.s.v.p. may be used, but they more generally appear on the informal invitation.

Is it necessary to request a reply when inviting people to a meal?

Actually no. It should be taken for granted by the recipient that when asked to dine an immediate reply is expected.

However, as people are apt to put off doing so, if not specifically told to, it is safer to request that answer. In the case of receptions, dances, et cetera, no reply is expected unless definitely asked for.

Is the address in the lower left-hand corner necessary?

Very much so. When the party is being held any place other than the home of the hosts, and an acknowledgment is requested, it is extremely important that the address where the reply is to be sent be indicated. If the party is to be given in the home, this, of course, is not necessary.

Must the question of what to wear always be indicated?

This is another case where it is better to be safe, thereby avoiding any chance of bringing embarrassment to your guests. Formerly, when nothing appeared on a formal invitation regarding clothes, it was taken for granted that it meant "white tie" or full dress for the gentlemen and evening clothes for the ladies. Today, so there will be no doubt in the minds of the guests, it is a kindness to clarify it for them. "Black tie" may also appear on the formal invitation. This indicates tuxedos and dinner dresses, and actually means that the function is to be of a semi-formal nature.

Must a specific form be followed when replying?

Yes. It should conform with the setup of the invitation itself. The reply should never be spaced as if it were a letter, and must always be handwritten.

Mr. and Mrs. Charles James Smith
accept with pleasure
the kind invitation of
Mr. and Mrs. Proper
to dinner
Monday, November tenth
eight o'clock
The Ritz Hotel

REMINDER: It is to be noted that on the invitation the full name of the hosts is given, and only the surname of the one invited. On the acknowledgment this is reversed.

Why is no mention made of the honor guests for whom a party is given?

This is not necessary. You are simply acknowledging your hosts' offer of hospitality.

What stationery should be used?

Only white (either single sheet or double) note paper will do. To use a calling card, informal fold-over card, colored stationery, or business letterhead is in extremely bad taste.

Must the reply always be handwritten?

Definitely *yes*. To use a typewriter is beyond the pale.

What wording is used if it is necessary to regret the invitation?

Replace "accept with pleasure" with, "regret that because of absence from town will be unable to accept," et cetera. Your reason for regretting may be "because of illness" or a "previous engagement." Whatever the cause, be clear as to why you can't make it. When regretting, it is not necessary to repeat the time, only the date.

How is the envelope addressed?

Until fairly recently it was directed to the hostess only. This is still preferred, but addressing it to "Mr. and Mrs." is not frowned upon today.

ENTERTAINING — AT-HOME CARD

Under what circumstances are these formal at-home cards issued?

They are suitable for debuts, weddings anniversaries, or for the formal afternoon tea or reception. Seldom, if ever, is a reply requested.

What paper is used?

A white, suède-finished card, measuring approximately five inches wide by four inches high, is preferred.

NOTE: Follow the same rules as those for the formal invitation (see page 161) with regard to engraving, lettering, et cetera.

Mr. and Mrs. Carroll James Gray
At Home

on Wednesday, December third
at four to six o'clock

Twenty-four Main Street

If the at-home card is used for a debut, how is the debut indicated?

The name of the daughter is included:

Mr. and Mrs. Carroll James Gray
Miss Elizabeth Mary Gray
At Home

   et cetera

NOTE: Should a party take the form of a tea dance or dance, the word "dancing" would be engraved or written in the lower right-hand corner.

What about a formal wedding anniversary celebration?

No indication of the anniversary need be made at all unless you wish. If you do, the years may be engraved on the upper right- and left-hand corners, above the invitation itself.

EXAMPLE: If for the twenty-fifth anniversary: 1934 on the left and 1959 on the right.

ENTERTAINING — SEMI-FORMAL AND INFORMAL INVITATIONS

Are informal parties more common today then they used to be?

During the last ten years parties have been leaning more and more to the informal ways of entertaining. Gone are the days when the formal dinner, and reception, for example, were the rule rather than the exception as they are now. The reasons are many for this trend. All of them make sense. To begin with, people in general enjoy the gay, informal parties more than the stiff, very formal ones. Also in these days of hard-to-get help and costly foods, it's much easier and less expensive for the hosts to entertain in this manner.

There are no rigid rules governing the issuing of invitations for the semi-formal and informal parties, such as there are for the formal. The main object is to make it clear to prospective guests, in a brief and courteous way, the kind of hospitality you are offering. The examples that follow are those that are in general use today. You can't go wrong if you adhere to them.

What forms of entertaining may come under the heading of "semi-formal or informal"?

Brunches, coffees, buffets, teas, cocktail parties, and cocktail buffets; semi-formal receptions (very close to cocktail buffets), semi-formal and informal dinners and evening get-togethers. (See Entertaining, page 186.)

May printed or plain white cards or stationery be used?

Yes. However, if you entertain quite often, the small expense of having your name and address engraved on cards is suggested. Reason: it's a little more dignified. If the information is written on a plain card, it should be done by hand, never typed. If a handwritten note, white stationery is best. There are also many attractive invitation cards for different types of parties that may be purchased at your stationer's. Two suggestions: be careful not to go overboard with too silly an approach to, for example, a cocktail party. Some of these cards border on the vulgar. Second: they should be used only for the very informal party.

Is it necessary that everything, including names, dates, and street numbers, be written out in full, as is the case with the formal invitation?

No. It is preferable to have only the name of the person issuing the invitation given in full (this should definitely be done if the card is engraved). Abbreviations may be used when wording the invitation itself. EXAMPLE: "Wed., Nov. 8th, cocktails 5 to 7."

Is it permissible to indicate that a party is being given in honor of someone?

Yes. While the formal phrase "in honor of" is sometimes used, the friendlier and less-formal phrases, "In compliment to" or "To meet" (followed by the name of the honoree), are preferred.

What invitation form, considered proper only for the semi-formal function in the past, is now used extensively for the informal as well?

Called the "fill in invitation," it has a wide variety of uses for those who entertain frequently. The words contained thereon should be engraved, using dignified lettering in black ink. The blank spaces are filled in by hand to fit the occasion. Usually a white card, measuring approximately 5½ inches by 4½ inches, is used.

Mr. and Mrs. Edward Coe Brown

request the pleasure of the company of

Mr. and Mrs. Smith

on Wednesday, November 7th

5 to 7 o'clock

R. s. v. p.   211 North Place

NOTE: The R.s.v.p. may or may not be engraved, as you see fit. If not, and the occasion arises when you do wish an answer, it is correct to handwrite these initials in the lower left-hand corner.

If your address is engraved on the card, and the party is being given someplace else, be sure to indicate where it is to be held, and in this case place the R.s.v.p. over the home address where you wish the acknowledgment to be sent.

How does the recipient answer this invitation?

It may be done in the same way as when replying to the very informal (see page 172). It is also correct to take a little more dignified approach and follow the setup of the invitation itself. Always written by hand, remember.

> *Mr. and Mrs. Daniel Dorn*
> *accept with pleasure*
> *the kind invitation of*
> *Mr. and Mrs. Brown*
> *for cocktails*
> *Wednesday, November 7th*
> *5 to 7 o'clock*

SPECIAL NOTICE:

For years the calling (or visiting) card has been used extensively for issuing informal invitations. Effective July 1, 1959, the Post Office Department passed a ruling that very small envelopes will no longer be accepted. They must measure 2¾ inches by 4 inches or more. As the largest sized calling cards never measure more than 2½ inches by 3½ inches, it seems clear that it would be wise to discontinue their use. However, if you still wish to use a calling card (the card itself is still correct), be sure to place it in an envelope the measurements of which comply with the Post Office regulation. Your invitation will land in the dead-letter office if you don't.

What is placed on the calling card if it is used?

The name and address are engraved; the invitation handwritten.

Wed. November 7th
Cocktails, 5 to 7

Mr. and Mrs. Edward Coe Brown

R.s. v. p.

221 North Place

What are other ways of issuing the informal invitation?

The large single card: This is an ideal replacement for the calling card, which perforce will be more or less dropped for this purpose. Measuring 4½ inches by 3½ inches, the address is engraved in the upper right-hand corner, and the name centered about one inch from the top, leaving a large space for the invitation itself.

221 North Place

Mr. & Mrs. Edward Coe Brown

Cocktails

Wednesday, Nov. 7th

5 to 7 o'clock

R.s. v. p.

The informal (or fold-over) card: Measuring 3 by 4 inches, this will safely pass the postal inspectors. On the outside, the name is engraved in the center and the address in the lower right-hand corner. The invitation is written on the inside, facing you.

Outside of card:

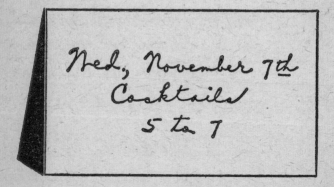

Inside of card:

The handwritten "note" invitation: The white medium-sized, folded-on-the-side note paper is best for this. The wording is up to you. The following is a suggestion:

October 20, 1958

Dear Mrs. Dorn:

We are having a small group in for cocktails on Wednesday, November 7th, from 5 to 7 o'clock, and would like so much to have you and Mr. Dorn join us.

Hoping that you can make it,

Sincerely,
Martha Brown

(*Mrs. Edward Brown*)

NOTE: The address should be written in the upper right-hand corner above the date if it is not engraved on the stationery.

ENTERTAINING — ACKNOWLEDGMENTS

What cards or stationery are used when replying to these invitations?

The rules regarding this are as flexible as those relative to the invitations themselves. Any of the following may be used: a calling card (advised against for reasons given on page 168); the large single card, the folded (or fold-over) card, or note paper.

What wording is used?

No rules govern this either. Just be gracious and polite. The following examples give a general idea. Handwrite on the large single card:

We are looking forward so much to seeing you on Nov. 7th.   Thank you for thinking of us.

or

> *Looking forward to seeing you on Wednesday, November 7th*
>
> ## Mr. and Mrs. Robert Black Dow
>
> 4132 Terrace Road

The regret might read:

> *Terribly sorry but we will be unable to come on Wednesday, November 7th, because of a previous engagement. You were so very kind to think of us.*

On the folded card: The same wording may be used and the message would be placed on the inside of the card.

NOTE: In either case the envelope can be addressed to the hostess only or to both her and her husband.

By handwritten note:

> 2722 Main Street
> October 23, 1958

> Dear Mrs. Brown:
> My husband and I will be delighted to join you on Wednesday, November 7th, between the hours of 5 and 7 o'clock.
> Looking forward to seeing you,
>
> Sincerely,
> Mary Dorn

(Mrs. John Dorn)

NOTE: If regretting, don't forget to give a reason why. The envelope would be addressed to the hostess only.

ENTERTAINING — REMINDERS

When is it necessary to send a reminder?

If an invitation is issued say two or three weeks in advance for a luncheon or dinner, it is wise to do so. This is particularly true if the invitation has been a telephoned one. People do forget, you know. For other functions, such as receptions, reminders are not necessary.

What form does a reminder take?

The very formal invitation should be followed up by a small, engraved "in blank" card, measuring approximately 3 x 3 inches.

To remind:
Mr. and Mrs. Philip John Proper
are expecting the pleasure of your company

on *monday, november tenth*
at *eight* o'clock

For the informal:

The large single card, with address at top right, or the fold-over card may be used. Simply handwrite:

To remind:
Luncheon, January 15th
1 o'clock

ENTERTAINING — POSTPONING A PARTY DATE

The formal:

Much the same procedure is followed as in the case of a cancellation. The printed wording would be:

> *Mr. and Mrs. Philip John Proper*
> *regret that it is necessary to*
> *postpone their invitation to*
> *dinner on Monday, November tenth*
> *to Friday, December fifth*
> *at eight o'clock*
> *The Ritz Hotel*
>
> *R.s.v.p.*

As in the case of the cancellation, should the time be very short, a telegram may be sent or a telephone call made.

The acknowledgment of such a change-of-date invitation is made in exectly the same way as it was done the first time. (See page 164.)

The semi-formal and informal:

Do exactly as you would when recalling such an invitation. (See below.)

ENTERTAINING — RECALLING AN INVITATION

The formal:

If illness, or death, or some other reason, causes the cancellation of a formal party, a printed card (there is not time to have it engraved) should immediately be sent to all those invited. The wording could be something like the following:

> *Mr. and Mrs. Philip John Proper*
> *because of the sudden illness of their daughter*
> *are obliged to recall their invitation*
> *for Monday, November tenth*

If the time is very short, a telegram may be sent or the message may be telephoned.

The semi-formal or informal:

If the group invited is small in number, it may be done by telephone. If fairly large, a short handwritten note on white note paper is preferred, although the use of the large single card or the folded card is not frowned upon in these cases.

ENTERTAINING — HOSTS

What is the first obligation of a host?

No entertainment, large or small, is ever successful unless the hosts are completely relaxed and at ease. The host who tries too hard, and thereby becomes tense and jittery, is doomed to failure. Also, to be successful, the host must want to give the party in the first place. It is bound to be obvious to all those present if you plan your party with a "hate to entertain but have to pay back those obligations" approach. Attitudes, like measles, are catching, and your guests will react according to the mood that you set for them. It is entirely up to you.

What is the first step to take when planning to entertain your friends?

Choose what type of entertainment it is to be. Base this on the family budget. Never attempt to "keep up with the Joneses" by entertaining beyond your means or in a way with which you are not familiar. Trying to give a formal dinner when you have neither the know-how nor the necessary equipment can only end in disaster.

What's next on the agenda?

The guest list. Whether it is to be two couples for dinner, or cocktails for a hundred, every effort should be made to make the group congenial. Perhaps some of those to whom you are obligated are not particularly appealing. Mix them with amusing, interesting friends, and their failings will be absorbed in the general gathering. Avoid playing Cupid by asking a divorced couple with a secret hope of patching things up. No feudists either, or political antagonists. Even if your parties are on the small side, add a new face or two once in a while. New ideas always help keep the conversational ball rolling. Never invite more people than you can comfortably fit into the space where the party is to be held. It is no compliment to your guests to pack them together like sardines. If your obligations have piled up, and they have a way of doing just that, make it two parties, say a week apart. As soon as you have decided on the type of party, get your invitations out as soon as possible, at least two weeks before the affair is to take place. Allow an even longer period of time if it is during a holiday season.

What is the next step?

Plan ahead. Make a list of everything that will be needed. Flowers, cigarettes, nuts, and candies, and the food should be carefully thought out, entirely dependent, of course, on the type of entertaining you have in mind. SUGGESTION: When planning your refreshments, don't attempt to serve something fancy. If at a club or hotel, go ahead, let your pocketbook be your guide. But if doing it yourself, stick to the tried-and-true recipes with which you are familiar. People enjoy simple food much more than badly prepared "gourmet delights."

Is it wise to ask close friends to help you?

Yes. Very definitely. If in the home, in these days when maids are few and far between, they are very valuable assistants in making a party a success. Ask two or three friends (the number depending upon the size of the party) to help make sure that no guest is left forlornly alone and not introduced to others; that they receive refreshments; that unsightly used glasses, dishes, and overflowing ash trays are removed. If the party is being given in a public place, these same helpful friends take over after the incoming guests have passed through the receiving line.

If a celebrity is among your guests, what should be your approach?

If asked as a guest, treat him as such and nothing else. It is inexcusable, for example, to plead with a famous singer for "just one little song." If you had expected him "to sing for his supper," and wanted him only for the purpose of entertaining the guests, you should have said so in the first place. Furthermore, you should expect to pay him his regular fee. Even if the performer is quite well known to you, handle it this way.

How do you greet your guests if there is no servant to open the front door?

Do it yourself, if possible. If the group is fairly large, ask one of the aforementioned friends to open the door for you. Make sure that you stay as near the door as you can, however, until all have arrived. Causing a guest to hunt for you is extremely rude. One way to get around this, even if the party is very informal, is to take a stand in one spot, say the entrance to the living room, greet each new arrival, and pass him on to your husband or a helping friend, who in turn will make sure that he is introduced to others and plied with refreshments.

In a public place such as a hotel or a club is a receiving line necessary?

Yes. Even if the entertainment being offered is very informal. While the words "receiving line" sound formal, their actual meaning isn't. It is "those who receive," even if it be only the hostess. She should always stand near the doorway of the room in which the party is being held. Her husband may or may not stand beside her. If he wishes, he may mingle with the guests. If the function is given in honor of a particular person or persons, they should be in the line. EXAMPLE: The hostess, Mrs. Guest of Honor, Mr. Guest of Honor, the host.

Is there any rule governing how many should stand in a receiving line?

No. But care should be taken not to have too many do so. Six at the most is suggested. If more people are to be honored, let them take turns rather than overdo it. This does not apply to the wedding-reception receiving line, for in that case the parents and members of the wedding party (with the exception of the best man and ushers) are expected to stand in the line.

How long should those receiving stand in line?

That depends. If, for example, it is a reception from six to eight, and people will be coming in all during that time, someone should be standing to greet them. Take turns stepping out of line and mingling with the guests, and then join the line again. For a dinner, or when a small group is expected, those in the line should stay there until all the guests have been received.

Is there any special thing to remember when bidding your guests good-by?

This also depends upon circumstances. If the group is small, the hosts escort them to the door, the guests having come first to you to say good-by. If there are several guests, divide it up—while the hostess is bidding one couple good-by, the host may be escorting another to the door. If entertaining in a public place, when people start to leave, it is the thoughtful hosts who make it a point to stand near the exit so that their guests will not have to hunt for them to express their thanks. A receiving line in reverse.

How do you avoid being a harried hostess?

No matter what goes wrong, keep your head. If the roast is burned to a crisp, open a can of something. Never greet your guests with a tale of woe. It's not their fault and your party is as ruined as the roast before it even gets going.

To excuse is to accuse. Therefore, no apologies for the food, the service, or anything else.

Supply several brands of cigarettes for your guests to choose from.

Provide large and obvious ash trays. Your guests will be happier and the furniture safer if you do. (When offering cigarettes, always pass them to the women first, and then the men.) If definitely allergic to smoking of any kind in your home, make it obvious that you do not approve by having no cigarettes or ash trays in evidence. Those of your guests who do smoke should take the hint.

Drink alcoholic beverages sparingly, if at all, at your own party.

By the way, never greet a guest with a drink in one hand and a cigarette in the other. You couldn't be ruder.

If liquid refreshments are being served, always include fruit juices and soft drinks. Not everyone prefers the alcoholic kind. If a guest refuses to imbibe, never urge him to do so. This is not only an infringement on his rights, it will probably embarrass him.

Do not allow your guests to settle down in large, ghastly, conversation-killing circles. Break a large group into small groups. Also don't permit men to huddle together around the bar while the ladies bunch themselves together in a corner. Tactfully mix your groups. Move from one to the other every now and then to make sure the conversational ball is rolling smoothly.

Don't urge your guests who want to go home early to stay on and on. If the shoe is on the other foot, don't indicate by your manner that you wish they would go home, either.

How do you handle the guest who imbibes too freely?

It's up to you to get him out as unobtrusively as possible, rather than have your other guests annoyed. The host should take care of this, but if he is tied up he should ask one of his friends to do so.

The smart aleck, who insists on telling off-color stories in mixed company?

Quietly take him aside and ask him to desist. If he doesn't, tell him to leave.

The person who picks an argument at the drop of a hat, or, if there is no hat, picks an argument anyway?

Tact really has to be used here. Step in and change the conversation. It may be tough going, and usually is, but change it.

The clumsy guest, or one who is just unfortunate?

Be nonchalant. If Great-Aunt Minnie's antique bowl is smashed, don't cry. Calm your guest by making it seem of small consequence, even if it is anything but. If a chicken leg skids off someone's plate and onto your best lace tablecloth, help with a hasty mopping up, a few quiet words of assurance to the unfortunate guest, and another chicken leg. It's the least you can do, and really the most.

The stay laters?

Getting them to go home simply cannot be done tactfully. Blunt frankness is the only recourse. Say something like, "I'm sorry, but my husband has a very early appointment tomorrow morning (or we have a dinner engagement), so I'm afraid we will have to say good night."

Under the heading of "stay laters" might also come those who weren't invited in the first place, but "just dropped in to say hello" around about five-thirty in the afternoon, and at seven are still placidly sitting on, completely ignoring the fact that you might want to get dinner started or perhaps have plans for the evening. This is an inexcusable habit. You can break down and invite them to dinner, but you are foolish if you do. Come right out and say you are sorry, but you must be excused, as you have other plans. If their feelings are ruffled, so be it. They deserve to be.

Those who get to the open door and chat on and on, letting the cold, or the bugs, in?

You need diplomacy here. Suggest that they come back in and sit down. This usually does it.

What are your obligations to an overnight (or longer) guest in your home?

When extending the invitation be definite as to the date, time of arrival, and tactfully tell him just how long you expect him to stay. Misunderstandings may develop if you aren't careful. The man who came to dinner and stayed a year may be an exaggeration—but no joke. It could happen to you.

Should usual family habits be changed to please the guest?

No—period. If friends stay under your roof, they should

fit themselves into your way of life. Naturally, make it pleasant, but don't upset the whole family.

If no maid, should you accept offers of help from the guest?

Within reason, yes. Granted it may be easier to do it yourself, don't give a blunt refusal. Soften it by letting him do a little here and there.

Do you plan entertainment for every second of the visit?

No. Never regiment a guest every second he is under your roof. He needs some time open when he may make his own plans. Maybe he would just like to be alone. We all do sometimes.

What do you do when the time set for the guest's departure arrives?

Let him go. Don't urge him to stay. Express your enjoyment of his visit, and hope he will come again.

What if the host is a bachelor?

When a bachelor plays the role of host his problems are few. There is no need to worry about who pays the check, nor is a hostess necessary.

What is the first thing a bachelor host must remember?

Never be in the kitchen mixing drinks as your guests arrive. Greet each and every one. After all are there, mingle with them. In order to do this, if no servant is on hand, designate a bachelor friend (more than one if needed) to pitch in and act as bartender, empty ash trays, and clear away used glasses, and generally make himself useful.

Is it necessary to ask someone to act as hostess?

No. If, however, you wish to have one, ask the wife of a married friend. (He will, of course, be among the guests.) Never invite an unattached woman to act in this capacity, unless you are formally engaged. Even then, it is better not to do so.

What is one important thing to remember if entertaining at a dinner at home or in a night club or hotel?

If asking an unmarried woman, she should be told to bring an escort. If not, provide her with one, to escort her to the party and also take her home. Remember a woman may be asked alone for a cocktail party, but you should never expect her to come and go on her own during the evening hours.

What must an unattached woman do when entertaining at home?

She follows the same rules as any other hostess. With one exception. If it is a seated dinner, the absence of a host may prove difficult. If you ask an unattached man to fill in this capacity (unless you are formally engaged), your friends' tongues undoubtedly will wag, predicting a romantic attachment. Avoid this by not designating any one man to play this role. The easiest thing to do is to act as host and hostess combined.

Is it all right for her to ask the assistance of a man guest to help out with mixing drinks, or helping to put away hats and coats?

Yes, if this is handled tactfully. He is not in the position of the host, but is merely a helping hand.

If she is a hostess to a mixed group in a restaurant or night club, what then?

This takes some doing. To avoid embarrassment on the part of the men present (with resultant argument about who foots the bill), make every effort to see that all financial arrangements are made before the party. If the menu is completely ordered prior to the dinner, then payment, including tips to the waiters, should be taken care of before the event. If the guests are each to place his own order, and the total expense of the party is unknown, give the headwaiter the approximate amount you think it will cost, asking him to take care of all details, and see that no check is presented to you at the end of the evening. A settlement with the headwaiter can be made next day. (By the way, while happy to give you this service, he should be tipped for his trouble, never less than $5.00 for a party of ten.)

If circumstances make it impossible to make these preparations beforehand, how does a single woman handle it?

Ask one of the men with whom you are fairly well acquainted to take care of it for you. Turn over to him the amount you think it is going to cost. This, of course, is done in private. As the party draws to a close, he can quietly excuse himself, go to the headwaiter, and unobtrusively settle things up.

How could one avoid all this financial planning?

If you entertain frequently, a credit card at your favorite hotel or restaurant is a great help. Sign the check, adding a tip to the waiter thereon, and that's all there is to it. In this way all chance of making your men guests uncomfortable is avoided.

How do you greet your guests when entertaining in public?

When extending your invitation, set a definite meeting place. Be sure to be there yourself a few minutes ahead of time just in case a guest is an early comer. When the guests all arrive, and have been greeted, notify the headwaiter, and he will lead them to your table. Your guests go first, and you come in last with your escort, who, in this case, is definitely not your host, but is merely escorting you.

How do you indicate where each person is to sit?

If there are only a few, you indicate where each guest should go. If the group is fairly large, to avoid confusion and delay, it facilitates things to use place cards.

ENTERTAINING — GUESTS

What is the first duty of a guest?

Acknowledge your invitation immediately, if a reply is asked for. Not to do so is to show extreme rudeness to the person who is offering to extend hospitality to you.

What should you say to the hostess when you arrive?

"How do you do? It's so very nice to be here," or words to that effect. Make your own speech. Just be nice and friendly.

If it is a fairly large group, and the hostess is nowhere in sight when you arrive, what do you do?

The only thing you can. Go look for her. Your hostess is at fault in this case, not you.

If there is a receiving line, and a woman is escorted by a man, who goes through the line first?

Always the woman.

What do you do when going through the line?

Shake hands with the first in line, saying "How do you do? I am Mrs. Green." Don't mention your given name. Of course, if you are well known to the hostess heading the line, mentioning your name is obviously superfluous. After your greeting to her, she will introduce you to the next in line. Should that person not catch your name, repeat the same thing that you said to the hostess in the first place, repeating your name, of course. By all means, leave chitchat until later. Don't hold up those following you. Keep moving.

Should you always express your appreciation before departing?

Of course. Never take it for granted that your hostess knows you had a good time. Maybe she does, but she likes to be told about it. Only if she is still in the receiving line when you take your departure is it considered anything but unpardonably rude not to say your "thank you." Always make every effort to find the host also. After all, he is giving the party, too.

How should you time your leave-taking?

This depends. However, if it is a luncheon, an hour and a half to two hours' total time is plenty. If it is a cocktail party, say from five to seven, regardless of the time you arrive, leave at seven. Your host may have other plans for the evening. If it is a dinner, ten o'clock, certainly not later than eleven. Remember, you were invited only for the evening, not to spend the night.

What if the party is given in your honor?

You have a special responsibility here. Arrive ahead of time, and remember no one else is supposed to make the move to go home before you do. So think of your fellow guests and don't make it end up in an endurance contest.

If you are not the guest of honor, and are forced to leave early, before she has done so, what do you do then?

Take your hostess aside and explain. She will, of course, understand, and should go with you when you say good-by to the guest of honor, which by all means you must do.

When is it possible to leave a party and not say farewell to everyone there?

Obviously it would be impossible to bid all the other guests good-by when attending any large gathering, such as a reception or a big cocktail party. Only when a group is fairly small should you attempt to express your pleasure at having seen every one of them.

Anything special to remember when leaving?

Most decidedly yes. Follow Shakespeare's admonition: "Stand not upon the order of your going, but go at once!" Those who drag out their departure provide an anticlimax to any party, large or small. They bore people, too. Once you are on your feet, keep moving—out the front door.

Is a verbal expression of appreciation when leaving a party all that is necessary?

It depends. For teas, cocktail parties, receptions and informal evening get-togethers, yes. For a meal, even if very informal, a telephone call to the hostess next day or a short handwritten note is never out of place, and is always appreciated. If the party was given in your honor, a note should definitely be written and, if possible, flowers sent the day after the event takes place.

What must guests never do?

Don't straggle in late, offering lame excuses that indicate you didn't try to be on time in the first place. Particularly when invited to a meal, arriving late is unpardonable, unless you have a valid excuse.

Don't act like a hermit crab and refuse to help make the party a success. If you do, you should have stayed at home. If you go to a party, join in. You at least owe your hosts that consideration. Don't overdo it. You don't have to be the life of the party, either.

Don't think it smart to tell that very off-color story in mixed company. If you want to attract attention, you undoubtedly will, but not the kind you want.

If you are a man, don't huddle in a corner, or at the bar with a group of the boys, and discuss golf, or tell stories to the exclusion of everyone else.

If you are a woman, don't gather with a group of the girls and discuss household affairs, your baby's cute sayings, your fight with the butcher. There is a time and place for everything. This is neither. You owe it to your hostess to mingle with other guests and keep the conversation going.

Avoid discussing controversial subjects, such as religion and politics. The ideal guest is one who talks of interesting and timely subjects. He doesn't foment civil strife, thereby bringing embarrassment upon the hostess.

Always determine what is moderate for you when it comes to the consumption of alcohol. To overindulge in the home of a friend is inexcusable.

Make sure you don't leave a cigarette burning where it might do some real harm. If the hostess has been so thoughtless as not to have provided sufficient ash trays, you still haven't a valid excuse. Better not smoke rather than use a plate from which you have been eating or a coffee cup as a dumping ground. Because your hostess has been thoughtless is no reason why you should be.

Never take Mrs. Visitor, who has just arrived in town, to a party to which you have been invited, without asking your hostess's permission. This is really unpardonable. It should never be done, no matter what kind of party. If you take an extra guest with you when invited for a meal, it is an inexcusable affront to your hostess, as her seating arrangements may all be set and ready and you place her in a position where she can do nothing but accept your rudeness as graciously as possible. If a cocktail party or buffet, you may conceivably ask your hostess if you can bring someone without overstepping the bounds. But do consider the hostess and ask this favor of her as seldom as possible.

Reversing this procedure, never tag along with someone who has been invited to a party, when you haven't. If you do, you are in the category of a "gate crasher." This is another inexcusable social blunder.

Don't make an unwanted guest of yourself by dropping in at odd hours at the home of a friend with no advance warning. You shouldn't, unless paying a formal call. Be fair—telephone first and see if it is convenient.

If a guest in someone's home, whether at a party or just visiting, do you hop up and replenish your drink without a by-your-leave from the host?

Let's hope you don't. Unless specifically told to do so by your host, it is extremely rude to barge into the kitchen, or wherever, and help yourself. If he is occupied for a few moments with other guests when you decide you would like a refill, control yourself and wait until he is free. Then, if he doesn't notice your empty glass, ask politely for what you want. This applies whether you are a close friend or a mere acquaintance.

How are the invitation and reply handled for a weekend visit?

The hostess should be specific about the date, the time of your arrival, and, tactfully, how long she expects you to stay. When replying, either verbally or by note, be sure to verify these three important questions so there will be no misunderstanding. It is confusing and embarrassing to everyone when you arrive in the wrong week.

Should you take a gift to your hostess?

If a frequent guest, a gift each time is not necessary, but an occasional one is a nice gesture. If a first-time visitor, an inexpensive gift, a book or flowers, should arrive with you.

If there are children in the family, a toy for them is sometimes better than a gift to the hostess, but think about it, and be careful not to take a toy that might prove dangerous to the child.

What is expected of you in your role of guest?

If there is no servant, keep your room tidied. Don't leave the bathroom looking as if a cyclone had struck it. Don't strew your belongings all over the house. Make every effort to act in accordance with the way in which the family live their daily lives. Offer your assistance to your hostess in preparing meals if no servant is present. If your offer is accepted, really help. If the offer is rejected, don't argue. You've done your part.

If it is necessary to make a long-distance call, how do you handle paying for it?

Tell the operator to call back the charges as soon as the call is completed and pay your hostess *then*. Remember, if you don't pay this debt, you are sponging on your hosts.

Is it all right to make outside plans without consulting your hostess?

No. While a good hostess will not tie you down to the last second with her own planning, it is only fair to discuss any of your own wishes with her before making them definite.

Do you tip servants, if any, when you depart?

Yes. Never less than a dollar for a weekend visit.

If urged to stay longer than was originally planned, should you?

No. Leave while you are ahead.

Should a thank-you note be written, even though you have expressed your appreciation verbally?

By all means, yes. Immediately upon your return home. Don't put it off.

ENTERTAINING — BRUNCHES AND "COFFEES"

What is a brunch?

A brunch is an informal meal served near the middle of the day, taking the place of both breakfast and lunch. Saturdays and Sundays are the most popular times for a brunch, Sunday after church being the most usual.

How is a brunch served?

It can be served either seated, or at a buffet. If seated, the table is set as for luncheon, except that coffee is served along with the meal. If at a buffet, coffee is often offered first, or is available to those who want it. Sherry or cocktails and fruit juices may also be offered to the guests on arriving.

What food is served at a brunch?

Bacon or sausages and scrambled eggs; or a creamed dish, such as chicken à la king or chipped beef with mushrooms. A cake or pastries should be on hand for those who have breakfasted earlier and do not care for the main dish.

How long do you stay at a brunch?

The departure time is not usually stated in the invitation; guests come and go as their convenience (and appetites) requires. An hour would be a reasonable length of time to stay, or less if necessary.

How do you invite people to a brunch?

By telephone, or by written invitation. "Brunch at 12 on Sunday the 10th" or "Come in after church next Sunday for brunch."

How does a brunch differ from a "coffee"?

A "coffee" is usually a get-together for women only, on a weekday morning. It is often a neighborhood affair, perhaps to introduce a newcomer to the group.

What is served at a "coffee"?

Sherry or fruit juices may be available for those who want them; coffee is poured in the living room by the hostess or someone asked to help her. Sweet rolls, brownies, and cookies are on plates on the table with the coffee, or conveniently placed around the room, with small plates nearby if needed.

How do you invite guests to a "coffee"?

Either by telephone or by written invitation.

How is the invitation worded?

It should be an informal note—either written out such as: "Dear Mrs. Doe: Can you drop by for coffee Thursday morning at 10 (or 10:30)? I'm having a few neighbors in to meet Mrs. Smith, who has recently moved into the red house on the hill," or use the folded informal card; at the top write, "To meet Mrs. George Smith"; under your engraved name write, "Coffee, Thursday morning the tenth, at 10:30."

How long does one stay?

Fifteen minutes to an hour.

Is there a receiving line?

No, the hostess greets the guest at the door and takes her to the honor guest, if there is one. Or a maid or friend answers the door, tells the guest where to put her coat, shows her into the living room, where she greets her hostess and is introduced around.

What does one wear to a "coffee"?

Sports clothes, without hat if you like; or, if going on to a luncheon or to shop, whatever is in order for that.

ENTERTAINING — LUNCHEONS

Do people entertain at luncheon nowadays?

There was a time when home luncheons with both men and women guests were a popular way to entertain. Except for weekends, home luncheons these days are usually women-only affairs, and even the occasional luncheon in which men are included on a Saturday or Sunday usually takes the form of a brunch or a buffet. Modern-day revision of the company luncheon in line with calorie counting and, often, limited help and equipment, calls for no more than three courses, and two can be sufficient.

What is usually served for a guest luncheon, seated?

A typical menu might be hot bouillon, a cold salad with muffins or cheese straws, a light dessert, and coffee. When salad is served as a main course, whether it is of the mixed-greens variety or in individual portions such as stuffed avocado or a mould, it is best arranged on the plates before it is brought to the table so that it will look more attractive. Dessert can be sherbet or pastry, or it could be a selection of cheeses served with toasted crackers, and coffee, of course.

What could be served for the two-course luncheon?

A creamed dish such as sea food or chicken on toast, dessert, and coffee. Or a cheese soufflé or rarebit, dessert, and coffee.

How is the table set and how is the food served?

Usually mats are used; no candles, unless needed for illumination, but daylight is more cheerful for luncheon, even on a gloomy day.

Bread-and-butter plates may be used, or hot rolls or muffins may be buttered in the kitchen and passed to the guests who place them on their luncheon plates. At luncheons the coffee is usually served at the table with the dessert, and full-size cups are used. Otherwise the service is the same as for semi-formal or informal dinners. Formerly there were luncheon-sized knives, forks, and plates, which were smaller than the dinner size. Nowadays most homes have only the luncheon size and use them for all occasions.

Is wine served with the luncheon?

It can be. At a ladies' luncheon the wineglasses could be filled and in place when the guests are seated. Or, if champagne is served, the waitress could pour it (from the right), or the hostess could pour from her place at table, asking for the glasses to be handed to her and passing back the filled glasses.

A SUGGESTION: If you wish, you may set your table in this same manner, and serve the luncheon "buffet style." The food may be placed on a sideboard from which the guests help themselves and then take their places at the table, which is, of course, completely set with the exception of the plates. They are placed by the food on the sideboard.

At a home luncheon, do the women guests keep on their hats?

Usually, but they may remove them if they wish.

What do you do with your gloves?

Usually leave them in your coat pocket; or put them in your handbag. And by the way, don't put your handbag on the table.

When you are invited to a home luncheon do you stay all afternoon?

Not unless card playing or some special thing such as a meeting or lecture is planned. You are at liberty to leave immediately after the luncheon. Don't stay more than a half-hour, or at the most an hour, after it is over.

ENTERTAINING — AFTERNOON TEA

How about afternoon tea?

The old custom of serving afternoon tea has faded some-what during recent years. However, as it is a delghtful and in-expensive way of entertaining, it is well to know the traditions that have come down to us on how to serve during the "tea hour." Very few changes have occurred in the ritual, and that's what it amounts to, of serving tea.

What is traditionally necessary for the serving of tea?

Many years ago only a large silver tray and service were considered proper. Today, except for the large formal teas, it is not considered bad taste to use a silver-plated chromium or tastefully decorated tin tray, with a tea set of china. The kettle in this case would be of non-breakable glass.

What does a "tea set" consist of?

A teapot, caddy containing the tea, strainer, waste bowl, cream pitcher, and sugar bowl, and a small plate with thin slices of lemon. The tea kettle of boiling water should be brought in at the last minute, and it is preferable to have a spirit lamp under it, to keep it boiling. (Never bring this in with the lamp lit. A serious accident can happen should it tip over. Light it after placing on the tray.)

What else is on the tea tray?

The abovementioned necessities are placed across the center of the top of the tray. On the left small plates are piled with a folded tiny tea napkin (like the filling in a sandwich) between each one. On the right cups on saucers, not too many, usually six at the most, because they should not be piled one upon the other. Side by side is the way to do it. Beside them are the teaspoons.

What refreshments are served at a tea?

This is up to the hostess. Just cookies and maybe some small thin bread-and-butter sandwiches are sufficient. For a large, more formal tea, where a bigger group is present, several varieties of "tea sandwiches," small cakes, or pastries may be served. Don't overdo it with heavy food. Remember, this is the afternoon.

What is the procedure when a small group is served at tea?

The hostess is seated behind a small table on which the tea service is placed. She first blends a pot of tea. The guests should then come to her one by one. The hostess asks, "How do you like your tea?" If the answer is, for example, "Weak with lemon," she blends the tea to the guest's liking, then hands her the cup and saucer, teaspoon, and a plate and napkin. The guest then helps herself to refreshments, returning to her chair. If men are present, they may correctly assist in getting tea and refreshments for the ladies, but usually each person procures his or her own.

Does the role of hostess differ when the group is a large one?

Yes. If many guests are present, the dining table is usually used. Often the tea service will be placed at one end and coffee at the other. If coffee is served, it is on a large silver tray, with the coffee urn placed in the center. Sugar and cream are on the left, and the cups and saucers and teaspoons to the right. The person assisting follows the same procedure as when serving tea, asking the guests their preferences.

Flowers are on the center of the table and small piles of plates and napkins are put in strategic places on both sides. In between them are platters containing the refreshments, from which the guests help themselves. Usually guests do not sit down at this type of tea.

As it is impossible when a large number have been invited for the hostess to greet her arriving guests and serve tea at the same time, she delegates friends to assist her in pouring either tea or coffee. It is considered a compliment to be asked to act in this capacity. The hostess must be certain, however, not to impose. If several ladies have been invited to assist her, she should make sure that they serve for only twenty or, at the most, thirty minutes during the afternoon. When asking someone to perform this duty, give a set time that she is to do so. "Mrs. Green, will you pour the tea between four and four-thirty?" Mrs. Brown is then told to relieve Mrs. Green at that time. This takes a little ahead-of-time planning. After you have set this schedule, call or write a note to the women in question, setting the time that you would like to have them assist.

TIP TO HOSTESS: Even when serving only a few, make arrangements with someone to help remove used plates, cups, and saucers. Also to replenish the refreshments, if necessary. If a maid is present, fine, if not, ask a close friend to pinch hit. For the large, formal tea it is wise to have paid assistance. If not, for some reason, several friends should be asked to do the job.

ENTERTAINING — BUFFETS

How about buffet entertaining?

It is by far the most popular way of entertaining today.

Easy on the hostess, in these days of little help, and invariably enjoyed by the guests. This informal way of extending hospitality can be done at any time of the day or night, inside or out: Brunches, luncheons, cocktail buffets, even semiformal receptions, dinners, and late evening suppers, all come under this heading. You do not necessarily have to have a large group to entertain in this manner, either. Six or sixty or more, it makes no difference.

No rules govern the setting of the buffet table. It is that flexible. Elaborate or plain, it's up to you when planning the kind of party you wish to give. The best china, glassware, silver, and linen may be used, and fancy dishes served. Or the simplest repast can be offered, placed on paper plates. It all depends on what you prefer to do. Servants may assist the guests in helping themselves, or the hosts can oversee the self-service.

How does one set and place the table for a buffet?

While there are no rules about setting a buffet table, bear two things in mind:

1. Balance it.
2. Don't overload it.

The table may be left in the center of the room, or pushed against a wall (this has the advantage of allowing more space to move about in). It may be covered by a cloth or it may have nothing on it at all, or only a small runner under the centerpiece.

REMINDER: Mats do not fit in here.

A centerpiece of flowers or fruit placed in the center of the table or against the wall makes it festive, no matter how informal.

The idea of a buffet is to have your guests start at one end of the table (cafeteria style) and end up at the other, completely equipped for their meal. FOR EXAMPLE: Place the forks in rows (please avoid fancy arrangements) at the left end of the table. As it is always advisable to serve food that need not be cut with a knife, carve a turkey or ham, et cetera, in the kitchen, and place on platters, so that knives will not be necessary. Beside the forks put the napkins, one overlapping the other, then the plates, in stacks (not too high—make two stacks if necessary). Now the food. If the table has been placed against the wall, arrange the food along the full length of the table. If the table is centered in the room, the food will be arranged on both sides of the centerpiece. Each platter or bowl of food should have its own serving utensils. To keep from overloading the table, condiments, relishes, et cetera, may be placed on a small table or sideboard nearby.

If just water or wine is served, it may be placed in a pitcher or decanter on the buffet table, with the glasses lined up beside it. If possible, however, it is better to use a small side table so as not to overcrowd the main table. Another way to handle this, if the guests are to sit after filling their plates, is to have a maid, or someone assisting, pass the water or wine after they are settled.

As guests can't handle the main meal and dessert at the same time, dessert should be brought in after the dinner plates and platters have been removed. This can be done in one of two ways. One, place spoons where the forks were, with dessert plates beside them, and put the dessert in the center of the table. This, of course, means that the guests help themselves. The other way: The dessert may be put on plates and handed around. Coffee may be self-service, or be passed.

How does one handle liquid refreshments at a buffet entertainment?

Be sure to make every effort to avoid a bottleneck between the buffet table and the one from which the liquid refreshments are being served. Get them as far apart as room will permit, so that one group will not trip over the other. If the guests are few in number, it is best to ask each his preference and then pass the drinks. If a large group, a table or bar may be set up, and a bartender or a friend designated to mix the drinks as requested by the guests. REMINDER: Always serve soft drinks, too.

How soon should you serve food at a cocktail buffet party?

When giving a party at which food is to be served after cocktails, don't hold up the food too long. Two or three hours of steady drinking will spoil the guests' enjoyment of the food, if indeed the long interval of waiting hasn't spoiled the food itself. It may also cause unpleasant episodes when those who can't drink without eating fairly soon thereafter act up. Never let a buffet, particularly, be delayed longer than an hour, or at the very most an hour and a half, after the first guest arrives. If all guests haven't put in an appearance, so be it. Get going.

How does one seat guests at a buffet?

It is almost impossible to make seating arrangements for

a very large group, so standing to eat is necessary. It is a kindness, however, if the room allows, to arrange places for your buffet guests to sit while eating. Card tables are ideal for this, and for the very small gathering little individual tables are handy. If card tables are used, they should be covered with a cloth or mats. Don't put unnecessary things on them. A flower or a candle will do. If only a few card tables are needed, the forks and napkins may be placed on them, rather than on the buffet table itself. This saves space on the main serving table.

ENTERTAINING — COCKTAIL PARTIES AND BUFFETS

Is the cocktail party a good way to entertain?

The cocktail party is by all means the most popular manner of informally entertaining both large and small groups, at home, or at a club or a hotel. It is gay, informal, allows guests to meet and mingle, and is not rigid in the matter of arrival or departure time during the hours stated. It's also easy on the hosts.

How are the invitations handled for a cocktail party?

No rules govern this. It's more or less up to you. Any of the following methods may be used to extend your invitation: by telephone, handwritten note, or on informal cards. A reply may or may not be requested. Due to the convenience and flexibility of the times set for the usual cocktail party, you can bank on a high percentage of those invited to attend. If you do wish an answer, however, the usual R.s.v.p. may be included. Another form being used today is to place your telephone number with "Please call" written above it. Yet another is to ask only those who are *not* coming to reply. This is done by writing "Please reply if unable to accept." Flexible to say the least! Guard against one thing—avoid overcute or silly cocktail invitations that may have pictures of roosters or what have you placed thereon. (See page 169 for invitation examples.)

What is the difference between a cocktail party and a reception?

When a party of this kind is given in honor of someone, particularly in the case of a dignitary or official of high rank, it is called a "reception," and may feature more elaborate food and a longer receiving line, although in all other ways it conforms to the cocktail-party pattern.

What are the hours for the cocktail party?

It may be planned for 5 to 7 P.M., 5:30 to 7:30, 5 to 8, or 6 to 8. The 6 to 8 P.M. cocktail party usually calls for more substantial food, since those going on to the theater or an evening engagement would not have time for dinner beforehand. However, so long as the event is designated simply as a cocktail party, mere "nibbling food" may be served just as appropriately at 6 to 8 parties as 5 to 7, if according to local custom.

What is necessary to the success of a cocktail party?

People enjoy a congenial crowd but not a crush; don't figure on additional room being created by guests "going and coming," for usually there's a period of time when they'll all be there together, regardless; so have plenty of standing, if not sitting, room. In fact, except in the case of the small party, guests do not sit; it's more sociable if they move around, and greetings and introductions are easier. Have plenty of bars and bar attendants, or waiters to pass the liquid refreshments. In ordering liquor, always overestimate the amount that may be needed. In different sections of the country special drinks are favored and these should, of course, be provided; however, most parties serve only scotch, bourbon (or rye), and martinis.

What if you do not care to drink liquor?

Many people do not, and for that reason the thoughtful hostess will provide soft drinks—cola, ginger ale, tomato juice. The event hinges on sociability purely and no one need apologize for not drinking, or stay away from a party at which drinks are served.

How can you let people know when you're going to serve a substantial buffet at your cocktail party?

Your invitations would read, "Cocktail buffet." Here it is more necessary that the invitation bear an R.s.v.p. so you'll know how many to plan for.

What is the difference in the food served at a cocktail party and at a cocktail buffet?

At a cocktail party, small dishes of salted nuts, cheese tidbits, and other appetizers are placed around the rooms; these are sufficient in themselves, or may be supplemented by bowls of "dip" surrounded by potato chips; caviar with toast; deviled eggs; stuffed celery; trays of hot or cold hors d'oeuvres, all "finger" foods. At a cocktail buffet, sliced ham or turkey or roast beef; a cold salmon with mayonnaise; salad or an aspic; small hot sausages; any or all of these plus the usual cocktail foods. Sometimes pastry and ice cream and coffee are included. At a cocktail buffet small plates with forks are provided.

At parties of this kind is it necessary to have a receiving line?

In a home the hostess stays near the door to greet guests as they are arriving; if there is a guest or guests of honor, they stand with her to be introduced. The host usually circulates, keeping an eye on things. In a club or hotel the host and hostess and the honor guests form a line near the door.

Is music or any special entertainment necessary at a cocktail party or cocktail buffet?

No in both cases. Particularly the music. Background music —such as a piano or recordings—may be used, but usually the music is not heard above the chatter after the party gets going—in fact it is a distraction. Be sure if music is played that it is soft and low so conversation may be heard above it.

What do you do about guests who linger too long after the stated departure time?

Close the bar; have the waiters start to gather up the dishes and put away the unused food. If the party is in your home, you may be stuck; if it's in a club or hotel, you can say, "I'm afraid they're closing up now, so I guess we'll have to go."

ENTERTAINING — WINES

When should one serve wine at a party?

Through the years the serving of wine has become associated with the pleasant things of life. The simplest meal assumes a glamorous air when wine is served. Also it usually accompanies important occasions in our lives—a wedding, an anniversary, a special dinner party.

What kind of wineglasses are needed?

Wineglasses of clear, uncolored glass, thin and of plain design, are best since the wine color is decoration in itself. It's preferable to have the wineglasses with stems so your hand won't warm the wine. If you're investing in only one kind of wineglass, buy the four-ounce, tulip-shaped, stemmed claret glasses. If you want an adequate supply, you'll need two more kinds of glasses: a tall stemmed two-and-a-half-ounce glass similar to the claret glass but smaller, which can be used for both white wines and sherry; and a champagne glass with hollow stem for sparkling wines. If you go this far you might as well add the V-shaped sherry glass, and your supply is complete. But never more than three, in addition to your water goblet, go on the table at one time.

How are the wineglasses placed on the table?

While rarely seen except at a formal banquet, the array is quite impressive: First, the water tumbler above the knives, at the right of the plate; next, the champagne glass; in front of these or in a straight line from the water tumbler the claret glass or the tall-stemmed glass for white wine; next to it, the V-shaped glass for sherry.

What wines are served with which foods?

Sherry, at room temperature, is served from a decanter with the soup; a white wine, such as chablis, chilled, is served with the fish; claret, a red wine, at room temperature, is served with the meat; or burgundy at room temperature with red meat as well as with duck and game. Champagne, chilled, of course, can be served with the fruit, cheese, and dessert.

Which wines are chosen when only one or two are to be served?

Sherry may be served with the first course, and champagne from then on. If only one wine is served, it may be champagne, a dry white wine, or claret, and it is served throughout the meal.

What are the "cocktail wines"?

Chilled dry sherry or dry champagne is often served instead of cocktails. A chilled dry white wine, such as a moselle, is preferred by some.

How is the serving of wine handled at dinner?

At the formal dinner wine is served by the waiters; if a guest does not care for wine he may merely say, "No, thank you." It is not proper to turn the wineglass upside down. The wineglass should never be poured more than two-thirds full. At the semi-formal dinner the opened bottle of wine is taken to the host by the waiter, who pours a little of the wine into the host's glass first, in case there are any particles of cork; the host tastes and smells the wine to see that it is sound; if so, he indicates to the waiter that it is to be served. If the wine does not meet his pleasure, another bottle must be produced, which, if the host is a connoisseur, makes it important that extra bottles be on hand, iced, if necessary.

At the informal dinner the host opens the bottle, which is in a cooler or on the table at his place, appraises the wine, then pours it himself, beginning with the lady on his right, asking that the empty glasses be passed to him and passing them back filled.

ENTERTAINING — RECEPTIONS

When is a party called a reception?

Receptions, large or small, take many forms and serve many purposes, yet they are all much alike in that they provide a means for entertaining large groups of people who may drop in and out of the gathering as their interest and convenience warrant. Receptions may be given at home, or at a club or a hotel. The hour is variable, depending on the occasion and the customs of the community. It might be at any time between 4 and 11 P.M. Four to 6, 5 to 7, and 6 to 8 are the favored times in most places.

Sometimes a "reception" differs only in its name from a regular cocktail party—the term "reception" being used because it has a more formal or dignified sound, especially if the party is a wedding celebration or is being given is someone's honor. In earlier days receptions were very formal and stiff affairs. The hostess greeted the guests as they arrived (her husband usually mingled with them). The guests circled the room exchanging polite remarks, perhaps were served a cup of punch, although refreshments of any kind were not necessarily present at these affairs. Then they made their departure perhaps after only a brief few minutes' stay. Nowadays we have come to expect some sort of refreshment, and its choice depends mainly on the reason for the event and the time chosen.

What are the different kinds of receptions?

A tea at which a large number of guests are present really comes under the heading of "reception." Usually held between the hours of 4 to 6 P.M., and most often attended by women only, the refreshments ordinarily consist of tea and coffee served in the traditional manner, small sandwiches, and cakes or pastry. (See Teas, 189.) Receptions held during the "cocktail hours," usually 5 to 7 or 6 to 8, may follow pretty much the same pattern as the so-called cocktail party, and of course alcoholic drinks and a punch are also included. Often the reception held between the hours of 6 and 8 really becomes a "reception buffet" and is much the same as a "cocktail buffet" (see page 196)—the only difference being it may be on a more elaborate scale. The menu served may include, for example, sliced turkey, ham, or roast beef, a hot dish or two, lobster newburg, chicken à la king, and sometimes even desserts. Evening receptions held after 9 (they usually start at 10) require formal dress and offer light food, such as small cakes, pastry, coffee, and champagne. Mixed drinks are also sometimes served. An after-the-theater reception would call for a fairly substantial midnight supper, with champagne or mixed drinks being served.

What about the receiving line?

This depends entirely upon the type of party. For example: Mrs. Host may greet her guests alone or Mr. Host may stand with her (she would be first). If entertaining in honor of a couple it would be "Mrs. Host, Mr. Guest, Mrs. Guest, Mr. Host." For special occasions, such as weddings or debuts, consult the Index.

How long does one stay at a reception?

The time specified on the invitation usually covers a two-hour period, although it may be one hour or three hours. But most people recognize that they are not expected to remain for the entire stretch of time indicated—they may arrive and leave sometime between the hours named. There is no particular rule as to the length of time one may stay, but out of consideration for other guests, if the room is crowded, one usually stays no more than one hour and may, of course, leave earlier than that. Just remember, if the time set is 5 to 7, see to it you are not among those present at 8!

Any particular points to be remembered when attending a reception?

Nothing special is required of guests other than greeting the hostess and those in the receiving line as they arrive, being friendly and charming to other guests, making introductions where needed, et cetera, not overindulging in food or drink, and being careful not to stay overtime. If the hostess is free, not greeting arriving guests when you leave, you may thank her for inviting you to the party; if she is still receiving newcomers, it is best, and not rude, to leave without interrupting her to say your good-bys. In this case, it is not necessary to wait until after the guest of honor (if there is one) has departed.

How does a tea dance differ from a reception?

The pattern is much the same with the exception that an orchestra and space for dancing are provided.

ENTERTAINING — TABLE SEATING

How can a hostess simplify getting her guests to their designated places at the formal dining table?

If a fairly large number have been invited, a lot of confusion can be avoided by the use of small escort cards and envelopes. These are placed on a table near where the gentlemen remove their overcoats. On the envelope is written the name of the man, and on the card enclosed the name of the lady he is to escort in to dinner.

EXAMPLE:

On the envelope: Mr. Smith
On the card: Mrs. Philips

When is it wise to have a "table diagram"?

At the very formal dinner, where many guests are present, chaos will be avoided if a neat diagram of the table is made on a large piece of white cardboard, showing just where each person is to sit. It should be placed on the table with the escort envelopes so that each man may see where he and his partner are to be placed. This does away with his being forced to hunt for their places upon reaching the dining table. This procedure is particularly advised if the guests are to be seated at more than one table.

How is it determined who escorts whom?

This is based on the way in which the table has been seated. Each man should escort the lady who will sit on his right, with one exception. The host always escorts Mrs. Guest of Honor, who would be seated on his right. *But* the hostess is taken in by Mr. Guest of Honor, and while he sits on her right, *she* is on his left at the table. This forces the man on the left of the hostess to escort the lady on the right of Mr. Guest of Honor. Slightly complicated but easy, once you get the hang of it.

Who leads the way into the dining room?

The host offers his right arm to Mrs. Guest of Honor, the

other guests follow two by two, the hostess and Mr. Guest of Honor bringing up the rear.

What is the first step when planning the seating of guests?

Make a rough diagram, drawing an oblong, square, or round shape to simulate whatever kind of table is to be used. Check your list of guests and if there is no one of official rank present, seat the table as you wish, always remembering to place those to whom deference should be shown "above the salt."

Where does the expression "above the salt" (or below) come from?

In olden times the salt was always placed in two holders, one at each end of the table. Important guests were seated near or "above" the salt—the "commoner" between or "below" the salt. Hence the expressions we use today, meaning those to whom special honor is to be given are placed at the ends of the table, while others step down to show respect and are seated in the middle.

If someone of official rank is present, what then?

Be sure that he is given the honor to which his relative position entitles him. To seat Mr. Low Rank above Mr. High Rank is actually insulting the latter and embarrassing the former. (See Protocol, page 259.)

What other rules should be followed?

Men and women should be seated alternately when dining. This custom has come down to us from the Middle Ages, when a man and his wife ate their food from the same wooden bowl. Today we have modified this tradition and believe that a man and a wife should not be seated together if it can be avoided, but we do alternate men and women at the table. It's nice if you can seat unattached men next to unattached women. An engaged couple should be together. Remember, too, that while attempting to abide by these rules every effort should also be made to seat together those who are congenial.

Why is it advisable to make every effort to avoid having the guests (including the hosts) reach a total divisible by four?

Because, try as you may, you will always end up with two men sitting together on one side of the table and two women on the other. (If you doubt this, try it and see!) If you do end up, however, with say twelve people, there is a way out. The hostess relinquishes her place at the end of the table, moving one place to the left. This puts the man on her right into her former position and places him opposite the host. Now your troubles are over and it will come out even.

The following diagram is an example of seating a table where official rank is not present. Notice the crisscross from one end of the table to the other. This facilitates separating husbands and wives.

THE GUEST LIST

THE HOST
1. *Mr. Honor Guest*
2. *Mr. Reverend Minister*
3. *Mr. Elderly*
4. *Mr. Middleage*
5. *Mr. Neighbor*
6. *Mr. Younger*

THE HOSTESS
1. *Mrs. Guest of Honor*
2. *Mrs. Minister*
3. *Mrs. Elderly*
4. *Mrs. Middleage*
5. *Mrs. Neighbor*
6. *Mrs. Younger*

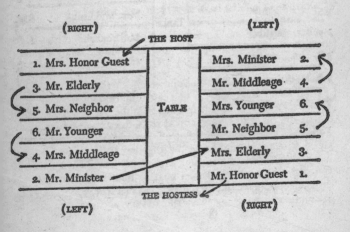

NOTE: The arrows indicate the lady each man escorted to the table.

This diagram shows how to seat a table when official rank is present. These officials are seated in accordance with the way in which they rank one another. (See Protocol, page 259.)

THE GUEST LIST

THE HOST
1. *The Secretary of State*
2. *Associate Justice Supreme Court*
3. *United States Senator*
4. *Mr. Reverend Minister*
5. *Mr. Elderly*
6. *Mr. Middleage*
7. *Mr. Neighbor*
8. *Mr. Younger*

THE HOSTESS
1. *Wife Secretary of State*
2. *Wife Associate Justice*
3. *Wife United States Senator*
4. *Mrs. Reverend Minister*
5. *Mrs. Elderly*
6. *Mrs. Middleage*
7. *Mrs. Neighbor*
8. *Mrs. Younger*

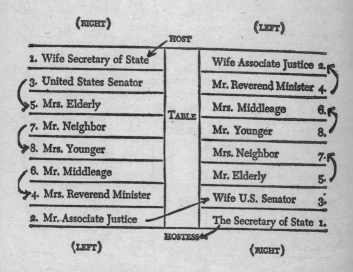

(RIGHT)   HOST   (LEFT)

	TABLE	
1. Wife Secretary of State		Wife Associate Justice 2.
3. United States Senator		Mr. Reverend Minister 4.
5. Mrs. Elderly		Mrs. Middleage 6.
7. Mr. Neighbor		Mr. Younger 8.
8. Mrs. Younger		Mrs. Neighbor 7.
6. Mr. Middleage		Mr. Elderly 5.
4. Mrs. Reverend Minister		Wife U.S. Senator 3.
2. Mr. Associate Justice		The Secretary of State 1.

(LEFT)   HOSTESS   (RIGHT)

NOTE: The arrows indicate the lady each man escorted to the table.

ENTERTAINING — THE FORMAL DINNER

What is a formal dinner?

The formal dinner is one at which traditional customs are carefully observed. With the exception of the dinner or ceremony where officials are involved and in the homes of those who stand very high in the social stratum, this form of entertainment is fast disappearing. The semi-formal dinner, at which it is not necessary to follow all the old customs and at which less equipment and fewer servants are required, has taken the place of the formal function.

What are the points to be observed in planning the formal dinner?

The formal dinner calls for a white damask cloth (with pad beneath) and large matching napkins. Lace or handkerchief linen may be used on the bare table, but damask is preferred. A centerpiece of flowers or fruit (it must be low enough to see over) occupies the exact center of the table; at exactly the same distance on either side are candelabra (some variance in decoration is permitted, depending on the size of the table, but the above is typical). Places must be set an equal distance apart—about two feet from plate center to plate center—so as not to make the serving of food difficult. To accomplish this, put the service plates (which are a must) in their positions around the table before any other equipment. The flat silver should be placed one inch from the edge of the table, exactly the same distance between each piece. Napkins should be folded square and flat (fancy shapes are in bad taste) and placed in the middle of the service plates. Place cards are never ornate—small stiff white board cards with gold edging are preferred. They are placed on the folded napkin in the center of the square. A folded or tent-shaped card is sometimes used, placed on the tablecloth at the top edge of the plate. There should be one serving man or maid for every three guests. Invitations to a formal dinner usually specify 8 o'clock; and guests are seated at 8:30.

What about the glassware?

The water goblet goes directly above the knives at the right of the plate; there should be no more than three wineglasses —these can be grouped to the right and in front of the water goblet, or can be set in line to its right. The service of wine is outlined in this chapter.

What is the purpose of the service plates?

Principally as decoration; also to conform to the traditional idea that the place before the guest must never be left bare. Food is never placed on the service plate. At the strictly formal dinner it is removed and replaced with another plate before the first course is brought in. Throughout the dinner, when one plate is removed it is always replaced with another (clean) plate.

What would the menu be at a formal dinner?

It might begin with soup, melon, or oysters; next, a fish course; after this, a roast, with vegetables; salad as a separate course; dessert; after-dinner coffee.

No bread and butter?

No butter—it never appears on the formal table. And no bread-and-butter plates. Rolls are passed after the soup course, are taken with the fingers, and placed on the tablecloth, to the upper left of the plate.

No relishes?

Radishes, olives, small celery or carrot curls may be passed after the soup is served; they are laid on the edge of the soup plate.

No pickles?

No; pickles are supposed to accompany cold meat only.

What about salt-and-pepper shakers?

Pepper pots and salt cellars (never shakers) are set between every other plate toward the center of the table. They are taken away after the salad course.

Is the hostess served first, so she may make sure the food is all right, and show how it is to be served?

Definitely not. A hostess is never served first unless she is the only woman present. She is served last.

Does the hostess hold up dinner for a guest who arrives late?

Not more than fifteen minutes; when the tardy guest arrives he quickly greets the hostess, makes his apologies quietly, and slips into his place at the table. He is then served with whatever course is being eaten by the other guests.

What is worn to the formal dinner?

The invitation undoubtedly will signify "white tie" in the lower left-hand corner. This indicates full evening clothes for the men and evening gowns for the ladies, who should also wear long gloves.

How do you time your conversations with the guests on either side of you?

Watch the hostess; when she turns from the guest on her right to talk with the one on her left, you do the same—not, of course, so suddenly as to be rude. Fifteen minutes is about the length of time to converse before changing.

How does the table break up?

When the hostess rises, so does everyone else. The hostess leads the women to a sitting room or the drawing room for coffee and liqueurs; the host takes the men to the library, or his den, or they simply stay at the table for their cigars, coffee, and liqueurs. After about twenty minutes they join the ladies.

Only one thing more: how do you get away?

As soon as the honor guests make the move to leave, you do the same. This may take place fifteen minutes after the men have joined the ladies, or by eleven o'clock at the latest.

ENTERTAINING — SEMI-FORMAL AND INFORMAL DINNERS

What is the difference between the semi-formal dinner and the informal dinner?

They are both seated dinners, with much similarity in preparation.

For the *semi-formal* dinner there must be a servant to do last-minute preparation and serving, even if the hostess does most of the cooking and sets her own table. It may consist of three or four courses, but three will be safer. Dinner jackets are worn by the men, dinner dresses by the women.

The *informal* dinner is served by the hostess without help entirely. Here advance preparation saves the day, with, of course, a simpler menu than the semi-formal dinner—no more than three courses. Usually the men are asked to wear business suits, the women afternoon dresses.

What are the similarities between the semi-formal dinner and the informal dinner?

If cocktails are served before either the semi-formal or the informal dinner, hot hors d'oeuvres should not be attempted. Only snacks. Cheese wafers, stuffed olives, and salted nuts are sufficient, but even these are not a necessity. Some hostesses prefer to eliminate these so-called "appetizers" entirely before a dinner—they curb the appetite and often delay the meal, also creating untidiness in the living room.

The first course, for either the semi-formal or the informal dinner, should be one that can be placed on the table in advance: fruit cocktail, sea food, antipasto, or a cold soup.

Either place mats or a table cloth may be used for the semi-formal as well as the informal dinner.

Place cards are not used for the informal dinner, only for the semi-formal dinner where there are ten or more people. The hostess should have the seating arrangement firmly in mind so that seating can be accomplished without confusion.

The woman guest of honor is seated on the host's right, the male guest of honor on the hostess's right. If there is no guest of honor, the persons new to the group are given the honor positions.

Then the semi-formal dinner and the informal dinner are the same, with the single exception that the former requires one servant?

No, here is a description of the semi-formal dinner. The first course, of the cold variety, is at each place when the guests go to the table. If service plates are used, they are removed as the first course is passed. When ready for the main course, warmed dinner plates replace those taken away. Carving may be done in the kitchen or at the table, or if there is not room on the dinner table, on a sideboard or side table. It depends on the skill the carver has and on the number of guests, but usually it works better for the host to slip out to the kitchen just before dinner is announced and do the carving, if the waitress cannot do it. (It works even better to serve something that doesn't *need* carving, of course!) If carving is done in the dining room, the host puts the first serving on the warmed dinner plate that has been put at his place, hands it to the waitress, who is at his left holding an extra dinner plate which she puts before the carver. She puts the filled plate before the lady on the host's right, removing the empty plate that was before that guest, and returns to the host's left, to repeat the process until everyone is served. Then she passes vegetables (serving from the left) —it saves time, if possible, to use a divided container or to arrange the vegetables attractively on a large platter. The waitress holds the hot dish on a folded napkin as it is passed.

If bread-and-butter plates crowd the table, buttered rolls may be passed, and they are placed on the side of the dinner plate, not on the table.

When the menu includes a fresh green vegetable and a good selection of relishes, a salad may not be necessary. However, if a salad is served, it should be a separate course before the dessert.

Before dessert, the table is crumbed; water glasses refilled; any unused silver removed; salt and pepper, relish dishes, et cetera, taken away. Dessert may be served in individual portions already on the plates, or plates with the necessary silver may be placed in front of the guests and the dessert offered to each by the waitress.

Usually finger bowls are omitted when one waitress does all the serving, unless the number at table is small. While the dessert is being eaten, the waitress brings in coffee, cups, and saucers; the hostess pours, and the waitress takes coffee to each place and offers cream and sugar (serving this time to the guest's right). Or when dessert is finished, the hostess may suggest that all go to the living room for a demitasse. While she pours, the host offers liqueurs.

Exactly how does the hostess manage to do the whole thing herself at the "informal" dinner?

The semi-formal and informal dinner can start out just alike, through cocktails and the first course. It is advisable to have the first course already on the table when the guests are seated. Or the hostess may prefer to serve the first course in the living room—shrimp with a sharp cocktail sauce or lobster "bites" with mayonnaise and lemon juice, passed during the last round of cocktails.

A serving table or tea cart conveniently within reach of her chair will simplify matters for the hostess. If the first course has been served at the table, the guests can pass their dishes to her to place on the cart, from which she then removes the warm dinner plates. The attempted plan is for the hostess to make only two trips to the kitchen: once to remove the used first-course plates and bring back the main course and vegetables, once to remove dishes and return with dessert and coffee.

The main course for the informal dinner should be one that involves little last-minute preparation and can "hold" for hours —chicken curry, beef Stroganoff, fried chicken, chicken divan, roast leg of lamb, boiled tongue are suggestions. Rice is easier to prepare and keep hot than potatoes. One green vegetable is sufficient. If relishes are served, they should be in two dishes, one for each side of the table. Bread sticks may be passed or may already have been placed on the bread-and-butter plates. Salads, if served at all, could have been on the table from the start, or the salad bowl may be passed to the guests after the main course is served.

At the informal dinner the meat dish is usually placed before the host (or on a small table at his left if the dining table is crowded). If the meat dish is to be served over rice, that, too, should be placed in front of him. The warm plates are at his left. When he fills the first one, he hands it to the woman on his right—"This is for you, Mrs. Jones—will you pass it on down to Helen (his wife) for vegetables?" When Helen has added the vegetables she hands the plate back to the person on her left, saying, "Will you pass this to Mrs. Jones, please?" The serving continues in turn down the right side of the table, then starting with the person on the host's left, down the left side (don't serve all the women first, then the men), with the hostess served next to last, the host last.

When everyone is ready for dessert, the hostess clears the table—she may pick up a plate in each hand, but does not stack the plates until she places them on the tea cart, or carries them into the kitchen. Dessert may be on individual plates ready to serve, or the hostess may distribute small plates and teaspoons and bring in a bowl of ice cream of various flavors which is passed from guest to guest. Coffee may be served at the table, poured by the hostess, and passed from guest to guest, or the tray previously set up may be taken into the living room as the guests leave the table, where the hostess might designate one of the women guests to pour while she quickly clears off the dining table, especially if it is where it may be seen from the living room.

NOTE: In a less sanctioned variation of the "informal" meal the plates for the main course are filled in the kitchen. While easier on the hostess, this is an unpopular way of serving because it smacks of restaurant service, but more importantly because it is embarrassing to leave food on the plate when it is more than can be eaten or of a kind that the guest cannot eat, or does not care for.

ENTERTAINING — FORMAL BALL versus SMALL DANCE

What is a formal ball?

This is strictly a "white-tie-and-long-gloves" affair. Few private homes have the space for such a party, and it is usually held in a club or a hotel. The formal ball may be a debut, or in honor of a person or a special occasion, but most often a money-raising affair for a charitable or civic organization.

At what time is the formal ball given?

Invitations to a formal ball may specify 10 P.M., 10:30 P.M., or even 11 P.M. The departure time, while not stated, is usually 2 A.M. (See Section on Invitations.)

What about the music?

If the room is large and several hundred people are invited (it is unlikely that a formal ball would be given under any other circumstances), two orchestras are engaged to provide continuous music.

Is there a receiving line?

The host and the hostess receive along with the honor guest or guests.

What about refreshments?

Liquor, champagne, punch, and soft drinks are available during the dancing, usually in another room. Small sandwiches may be served along with the beverages. A buffet or seated supper may be served at one o'clock. It is usually a buffet, and tables are provided, set with silver, to which the guests carry their plates. They make up their own tables. There are no place cards.

How does a formal ball differ from a small dance?

In several ways; anything less than a formal ball is referred to on the invitation as "A small dance," even if 300 people are invited. The "small dance" (see Invitations) may start as early as 9 P.M., and end by midnight; one orchestra will do; otherwise it is handled in about the same way as the formal ball. Beverages are available during the dancing; a buffet supper may or may not be, but usually is, served at midnight.

If there a difference in the clothes that should be worn to these two functions?

Yes. The formal ball invariably means full-dress evening clothes (white tie and tails) for the men and ball gowns (ankle or floor length) for the ladies, always accompanied by long, above-elbow-length gloves. The so-called "small dance" requires tuxedos (black tie) and less elaborate evening gowns, which may be either ankle length or ballerina. Gloves may or may not be worn. If they are, the elbow length is correct.

ENTERTAINING — DEBUTS

How are debuts handled today?

The origin and meaning of "debut" is not only interesting, in a way it hints of things to come. The word is from the French *débuter,* which means to make the first stroke in a game. Now while the admitted reason behind presenting a young girl to society is not to "catch a man"—it is to announce that she is now grown up and may join adult society—it invariably leads to the "game" of choosing her life's partner. (Aside to parents: In years past the young lady never "came-out" until she reached the age of eighteen. Now some do so when they are sixteen and barely started in the first year of college. Think twice before bringing your daughter out at this early age. First, she is not ready for it, and second, when she becomes eighteen or nineteen she is all too apt to be "on the shelf" because of her post-deb status.)

Back in the gay nineties and for many years before the presentation of a young lady followed a very formal pattern. The most general forms of entertaining were an afternoon tea or reception. Only the friends of the parents were invited to attend. The mother officiated by greeting them and "introducing" her daughter. No young friends of the girl herself were included. Later, a tea dance, small dance, or ball was given by the family for the younger group. This procedure is still followed by many today. More often than not, however, only one party is given and the guest list includes more young people than oldsters; the parties themselves are much less formal than heretofore; Dad, instead of merely being in the background, now has become, in most cases, part of the proceedings.

What types of entertaining are usually held when presenting a young girl to society?

Luncheons, teas, tea dances, receptions, both afternoon and evening, dinners, dances, and balls. Any and all of these may be held in the home, at a club, or a hotel.

Is is necessary to have a professional social secretary handle all details?

This all depends. If a large affair is planned, her services will be invaluable. She can guide you on choosing a date that will not conflict with others; help you compile the guest list, and, if necessary, add to the young men to be invited from her own well-screened list of eligible men that she can recommend (yes, it is perfectly proper to invite young men whom you do not know under these conditions), and also handle all details for the actual party itself. If the debut is taking place in the home, her services may not be necessary. They are really necessary, however, if your daughter is participating in a "group" debut. This is where several young girls are presented at the same time. The sensible thing to do in this case, and the usual one, is to appoint one social secretary to represent the whole group and oversee the entire proceedings. Not to do so is bound to end in chaos.

What special custom differentiates a debutante party from other kinds of parties?

The receiving line. Until about fifteen years ago only the mother presented her daughter to those arriving. Dad mingled with the guests. Today he is often "in the line," too, and rightfully so. After all, she is his daughter, also! Either is correct, however. If only mother and daughter, Mother is first—if both parents, Mother, daughter, then Dad.

Do those invited send flowers?

Yes. It is a tribute for them to do so. They are addressed to the young girl at the place where the party is being held. Either baskets or cut flowers are preferred. Be thoughtful. If they are cut flowers, have the florist place them in containers. Otherwise, there is usually a last-minute hassle trying to find vases to put them in. REMINDER: Remove all cards as soon as the flowers are received, and make a careful list of those to be thanked.

Is it proper to send gifts rather than flowers?

Only recently has presenting a gift become more or less regular practice. It is advised, however, that only relatives and close friends follow this trend. Acquaintances should stick to the floral tributes.

Are the young men on the "stag list" who may attend many parties during the season expected to send flowers to each debutante?

Heavens, no. All that is expected of them is to help make the party a success by making every effort to join it. Dance with all the "wallflowers," be polite to their elders, don't overdo at the punch bowl, and never give the impression by their actions that they are having a whale of a good time at someone else's expense for which they are giving nothing.

What is the proper attire for the debutante? For her mother?

For an evening party (after six o'clock) a filmy white dress is usually chosen (one of a soft pastel color is also sometimes worn) by the debutante. It may be full skirted, of floor or ballerina length. A strapless gown may be worn today, although in past years one without at least a suggestion of sleeves was severely frowned upon. Make the décolletage modest by all means. For this party the mother would wear an evening dress in a pastel shade, never black.

At a luncheon dressy daytime frocks are worn by mother and debutante, with hats if the party is given in a club or a hotel. At an afternoon (before six o'clock) affair, the debutante may wear a filmy white dress, or one in a pastel shade (but not with bare top) floor or ballerina length; the mother would wear a dressy frock in a pastel shade of either length.

How should the guests dress?

In clothing suitable for the time of day—hats and gloves if before 6 P.M. If the debut is an evening affair, the invitation will state whether black ties or white, which in terms of women's attire means dinner clothes or more formal evening dress.

HOW TO ADDRESS: FROM DIGNITARIES TO JUST PLAIN MR. (over)

The Person	Address on envelope	Salutation	Complimentary Close
The President	The President	The President: (very formal, official) Mr. President: (formal) My dear Mr. President: (informal)	Respectfully, (formal, official) Faithfully yours, (informal, official) Very respectfully, (private individuals)
His wife	Mrs. Doe[1]	My dear Mrs. Doe:	Sincerely yours,
Addressed together	The President and Mrs. Doe		
The Vice-President	The Vice-President	Sir: (formal) My dear Mr. Vice-President: (informal)	Very truly yours, (formal) Sincerely yours, (informal)
His wife	Mrs. Doe	My dear Mrs. Doe:	Sincerely yours,
Addressed together	The Vice-President and Mrs. Doe		
The Chief Justice	The Chief Justice	Sir: (formal) My dear Mr. Chief Justice: (informal)	Very truly yours, (formal) Sincerely yours, (informal)
His wife	Mrs. Doe	My dear Mrs. Doe:	Sincerely yours,
Addressed together	The Chief Justice and Mrs. Doe		

[1] No given name is used when addressing wives of high officials.

On Invitation	Place Card	Speaking to	Introducing
The President	The President	Mr. President or Sir	[2] Mr. President, may I have the honor to present Mrs. Jones (Mr. Jones)
Mrs. Doe The President and Mrs. Doe	Mrs. Doe	Mrs. Doe	Mrs. Doe
The Vice-President	The Vice-President	Mr. Vice-President or Sir	Mr. Vice-President
Mrs. Doe The Vice-President and Mrs. Doe	Mrs. Doe	Mrs. Doe	Mrs. Doe
The Chief Justice	The Chief Justice	Mr. Chief Justice or Sir	Mr. Chief Justice
Mrs. Doe The Chief Justice and Mrs. Doe	Mrs. Doe	Mrs. Doe	Mrs. Doe

[2] This form is always followed when making introductions to high officials.

The Person	Address on envelope	Salutation	Complimentary Close
Associate Justice of The Supreme Court	Mr. Justice Doe	Sir: (formal) My dear Mr. Justice: (informal)	Very truly yours, (formal) Sincerely yours, (informal)
His wife	Mrs. Doe	My dear Mrs. Doe:	Sincerely yours,
Addressed together	Mr. Justice Doe and Mrs. Doe		
Former President	The Honorable John Edward Doe	Sir: (formal) My dear Mr. Doe: (informal)	Very truly yours, (formal) Sincerely yours, (informal)
His wife (or widow)	Mrs. John Edward Doe	My dear Mrs. Doe:	Sincerely yours,
Addressed together	The Honorable John Edward Doe and Mrs. Doe		
The Speaker of The House of Representatives	The Honorable John Edward Doe, The Speaker of The House of Representatives	Sir: (formal) My dear Mr. Speaker: (informal)	Very truly yours, (formal) Sincerely yours, (informal)
His wife	Mrs. Doe	My dear Mrs. Doe:	Sincerely yours,
Addressed together	The Honorable The Speaker of The House of Representatives and Mrs. Doe		

On Invitation	Place Card	Speaking to	Introducing
Mr. Justice Doe	Mr. Justice Doe	Mr. Justice or Sir	Mr. Justice Doe
Mrs. Doe	Mrs. Doe	Mrs. Doe	Mrs. Doe
Mr. Justice Doe and Mrs. Doe			
Mr. Doe	Mr. Doe	Mr. Doe or Sir	Mr. Doe
Mrs. Doe	Mrs. Doe	Mrs. Doe	Mrs. Doe
Mr. and Mrs. Doe			
The Speaker	The Speaker	Mr. Speaker or Sir	Mr. Speaker
Mrs. Doe	Mrs. Doe	Mrs. Doe	Mrs. Doe
The Speaker and Mrs. Doe			

217

The Person	Address on envelope	Salutation	Complimentary Close
[1] Cabinet Member (man)	The Honorable John Edward Doe, The Secretary of State	Sir: (formal) My dear Mr. Secretary: (informal)	Very truly yours, (formal) Sincerely yours, (informal)
Cabinet Member (woman)	The Honorable Jane Mary Doe, The Secretary of Labor	Madam: (formal) My dear Madam Secretary: (informal)	Very truly yours, (formal) Sincerely yours, (informal)
His wife (or her husband)	Mrs. (or Mr.) Doe	My dear Mrs. (or Mr.) Doe:	Sincerely yours,
Under or Deputy Secretary	The Honorable John Edward Doe, The Under Secretary of State	Sir: (formal) My dear Mr. Under Secretary: (informal)	Very truly yours, (formal) Sincerely yours, (informal)
His wife	Mrs. John Edward Doe	My dear Mrs. Doe:	Sincerely yours,
Addressed together	The Honorable The Under Secretary of State and Mrs. Doe		
Assistant Secretary or Legal Adviser	The Honorable John Edward Doe, Assistant Secretary of State	My dear Mr. Doe:	Sincerely yours,
His wife	Mrs. John Edward Doe	My dear Mrs. Doe:	Sincerely yours,
Addressed together	The Honorable John Edward Doe and Mrs. Doe		

[1] All but two Cabinet members use the title "Secretary"; exceptions: The Attorney
EXAMPLE: on envelope, The Attorney General; in speaking to, Mr. Attorney General.

On Invitation	Place Card	Speaking to	Introducing
The Secretary of State	The Secretary of State	Mr. Secretary or Sir	Mr. Secretary
The Secretary of Labor	The Secretary of Labor	Madam Secretary	Madam Secretary
Mrs. (or Mr.) Doe	Mrs. (or Mr.) Doe	Mrs. (or Mr.) Doe	Mrs. (or Mr.) Doe
The Under Secretary of State	The Under Secretary of State	Mr. Under Secretary or Sir	Mr. Under Secretary
Mrs. Doe	Mrs. Doe	Mrs. Doe	Mrs. Doe
The Under Secretary of State and Mrs. Doe			
Mr. Doe	Mr. Doe	Mr. Doe	Mr. Doe
Mrs. Doe	Mrs. Doe	Mrs. Doe	Mrs. Doe
Mr. and Mrs. Doe			

General and The Postmaster General. Their full titles are used when addressing them.

The Person	Address on envelope	Salutation	Complimentary Close
Senator (man)	The Honorable John Edward Doe, United States Senate	Sir: (formal) My dear Senator Doe: (informal)	Very truly yours, (formal) Sincerely yours, (informal)
Senator (woman)	The Honorable Jane Mary Doe, United States Senate	Madam: (formal) My dear Senator Doe: (informal)	Very truly yours, (formal) Sincerely yours, (informal)
His wife (or her husband)	Mrs. (or Mr.) John Edward Doe	My dear Mrs. (or Mr.) Doe:	Sincerely yours,
Addressed together	The Honorable John Edward Doe and Mrs. Doe		
Representative (man)	The Honorable John Edward Doe, United States House of Representatives	Sir: (formal) My dear Mr. Doe: (informal)	Very truly yours, (formal) Sincerely yours, (informal)
His wife	Mrs. John Edward Doe	My dear Mrs. Doe:	Sincerely yours,
Addressed together	The Honorable John Edward Doe and Mrs. Doe		
Representative (woman)	The Honorable Jane Mary Doe, United States House of Representatives	Madam: (formal) My dear Miss (Mrs.) Doe: (informal)	Very truly yours, (formal) Sincerely yours, (informal)
Woman Representative with husband	Mr. and Mrs. John Edward Doe		

On Invitation	Place Card	Speaking to	Introducing
Senator Doe	Senator Doe	Senator Doe or Sir	Senator Doe from Ohio
Senator Doe	Senator Doe	Senator Doe	Senator Doe from Ohio
Mrs. (or Mr.) Doe	Mrs. (or Mr.) Doe	Mrs. (or Mr.) Doe	Mrs. (or Mr.) Doe
Senator and Mrs. Doe			
Mr. Doe	Mr. Doe	Mr. Doe or Sir	Mr. Doe, Representative from Ohio
Mrs. Doe	Mrs. Doe	Mrs. Doe	Mrs. Doe
Mr. and Mrs. Doe			
Miss (Mrs.) Doe	Miss Doe	Miss Doe	Miss Doe, Representative from Ohio
Mr. and Mrs. Doe			

The Person	Address on envelope	Salutation	Complimentary Close
Assistant to The President	The Honorable John Edward Doe, The Assistant to The President	Sir: (formal) My dear Mr. Doe: (informal)	Very truly yours, (formal) Sincerely yours, (informal)
His wife	Mrs John Edward Doe	My dear Mrs. Doe:	Sincerely yours,
Addressed together	The Honorable John Edward Doe and Mrs. Doe		
Secretary to The President	The Honorable John Edward Doe, Secretary to The President	Sir: (formal) My dear Mr. Doe: (informal)	Very truly yours, (formal) Sincerely yours, (informal)
His wife	Mrs. John Edward Doe	My dear Mrs. Doe:	Sincerely yours,
Addressed together	The Honorable John Edward Doe and Mrs. Doe		
Director of a Bureau and Head of Independent Federal Agency	The Honorable John Edward Doe, Director, Bureau of the Budget	Sir: (formal) My dear Mr. Doe: (informal)	Very truly yours, (formal) Sincerely yours, (informal)
His wife	Mrs. John Edward Doe	My dear Mrs. Doe:	Sincerely yours,
Addressed together	The Honorable John Edward Doe and Mrs. Doe		

On Invitation	Place Card	Speaking to	Introducing
Mr. Doe	Mr. Doe	Mr. Doe or Sir	Mr. Doe, The Assistant to The President
Mrs. Doe	Mrs. Doe	Mrs. Doe	Mrs. Doe
Mr. and Mrs. Doe			
Mr. Doe	Mr. Doe	Mr. Doe or Sir	Mr. Doe, Secretary to The President
Mrs. Doe	Mrs. Doe	Mrs. Doe	Mrs. Doe
Mr. and Mrs. Doe			
Mr. Doe	Mr. Doe	Mr. Doe or Sir	Mr. Doe
Mrs. Doe	Mrs. Doe	Mrs. Doe	Mrs. Doe
Mr. and Mrs. Doe			

The Person	Address on envelope	Salutation	Complimentary Close
Governor of a state	The Honorable John Edward Doe, Governor of Ohio	Sir: (formal) My dear Governor Doe: (informal)	Very truly yours, (formal) Sincerely yours, (informal)
His wife	Mrs. John Edward Doe	My dear Mrs. Doe	Sincerely yours,
Addressed together	The Honorable John Edward Doe and Mrs. Doe		
Secretary of State of a state	The Honorable John Edward Doe, Secretary of State of Ohio	Sir: (formal) My dear Mr. Doe: (informal)	Very truly yours, (formal) Sincerely yours, (informal)
His wife	Mrs. John Edward Doe	My dear Mrs. Doe:	Sincerely yours,
Addressed together	The Honorable John Edward Doe and Mrs. Doe		
State Legislator	The Honorable John Edward Doe	Sir: (formal) My dear Mr. Doe: (informal)	Very truly yours, (formal) Sincerely yours, (informal)
His wife	Mrs. John Edward Doe	My dear Mrs. Doe:	Sincerely yours,
Addressed together	The Honorable John Edward Doe and Mrs. Doe		

On Invitation	Place Card	Speaking to	Introducing
The Governor of Ohio	Governor Doe	Governor Doe or Sir	Governor Doe of Ohio
Mrs. Doe	Mrs. Doe	Mrs. Doe	Mrs. Doe
Governor and Mrs. Doe			
Mr. Doe	Mr. Doe	Mr. Doe or Sir	Mr. Doe
Mrs. Doe	Mrs. Doe	Mrs. Doe	Mrs. Doe
Mr. and Mrs. Doe			
Mr. Doe	Mr. Doe	Mr. Doe or Sir	Mr. Doe
Mrs. Doe	Mrs. Doe	Mrs. Doe	Mrs. Doe
Mr. and Mrs. Doe			

The Person	Address on envelope	Salutation	Complimentary Close
Mayor of a city	The Honorable John Edward Doe, Mayor of New York	Sir: (formal) My dear Mayor Doe: (informal)	Very truly yours, (formal) Sincerely yours, (informal)
His wife	Mrs. John Edward Doe	My dear Mrs. Doe:	Sincerely yours,
Addressed together	The Honorable John Edward Doe and Mrs. Doe		
Presiding Justice of a State Supreme Court	The Honorable John Edward Doe, Presiding Justice Supreme Court	Sir: (formal) My dear Mr. Justice: (informal)	Very truly yours, (formal) Sincerely yours, (informal)
His wife	Mrs. John Edward Doe	My dear Mrs. Doe:	Sincerely yours,
Addressed together	The Honorable John Edward Doe and Mrs. Doe		
Judge of a court	The Honorable John Edward Doe, Judge of (name of court)	Sir: (formal) My dear Judge Doe: (informal)	Very truly yours, (formal) Sincerely yours, (informal)
His wife	Mrs. John Edward Doe	My dear Mrs. Doe:	Sincerely yours,
Addressed together	The Honorable John Edward Doe and Mrs. Doe		
Clerk of a court	Mr. John Edward Doe Clerk of the (name of court)	Sir: (formal) My dear Mr. Doe: (informal)	Very truly yours, (formal) Sincerely yours, (informal)

On Invitation	Place Card	Speaking to	Introducing
Mayor Doe	Mayor Doe	Mayor Doe or Sir	Mayor Doe
Mrs. Doe	Mrs. Doe	Mrs. Doe	Mrs. Doe
Mayor and Mrs. Doe			
Mr. Justice Doe	Mr. Justice Doe	Mr. Justice Doe or Sir	Mr. Justice Doe
Mrs. Doe	Mrs. Doe	Mrs. Doe	Mrs. Doe
Mr. Justice Doe and Mrs. Doe			
Judge Doe	Judge Doe	Judge Doe or Sir	Judge Doe
Mrs. Doe	Mrs. Doe	Mrs. Doe	Mrs. Doe
Judge and Mrs. Doe			
Mr. Doe	Mr. Doe	Mr. Doe or Sir	Mr. Doe

The Person	Address on envelope	Salutation	Complimentary Close
Chief of Staff	General John Doe, Chief of Staff United States Army	Sir: (formal) My dear General Doe: (informal)	Very truly yours, (formal) Sincerely yours, (informal)
His wife	Mrs. John Doe	My dear Mrs. Doe:	Sincerely yours,
Addressed together	General, U.S.A., and Mrs. John Doe		
Admiral of United States Navy	Admiral John Doe, U.S.N.	Sir: (formal) My dear Admiral Doe: (informal)	Very truly yours, (formal) Sincerely yours, (informal)
His wife	Mrs. John Doe	My dear Mrs. Doe:	Sincerely yours,
Addressed together	Admiral, U.S.N., and Mrs. John Doe		
Colonel, United States Marine Corps	Colonel John Doe, U.S.M.C.	Sir: (formal) My dear Colonel Doe: (informal)	Very truly yours, (formal) Sincerely yours, (informal)
His wife	Mrs. John Doe	My dear Mrs. Doe:	Sincerely yours,
Staff Sergeant, United States Air Force	S/Sgt. John Doe, U.S.A.F.	My dear Sergeant Doe: or My dear Mr. Doe:	Sincerely yours,
Private First Class	Pfc. John Doe, U.S.A.	My dear Mr. Doe:	Sincerely yours,

On Invitation	Place Card	Speaking to	Introducing
General Doe	General Doe	General Doe or Sir	General Doe
Mrs. Doe	Mrs. Doe	Mrs. Doe	Mrs. Doe
General and Mrs. Doe			
Admiral Doe	Admiral Doe	Admiral Doe or Sir	Admiral Doe
Mrs. Doe	Mrs. Doe	Mrs. Doe	Mrs. Doe
Admiral and Mrs. Doe			
Colonel Doe	Colonel Doe	Colonel Doe or Sir	Colonel Doe
Mrs. Doe	Mrs. Doe	Mrs. Doe	Mrs. Doe
Mr. Doe	Mr. Doe	Mr. Doe	Mr. Doe
Mr. Doe	Mr. Doe	Mr. Doe	Mr. Doe

The United Nations

The Person	Address on envelope	Salutation	Complimentary Close
The Secretary General	His Excellency John Edward Doe, Secretary General of the United Nations	Excellency: (formal) My dear Mr. Secretary General: (informal)	Very truly yours, (formal) Sincerely yours, (informal)
His wife	Madame (or Mrs.) Doe	My dear Madame Doe:	Sincerely yours,
Addressed together	His Excellency, The Secretary General of the United Nations and Madame Doe		
Under Secretary of the United Nations	The Honorable John Edward Doe, Under Secretary of the United Nations Secretariat	Sir: (formal) My Dear Mr. Doe: (informal)	Very truly yours, (formal) Sincerely yours, (informal)
His wife	Mrs. John Edward Doe	My dear Mrs. Doe:	Sincerely yours,
Addressed together	The Honorable John Edward Doe and Mrs. Doe		
Foreign Representative with personal rank of Ambassador	His Excellency John Edward Doe, Representative of (country) to the United Nations	Excellency: (formal) My Dear Mr. Ambassador: (informal)	Very truly yours, (formal) Sincerely yours, (informal)
His wife	Madame Doe	My dear Madame Doe:	Sincerely yours,
Addressed together	His Excellency, The Representative of (country) to the United Nations and Madame Doe		

On Invitation	Place Card	Speaking to	Introducing
The Secretary General of the United Nations	The Secretary General of the United Nations	Excellency, Mr. Secretary General or Sir	Mr. Secretary General
Madame Doe	Madame Doe	Madame Doe	Madame Doe
The Secretary General of the United Nations and Madame Doe			
Mr. Doe	Mr. Doe	Mr. Doe or Sir	Mr. Doe
Mrs. Doe	Mrs. Doe	Mrs. Doe	Mrs. Doe
Mr. and Mrs. Doe			
Ambassador Doe	Ambassador Doe	Mr. Ambassador or Sir	Mr. Ambassador
Madame Doe	Madame Doe	Madame Doe	Madame Doe
Ambassador and Madame Doe			

The Person	Address on envelope	Salutation	Complimentary Close
United States Representative to the United Nations	The Honorable John Edward Doe, United States Representative to the United Nations	Sir: (formal) My dear Mr. Ambassador: (informal)	Very truly yours, (formal) Sincerely yours, (informal)
His wife	Mrs. John Edward Doe	My dear Mrs. Doe:	Sincerely yours,
Addressed together	The Honorable John Edward Doe and Mrs. Doe		
Representative to a Council of the United Nations	The Honorable John Edward Doe, United States Representative on the (Council) of the United Nations	Sir: (formal) My dear Mr. Doe: (informal)	Very truly yours, (formal) Sincerely yours, (informal)

Organization of American States

The Secretary General	The Honorable (unless entitled to His Excellency) John Edward Doe, Secretary General of the Organization of American States	Sir: (Excellency) (formal) My dear Mr. Secretary General: (informal)	Very truly yours, (formal) Sincerely yours, (informal)
His wife	Madame Doe	My dear Madame Doe:	Sincerely yours,
Addressed together	The Honorable (His Excellency) The Secretary General of the Organization of American States and Madame Doe		

On Invitation	Place Card	Speaking to	Introducing
Ambassador Doe	Ambassador Doe	Mr. Ambassador or Sir	Mr. Ambassador
Mrs. Doe	Mrs. Doe	Mrs. Doe	Mrs. Doe
Ambassador and Mrs. Doe			
Mr. Doe	Mr. Doe	Mr. Doe or Sir	Mr. Doe
The Secretary General of the Organization of American States	The Secretary General of the Organization of American States	Mr. Secretary General or Sir	Mr. Secretary General
Madame Doe	Madame Doe	Madame Doe	Madame Doe
The Secretary General of the Organization of American States and Madame Doe			

The Person	Address on envelope	Salutation	Complimentary Close
Foreign Representative to the Organization of American States	His Excellency John Edward Doe, The Ambassador of (country) to the Organization of American States	Excellency: (formal) My dear Mr. Ambassador: (informal)	Very truly yours, (formal) Sincerely yours, (informal)
His wife	Madame Doe	My dear Madame Doe:	Sincerely yours,
Addressed together	His Excellency The Ambassador of (country) to the Organization of American States and Madame Doe		
United States Representative to the Organization of American States	The Honorable John Edward Doe, United States Representative to the Organization of American States	Sir: (formal) My dear Mr. Ambassador: (informal)	Very truly yours, (formal) Sincerely yours, (informal)
His wife	Mrs. John Edward Doe	My dear Mrs. Doe:	Sincerely yours,
Addressed together	The Honorable The United States Representative to the Organization of American States and Mrs. Doe		

On Invitation	Place Card	Speaking to	Introducing
The Ambassador of (country) to the Organization of American States	Ambassador Doe	Mr. Ambassador or Sir	Mr. Ambassador
Madame Doe	Madame Doe	Madame Doe	Madame Doe
His Excellency The Ambassador of (country) to the Organization of American States and Madame Doe			
The United States Representative to the Organization of American States	Ambassador Doe	Mr. Ambassador or Sir	Mr. Ambassador
Mrs. Doe	Mrs. Doe	Mrs. Doe	Mrs. Doe
The United States Representative to the Organization of American States and Mrs. Doe			

United States Representatives to Foreign Countries

The Person	Address on envelope	Salutation	Complimentary Close
Ambassador (man)	The Honorable John Edward Doe, American Ambassador	Sir: (formal) My dear Mr. Ambassador: (informal)	Very truly yours, (formal) Sincerely yours, (informal)
Ambassador (woman)	The Honorable Jane Mary Doe, American Ambassador	Madam: (formal) My dear Madam Ambassador: (informal)	Very truly yours, (formal) Sincerely yours, (informal)
His wife (or her husband)	Mrs. (or Mr.) John Edward Doe	My dear Mrs. (or Mr.) Doe:	Sincerely yours,
Addressed together	The Honorable John Edward Doe and Mrs. Doe		
Minister	The Honorable John Edward Doe, American Minister	Sir: (formal) My dear Mr. Minister: (informal)	Very truly yours, (formal) Sincerely yours, (informal)
His wife	Mrs. John Edward Doe	My dear Mrs. Doe:	Sincerely yours,
Addressed together	The Honorable John Edward Doe and Mrs. Doe		
Consul General	Mr. John Edward Doe, American Consul General	Sir: (formal) My dear Mr. Doe: (informal)	Very truly yours, (formal) Sincerely yours, (informal)

On Invitation	Place Card	Speaking to	Introducing
Ambassador Doe	Ambassador Doe	Mr. Ambassador or Sir	Mr. Doe, our Ambassador to France
Ambassador Doe	Ambassador Doe	Madame Ambassador	Madame Doe, our Ambassador to France
Mrs. (or Mr.) Doe	Mrs. (or Mr.) Doe	Mrs. (or Mr.) Doe	Mrs. (or Mr.) Doe
Ambassador and Mrs. Doe			
Mr. Doe	Mr. Doe	Mr. Minister, Mr. Doe or Sir	Mr. Doe, our Minister to France
Mrs. Doe	Mrs. Doe	Mrs. Doe	Mrs. Doe
Mr. and Mrs. Doe			
Mr. Doe	Mr. Doe	Mr. Doe or Sir	Mr. Doe

Foreign Representatives to the United States

The Person	Address on envelope	Salutation	Complimentary Close
Ambassador	His Excellency, John Edward Doe, Ambassador of France	Excellency: (formal) My dear Mr. Ambassador: (informal)	Respectfully yours, (formal) Sincerely yours, (informal)
Ambassador with royal title	His Royal Highness, Prince John Doe, The Ambassador of (country)	Your Royal Highness: (formal) My dear Mr. Ambassador: (informal)	Respectfully yours, (formal) Sincerely yours, (informal)
Ambassador with personal title	His Excellency, Count John Doe, The Ambassador of (country)	Excellency: (formal) My dear Mr. Ambassador: (informal)	Respectfully yours, (formal) Sincerely yours, (informal)
His wife	Madame Doe, Mrs. Doe, or Señora de Doe (according to custom of the country)	My dear Madame Doe:	Sincerely yours,
Addressed together	His Excellency, The Ambassador of France, and Madame Doe		
Ministers	His Excellency John Edward Doe, Minister of (country)	Sir: (formal) My dear Mr. Minister: (informal)	Respectfully yours, (formal) Sincerely yours, (informal)
His wife	Madame Doe	My dear Madame Doe:	Sincerely yours,
Addressed together	The Honorable The Minister of (country), and Madame Doe		

On Invitation	Place Card	Speaking to	Introducing
His Excellency, The Ambassador of France	The Ambassador of France	Mr. Ambassador or Sir	Mr. Ambassador
His Royal Highness, The Ambassador of (country)	The Ambassador of (country)	Your Royal Highness or Sir	Your Royal Highness
His Excellency, The Ambassador of (country)	The Ambassador of (country)	Your Excellency, Mr. Ambassador or Sir	Your Excellency
Madame Doe	Madame Doe	Madame Doe	Madame Doe
His Excellency, The Ambassador of France and Madame Doe			
The Minister of (country)	The Minister of (country)	Mr. Minister or Sir	Mr. Minister
Madame Doe	Madame Doe	Madame Doe	Madame Doe
The Minister of (country) and Madame Doe			

The Person	Address on envelope	Salutation	Complimentary Close
Chargé d'Affaires ad interim	Mr. John Edward Doe, Chargé d'Affaires ad interim of (country)	Sir: (formal) My dear Mr. Chargé d'Affaires: (informal)	Respectfully yours, (formal) Sincerely yours, (informal)
His wife	Madame or Mrs. John Edward Doe	My dear Madame Doe:	Sincerely yours,
Addressed together	The Chargé d'Affaires ad interim of (country) and Madame Doe		

On Invitation	The Chargé d'Affaires of (country)	Speaking to	Introducing
The Chargé d'Affaires ad interim of (country)		Mr. Doe or Sir	Mr. Chargé d'Affaires
	Madame Doe		
Madame Doe	Place Card	Madame Doe	Madame Doe
The Chargé d'Affaires ad interim of (country) and Madame Doe			

Roman Catholic Church

The Person	Address on envelope	Salutation	Complimentary Close
Apostolic Delegate	His Excellency, The Most Reverend John Doe, The Apostolic Delegate	Your Excellency: or Most Reverend Sir:	Respectfully yours,
Cardinal	His Eminence John Cardinal Doe, Cardinal Archbishop of New York	Your Eminence: (formal) My dear Cardinal Doe: (informal)	Respectfully yours, (formal) Sincerely yours, (informal)
Archbishop or Bishop	His Excellency, The Most Reverend John Doe, S.T.D., Archbishop of (diocese)	Your Excellency: (formal) My dear Arch-bishop: (informal)	Respectfully yours, (formal) Sincerely yours, (informal)
Monsignor	The Right Reverend John Doe	Monsignor: (formal) My dear Monsignor Doe: (informal)	Respectfully yours, (formal) Sincerely yours, (informal)
Priest	The Reverend John Doe	Reverend Sir: (formal) My dear Father Doe: (informal)	Very truly yours, (formal) Sincerely yours, (informal)
Mother Superior	Mother Superior (name of institution)	My dear Mother Superior:	Sincerely yours,
Sister	Sister (name) (name of institution)	My dear Sister (name):	Sincerely yours,
Brother	Brother (given name) F.S.C., Superior (name of institution)	My dear Brother (name):	Sincerely yours,
Abbot	The Right Reverend John Doe, Abbot of (——)	My dear Father Doe:	Sincerely yours,

On Invitation	Place Card	Speaking to	Introducing
His Excellency, The Apostolic Delegate	The Apostolic Delegate	Your Excellency or Sir	Your Excellency
His Eminence, Cardinal Doe	Cardinal Doe	Cardinal Doe or Sir	Your Eminence or Cardinal Doe
His Excellency, The Archbishop of (diocese)	The Archbishop of (diocese)	Your Excellency or Sir	Your Excellency
Monsignor Doe	Monsignor Doe	Monsignor Doe or Sir	Monsignor Doe
Father Doe	Father Doe	Father Doe or Sir	Father Doe
Mother Superior	Mother Superior	Mother Superior	Mother Superior
Sister (name)	Sister (name)	Sister (name)	Sister (name)
Brother (name)	Brother (name)	Brother (name)	Brother (name)
Father Doe	Father Doe	Father Doe	Father Doe

Protestant Episcopal Church

The Person	Address on envelope	Salutation	Complimentary Close
Presiding Bishop	The Most Reverend, John Edward Doe, D.D., LL.D., Presiding Bishop of the Protestant Episcopal Church in America	Most Reverend Sir: (formal) My dear Bishop Doe: (informal)	Respectfully yours, (formal) Sincerely yours, (informal)
His wife	Mrs. John Edward Doe	My dear Mrs. Doe:	Sincerely yours,
Addressed together	The Most Reverend John Edward Doe and Mrs. Doe		
Other bishops	The Right Reverend John Edward Doe, DD., LL.D., The Bishop of Washington	Right Reverend Sir: (formal) My dear Bishop Doe: (informal)	Respectfully yours, (formal) Sincerely yours, (informal)
His wife	Mrs. John Edward Doe	My dear Mrs. Doe:	Sincerely yours,
Addressed together	The Right Reverend John Edward Doe and Mrs. Doe		
Archdeacon	The Venerable John Edward Doe, D.C., The Archdeacon of (diocese)	Venerable Sir: (formal) My dear Arch- deacon: (informal)	Very truly yours, (formal) Sincerely yours, (informal)
His wife	Mrs. John Edward Doe	My dear Mrs. Doe:	Sincerely yours,
Addressed together	The Venerable John Edward Doe and Mrs. Doe		

On Invitation	Place Card	Speaking to	Introducing
Bishop Doe	Bishop Doe	Bishop Doe or Sir	Bishop Doe
Mrs. Doe	Mrs. Doe	Mrs. Doe	Mrs. Doe
Bishop and Mrs. Doe			
Bishop Doe	Bishop Doe	Bishop Doe or Sir	Bishop Doe
Mrs. Doe	Mrs. Doe	Mrs. Doe	Mrs. Doe
Bishop and Mrs. Doe			
Archdeacon Doe	Archdeacon Doe	Archdeacon Doe	Archdeacon Doe
Mrs. Doe	Mrs. Doe	Mrs. Doe	Mrs. Doe
Archdeacon and Mrs. Doe			

Protestant Episcopal Church (continued)

The Person	Address on envelope	Salutation	Complimentary Close
Dean	The Very Reverend John Edward Doe, D.C., Dean of Washington Cathedral	Very Reverend Sir: (formal) My dear Dean Doe: (informal)	Very truly yours, (formal) Sincerely yours, (informal)
His wife	Mrs. John Edward Doe	My dear Mrs. Doe:	Sincerely yours,
Addressed together	The Very Reverend John Edward Doe and Mrs. Doe		
Canon	The Reverend John Edward Doe, D.C., LL.D., Canon of Washington Cathedral	Reverend Sir: (formal) My dear Canon Doe: (informal)	Very truly yours, (formal) Sincerely yours, (informal)
His wife	Mrs. John Edward Doe	My dear Mrs. Doe:	Sincerely yours,
Addressed together	The Reverend John Edward Doe, and Mrs. Doe		
Priest (High Church)	The Reverend John Edward Doe, DD., LL.D.	Reverend Sir: (formal) My Dear Dr. Doe: (informal)	Very truly yours, (formal) Sincerely yours, (informal)
His wife	Mrs. John Edward Doe	My dear Mrs. Doe:	Sincerely yours,
Addressed together	The Reverend John Edward Doe and Mrs. Doe		

On Invitation	Place Card	Speaking to	Introducing
Dean Doe	Dean Doe	Dean Doe or Sir	Dean Doe
Mrs. Doe	Mrs. Doe	Mrs. Doe	Mrs. Doe
Dean and Mrs. Doe			
Canon Doe	Canon Doe	Canon Doe	Canon Doe
Mrs. Doe	Mrs. Doe	Mrs. Doe	Mrs. Doe
Canon and Mrs. Doe			
Dr. Doe	Dr. Doe	Dr. Doe	Dr. Doe
Mrs. Doe	Mrs. Doe	Mrs. Doe	Mrs. Doe
The Reverend and Mrs. Doe			

Other Protestant Bishops

The Person	Address on envelope	Salutation	Complimentary Close
Methodist Bishop	The Reverend John Edward Doe, D.C., Methodist Bishop	Reverend Sir: (formal) My dear Bishop Doe: (informal)	Very truly yours, (formal) Sincerely yours, (informal)
His wife	Mrs. John Edward Doe	My dear Mrs. Doe:	Sincerely yours,
Addressed together	The Reverend John Edward Doe and Mrs. Doe		
Mormon Bishop	Mr. John Edward Doe, Church of Jesus Christ of Latter-Day Saints	Sir: (formal) My dear Mr. Doe: (informal)	Very truly yours, (formal) Sincerely yours, (informal)
His wife	Mrs. John Edward Doe	My dear Mrs. Doe:	Sincerely yours,
Addressed together	Mr. and Mrs. John Edward Doe		

Protestant Ministers

With a scholastic degree	The Reverend John Edward Doe, D.D., Litt.D.	Reverend Sir: (formal) My dear Dr. Doe: (informal)	Very truly yours, (formal) Sincerely yours, (informal)
Without a scholastic degree	The Reverend John Edward Doe	Reverend Doe: (formal) My dear Mr. Doe: (informal)	Very truly yours, (formal) Sincerely yours, (informal)

On Invitation	Place Card	Speaking to	Introducing
Bishop Doe	Bishop Doe	Bishop Doe	Bishop Doe
Mrs. Doe	Mrs. Doe	Mrs. Doe	Mrs. Doe
Bishop and Mrs. Doe			
Mr. Doe	Mr. Doe	Mr. Doe	Mr. Doe
Mrs. Doe	Mrs. Doe	Mrs. Doe	Mrs. Doe
Mr. and Mrs. Doe			
Dr. Doe	Dr. Doe	Dr. Doe	Dr. Doe
Mr. Doe	Mr. Doe	Mr. Doe	Mr. Doe

The Person	Address on envelope	Salutation	Complimentary Close
Greek Archbishop	The Most Reverend John Doe Archbishop of the Greek Orthodox Church of North and South America	Most Reverend Sir: (formal) My Dear Archbishop Doe: (informal)	Respectfully yours, (formal) Sincerely yours, (informal)
His wife	Mrs. John Doe	My dear Mrs. Doe:	Sincerely yours,
Addressed together	The Most Reverend John Doe and Mrs. Doe		
Jewish Rabbi	Rabbi John Doe	Sir: (formal) My dear Rabbi Doe: (informal)	Very truly yours, (formal) Sincerely yours, (informal)
His wife	Mrs. John Doe	My dear Mrs. Doe:	Sincerely yours,
Addressed together	Rabbi and Mrs. John Doe		
Chaplain in the Armed Services			
Chief of Chaplains	The Chief of Chaplains, Department of the Army	Reverend Sir:	Very truly yours,
Individual chaplains	Chaplain John Doe, Captain, U.S.N.	My dear Chaplain Doe:	Sincerely yours,
His wife	Mrs. John Doe	My dear Mrs. Doe:	Sincerely yours,
Addressed together	Captain, U.S.N., and Mrs. John Doe		

On Invitation	Place Card	Speaking to	Introducing
Archbishop Doe	Archbishop Doe	Archbishop Doe or Sir	Archbishop Doe
Mrs. Doe	Mrs. Doe	Mrs. Doe	Mrs. Doe
Archbishop and Mrs. Doe			
Rabbi Doe	Rabbi Doe	Rabbi Doe or Sir	Rabbi Doe
Mrs. Doe	Mrs. Doe	Mrs. Doe	Mrs. Doe
Rabbi and Mrs. Doe			
The Chief of Chaplains	Chaplain Doe	Chaplain Doe or Sir	Chaplain Doe
Chaplain Doe	Chaplain Doe	Chaplain Doe or Sir	Chaplain Doe
Mrs. Doe	Mrs. Doe	Mrs. Doe	Mrs. Doe
Chaplain and Mrs. Doe			

The Person	Address on envelope	Salutation	Complimentary Close
President of a university	John Doe, LL.D., Ph.D., President, Ohio State University	My dear Dr. Doe:	Sincerely yours,
His wife	Mrs. John Doe	My dear Mrs. Doe:	Sincerely yours,
Addressed together	[1] Dr. and Mrs. John Doe		
Roman Catholic priest (President of a university)	The Very Reverend John Doe, S.J., D.D., Ph.D., President, Georgetown university	My dear Father Doe:	Sincerely yours,
Dean of a university with a scholastic degree	John Doe, LL.M., Jur. Sc.D., Dean Law Department Harvard University	My dear Dr. Doe:	Sincerely yours,
His wife	Mrs. John Doe	My dear Mrs. Doe:	Sincerely yours,
Addressed together	Dr. and Mrs. John Doe		
Dean of a university without a scholastic degree	Dean John Doe, Law Department, Harvard University	My dear Dean Doe:	Sincerely yours,

[1] If both man and wife have a scholastic degree, the wife drops title when addressed together. EXAMPLE: Dr. and Mrs. John Doe.

On Invitation	Place Card	Speaking to	Introducing
Dr. Doe	Dr. Doe	Dr. Doe or Sir	Dr. Doe
Mrs. Doe Dr. and Mrs. Doe	Mrs. Doe	Mrs. Doe	Mrs. Doe
Reverend Dr. Doe	Father Doe	Father Doe or Sir	Father Doe
Dr. Doe	Dr. Doe	Dr. Doe or Sir	Dr. Doe
Mrs. Doe Dr. and Mrs. Doe	Mrs. Doe	Mrs. Doe	Mrs. Doe
Dean Doe	Dean Doe	Dean Doe or Sir	Dean Doe

The Person	Address on envelope	Salutation	Complimentary Close
Professor with scholastic degree	John Doe, Ph.D., Ohio State University	My dear Dr. Doe:	Sincerely yours,
His wife	Mrs. John Doe	My dear Mrs. Doe:	Sincerely yours,
Addressed together	Dr. and Mrs. John Doe		
Professor without scholastic degree	Professor John Doe, Department of English, Ohio State University	My dear Professor Doe:	Sincerely yours,
Doctor of Medicine	John Doe, M.D.	My dear Dr. Doe:	Sincerely yours,
Lawyer	Mr. John Doe, Attorney at Law	My dear Mr. Doe:	Sincerely yours,

On Invitation	Place Card	Speaking to	Introducing
Dr. Doe	Dr. Doe	Dr. Doe or Sir	Dr. Doe
Mrs. Doe	Mrs. Doe	Mrs. Doe	Mrs. Doe
Dr. and Mrs. Doe			
Professor Doe	Professor Doe	Professor Doe or Sir	Professor Doe
Dr. Doe	Dr. Doe	Dr. Doe	Dr. Doe
Mr. Doe	Mr. Doe	Mr. Doe	Mr. Doe

The Person	Address on envelope	Salutation	Complimentary Close
Man	Mr. John Doe	My dear Mr. Doe:	Sincerely yours,
Married woman	Mrs. John Doe	My dear Mrs. Doe:	Sincerely yours,
Widow	Mrs. John Doe	My dear Mrs. Doe:	Sincerely yours,
Divorcee	[1] Mrs. Jones Doe or Mrs. Mary Jones Doe	My dear Mrs. Doe:	Sincerely yours,
Unmarried woman	Miss Mary Jane Doe	My dear Miss Doe:	Sincerely yours,

[1] A divorcee uses her maiden surname and the surname of her former husband, or her Christian name with maiden surname and the surname of her former husband. The first form is preferred.

On Invitation	Place Card	Speaking to	Introducing
Mr. Doe	Mr. Doe	Mr. Doe	Mr. Doe
Mrs. Doe	Mrs. Doe	Mrs. Doe	Mrs. Doe
Mrs. Doe	Mrs. Doe	Mrs. Doe	Mrs. Doe
Mrs. Doe	Mrs. Doe	Mrs. Doe	Mrs. Doe
Miss Doe	Miss Doe	Miss Doe	Miss Doe

PROTOCOL

What is protocol?

It is not a social affectation, as many would have you believe. Webster's dictionary defines it as: "the rules prescribing the etiquette in the ceremonies of state" and "the code prescribing deference to rank and strict adherence to due order of preference and correct procedure, as in diplomatic exchange and ceremonies."

Believe it or not, nations have come to the verge of war for failing to conform to the procedures that have been established through the centuries. Actually, protocol between nations is based on consideration and mutual respect, one to the other. Sounds familiar, doesn't it? Those of us not in official life follow the same principle in our daily contacts with one another. For example: a man opens a door, steps back, and allows a woman to enter first; we give special deference to the elderly; a man is introduced to a woman, rather than she to him. All these are really "protocol."

Protocol in itself has many facets. It would be impossible to cover them all here. Therefore, chief consideration herein is given to the question of "who outranks whom" and why.

How are the comparative ranks of those in official life determined?

Definitely not, as the old saying has it, "because God made us so that we cannot all get through a door at the same time therefore precedence." When the powers-that-be determine where an official should rank, their object is to be sure that the man holding a certain position be given the honor and respect to which he is entitled. Where he is placed in precedence rankings depends entirely upon the importance of the position he holds with relation to other officials. One thing is sure: knowing the results of their decisions on where to seat an official correctly at table will avoid embarrassment (or worse). This knowledge definitely simplifies—not complicates.

NOTE: Those who scoff at this practice should ask themselves: Would I rank a private in the Army ahead of a general?

PROTOCOL — REMINDERS

Is it necessary to follow protocol at all times?

The necessity of following protocol when government officials are present is of momentous importance. Do not belittle it.

It is also important to know how to speak correctly to an official. EXAMPLE: All officials from the President through the Cabinet (with one exception) do not have surnames. They are addressed by their titles alone. The name should never be mentioned. Reason? Only one man holds the position and bears the title in each case. The name is superfluous. The exception is a member of the Supreme Court of the United States. As more than one man bears the title, the use of the surname is necessary.

If in a prolonged conversation with any official (including the President) it is perfectly proper that he be addressed as "Sir" rather than by his title. This is particularly helpful when the title is a long one, such as "Mr. Postmaster General."

Never forget that the wife of an official always assumes the rank held by her husband, whether he is present or not. Following this same ruling, the husband of a woman official assumes the rank held by his wife.

Widows of former officials have no rank at all but are usually given a courtesy position. This is not obligatory, however. The only exceptions to this ruling are that the wife of a former President of the United States and the widow of one have a definite ranking in official precedence.

When there is doubt as to which of two people bears the higher rank, it is the part of wisdom never to invite them to dinner at the same time.

Remember that personal friendships do not count in official life. The rank of one's guest must be the deciding factor at all times.

PROTOCOL — UNOFFICIAL TABLE OF PRECEDENCE

THIS LIST OF "WHO OUTRANKS WHOM" IS SUBJECT TO CHANGES AT ANY TIME

The President of the United States

The Vice-President of the United States
The Chief Justice of the United States
Former Presidents of the United States
Retired Chief Justices of the United States
The Speaker
Ambassadors of Foreign Powers
Widows of Presidents of the United States
The Secretary of State
United States Representative to the United Nations
Ministers of Foreign Powers
Associate Justices of the Supreme Court and retired Associate Justices
The Cabinet (ranked according to when the Department they represent was founded)

1. The Secretary of the Treasury
2. The Secretary of Defense
3. The Attorney General
4. The Postmaster General
5. The Secretary of the Interior
6. The Secretary of Agriculture
7. The Secretary of Commerce
8. The Secretary of Labor
9. The Secretary of Health, Education, and Welfare

The Assistant to the President
Chairman, Atomic Energy Commission
Director of the Bureau of the Budget
Director of Defense Mobilization
The President pro tem of the Senate
The Senate
Governors of States
Acting Heads of Executive Departments (when Secretary is absent)
Former Vice-Presidents of the United States
The House of Representatives and Delegates from United States Territories
Widows of Vice-Presidents of the United States
Under Secretary of State
Deputy Secretary of Defense
Chargés d'Affaires of Foreign Powers
Chairman, Council of Economic Advisors
Secretaries of the Army, Navy, and Air Force
Under Secretaries of the Executive Departments and Deputy Secretaries

Chairman, Joint Chiefs of Staff
Chiefs of Staff of the Army, Naval Operations, and Air Force
Generals of the Army and Fleet Admirals (five stars)
Director, Central Intelligence Agency
Director, International Cooperation Administration
Administrator, General Services
Federal Civil Defense Administrator
Director, United States Information Agency
Deputy Assistant to the President
Secretaries to the President
Special Counselor to the President
Chairman, Civil Service Commission
The Secretary General of the United Nations
The Secretary General of the Pan American Union
Judges, United States Court of Appeals
Chairman, Federal Reserve Bank
Special Assistants to the President
Deputy Under Secretaries of the Executive Departments
Assistant Secretaries of the Executive Departments
Judge, Court of Military Appeals
Active United States Ambassadors to Foreign Countries (when
    in the United States)
The Chief of Protocol
Administrative Assistants to the President
Under Secretaries of the Army, Navy, and Air Force
Active United States Ministers to Foreign Countries (when in
    the United States)
Commandant of the Marine Corps
Generals and Admirals (four stars)
Assistant Secretaries of the Army, Navy, and Air Force
Lieutenant Generals and Vice Admirals (three stars)
Chairman of the Red Cross
Archbishops and Bishops
Former United States Ambassadors and Ministers to Foreign
    Countries
The Treasurer of the United States
Ministers of Foreign Powers (not accredited)
Staff Assistants and Staff Secretaries to the President
Deputy Assistant Secretaries to the Executive Departments
Deputy Chief of Protocol
Directors of Offices of the Executive Departments
Counselors of Foreign Powers
Consuls General of Foreign Powers
Major Generals and Rear Admirals (two stars)

Surgeon General of the United States Public Health Service
Judges, United States Court of Claims, Customs, and Patent
    Appeals and Tax Court
Judges, United States District Court for District of Columbia
Brigadier Generals and Commodores (one star)
Judges, Municipal Courts
First Secretaries of Foreign Powers
Assistant Chiefs of Protocol
The Secretary of the Senate

What is "The Line of Succession"?

Should the President of the United States die, or for any
reason be unable to continue his duties, a bill, passed by the
Congress of the United States, provides that the men holding
the following high positions in our Government would succeed him in this order:

The Vice-President, the Speaker of the House of Representatives, the President Pro-tempore of the United States
Senate, the members of the Cabinet (ranking one another
according to the year when the Executive Department they
represent was founded).

Why were the men in these positions chosen?

Because all were voted for their positions by the people of
the United States, with the exception of those in the Cabinet,
who are nominated by the President and confirmed by the
Senate.

NOTE: Actually, it is obvious that only in the case of a
major disaster would more than the first, or at most the
second, be called upon to serve.

PROTOCOL — THE VICE-PRESIDENT

What is the role played by the Vice-President in relation to the President?

The Vice-President holds the office of President of the
Senate, over which he presides. Socially, his role is to replace
the President in the political-social life from which the latter
is necessarily exempt.

What other title does the Vice-President hold other than "Mr. Vice-President"?

When presiding over the Senate, he is always addressed as
"Mr. President."

Who precedes the Vice-President at social functions?

In the absence of the President of the United States, the Vice-President precedes everyone at all times.

In the event of the death of the President, where does the Vice-President stand in the line of succession?

He is first in line to the President.

PROTOCOL — THE SUPREME COURT OF THE UNITED STATES

Who presides over the Supreme Court?

The Chief Justice of the United States.

How does his title differ from that of "Associate Justices"?

He is Chief Justice of the United States. They are Associate Justices of the Supreme Court.

How is precedence ranking of the Chief Justice determined?

The Chief Justice follows the Vice-President of the United States in precedence ranking. For many years the Chief Justice and Ambassadors of Foreign Powers were considered of comparable rank. It was therefore considered incorrect to invite the Chief Justice and an Ambassador to the same dinner. Upon occasions where they were, through necessity, the Ambassador was given the prior rank because of "courtesy to the foreigner." The ruling was finally handed down that the Chief Justice outranked an Ambassador of a Foreign Power, thereby removing this problem from precedence rankings.

How are the precedence rankings of the eight members of the Supreme Court determined?

The Justices of the Supreme Court take precedence, one to the other, according to length of service, except, of course, the Chief Justice, who ranks them all, no matter what the date of his appointment.

What is the rank of an Associate Justice with relation to a Minister of a Foreign Power?

At the same time the decision was handed down that the Chief Justice of the United States outranked an Ambassador of a Foreign Power, the edict was given that a Minister of a Foreign Power ranked *above* an Associate member of the Supreme Court.

PROTOCOL — SPEAKER OF THE HOUSE
OF REPRESENTATIVES

What is the role played by the Speaker of the House of Representatives?

He presides over that body of legislators.

What is his relative position in precedence rankings?

He is fourth ranking man in our government.

Where does he stand in line of succession?

Second in line.

PROTOCOL — THE CABINET

How do members of the Cabinet rank one another?

Seniority in the Cabinet is determined by the date of the founding of the different departments they represent. Length of service has nothing to do with it.

Based on the founding of the Executive Departments (with one exception), in what order do they come?

State; Treasury; Defense; Justice; Post Office; Interior; Agriculture; Commerce; Labor; and Health, Education and Welfare.

What is the exception?

In September 1947 the War and Navy Departments, then in third and fourth place, were consolidated into the Department of Defense. In former years, new Executive Departments were placed at the bottom of the line, but in this case, because of the vital importance of the military, the Department of Defense was placed third in line in the Executive Departments.

Do members of the Cabinet come under the line of succession?

Yes, fourth in line, in order of the founding of the department they represent.

What position does an Under Secretary of an Executive Department assume if the Secretary is out of town?

He becomes "Acting Secretary" and assumes the precedence ranking of the Secretary.

When Under Secretaries representing several Executive Departments are present, how is relative rank determined?

They are ranked in order of the founding of the Department they represent.

When two or more Assistant Secretaries from the same Executive Department are present, how is their relative rank arrived at?

It is based upon their individual length of service.

If Assistant Secretaries from several Departments are present, how is their rank determined?

It is based on the date of the founding of the Department they represent.

PROTOCOL — THE SENATE

Who serves as President of the Senate?

The Vice-President of the United States.

Who serves in his place should he be absent?

The President pro tempore, who outranks all other Senators regardless of length of service. He is also third in line of succession.

How do Senators rank one another?

Highest ranking is given to the Senator who has served the greatest number of years. In the instance of several Senators being present, all of whom were sworn in on the same date, precedence is determined alphabetically.

Is this a different procedure than in former years?

Yes. Heretofore Senators sworn in upon the same date were ranked according to the date when the State they represented entered the Union. This form has been dropped.

How is the rank of a woman Senator determined?

In exactly the same manner as that of her male colleagues.

Does the wife of a Senator outrank a woman Senator if her husband has served a greater length of time than the woman official?

Yes. It is to be remembered that a wife carries her husband's rank at all times.

How does a Senator rank a member of the House of Representatives who has served as long or longer than he?

With the exception of the Speaker, a Senator always outranks a member of the House of Representatives, regardless of length of service.

PROTOCOL — THE HOUSE OF REPRESENTATIVES

Who presides over the House of Representatives?
The Speaker.

How do Representatives rank one another?
Highest ranking is given to the Representative who has served the greatest number of years. In the instance of several Representatives being present, all of whom were sworn in on the same date, precedence is determined alphabetically.

How is the rank of a woman Representative determined?
In exactly the same manner as that of her male colleagues.

Does the wife of a Representative outrank the woman Representative if the former's husband has served longer than the woman official?
Yes. Because the woman carries the rank of her husband at all times.

Does a Representative outrank a Senator when he has served a longer term in office?
No. A Senator always outranks a Representative (with the exception of the Speaker), regardless of length of service.

PROTOCOL — THE ARMED SERVICES

What should be especially remembered about the Department of Defense?
In September 1947 the Department of Defense replaced the War and Navy Departments. It is a consolidation of the Army, the Navy, and the Air Force and ranks third among the Executive Departments.

The Department of Defense is represented in the Cabinet by the Secretary of Defense, who ranks third among the Cabinet officials.

A Deputy Secretary of Defense assumes the rank of an Under Secretary. Normally, he would be placed third in relation to Under Secretaries of other Executive Departments. However, a special ruling ranks him second in line, immediately following the Under Secretary of State.

Assistant Secretaries of Defense rank third among Assistant Secretaries of other Executive Departments.

It is well to remember that the heads of the three military

departments of the Department of Defense do *not* have Cabinet rank.

They are the Secretary of the Army, the Secretary of the Navy, and the Secretary of the Air Force, who rank one another in that order (based on the date when the service they represent was founded).

The Under Secretaries and Assistant Secretaries of the three military departments rank *below* the Under Secretaries and Assistant Secretaries of the Executive Departments.

The Chairman of the Joint Chiefs of Staff takes precedence over all other officers of the Armed Services while holding such office.

The Chief of Staff of the Army, the Chief of Naval Operations, and the Chief of Staff of the Air Force rank one another in accordance with date of appointment. Their precedence ranking is below that of the Chairman of the Joint Chiefs of Staff.

PROTOCOL — THE DIPLOMATIC CORPS

What should be especially remembered about the Diplomatic Corps?

The Diplomatic Corps consists of the representatives of Foreign Powers, and their staffs within the capital of any country.

An Ambassador, Extraordinary and Plenipotentiary, is a diplomatic agent who is the personal representative of the head of state of his country.

A Minister, Extraordinary and Plenipotentiary, is a diplomatic agent representing the government of his country.

The Ambassadors of Foreign Powers rank one another according to length of continuous service in Washington. Comparative rankings are based on the date upon which an Ambassador presented his credentials to the President of the United States.

The Ambassador who has had the longest continuous service is known as "The Dean of the Diplomatic Corps." He, of course, outranks all others.

This same rule applies with regard to the ranking of Ministers.

However, it is to be remembered that an Ambassador outranks a Minister at all times, regardless of length of service.

PROTOCOL — VISITING CARDS OF
HIGH-RANKING OFFICIALS

What are the correct forms for visiting cards of high-ranking officials?

The President of the United States:

Actually the cards of the President and his wife do not come under the heading of "visiting cards." Never, under any circumstances, do they ever pay a call (or visit) or return one. Their cards are used only upon the occasions when they present gifts or send flowers. The cards are as follows:

The President:

The President

His wife:

Mrs. Doe

Their joint card:

> The President
> and Mrs. Doe

NOTE: It is interesting to know that until President Eisenhower assumed office the joint card had never before been used by a chief executive.

The Vice-President of the United States:

> The Vice President

The Chief Justice of the United States:

> ## The Chief Justice

It is to be noted that no surname is included for those hold-ing the highest offices in our government. The title itself is sufficient. The card of the wife of such an official contains only the surname. EXAMPLE: "Mrs. Doe." Given names and addresses should never be included.

NOTE: In the above and the examples following the joint card of an official and his wife would follow the same pattern: "The Vice-President and Mrs. Doe."

The Speaker of the House of Representatives:

> ## The Speaker

An Associate Justice of the Supreme Court[1]:

> Mr. Justice Doe
> United States Supreme Court

A member of the Cabinet:

> The Secretary of The Treasury

For a Senator:

> John Francis Brown
>
> United States Senate   New York

[1] The surname is used in this instance because more than one man bears the title. His wife's card would contain only "Mrs. Doe."

For a member of the House of Representatives:

> ### James Thomas Green
>
> United States   Third District
> House of Representatives   New York

In both of the above cases the card of the wife would be, for example, "Mrs. John Francis Brown," the home address appearing in the lower right-hand corner.

For an Under Secretary of an Executive Department:

> ### The Under Secretary of Labor

His wife's card would read "Mrs. Doe," using the surname only. No address given.

For an Assistant Secretary of an Executive Department[2]:

> **David Allan Jones**
> Assistant Secretary of Defense

The wife of an Assistant Secretary would place on her card the full name: "Mrs. David Allan Jones," and the address would appear in the lower right-hand corner.

What are the correct forms for visiting cards of the Armed Services?

Officers are under no official restrictions relative to the engraving to be placed upon their cards. It is entirely up to the individual. The two forms given below are considered correct. The first example is the one most generally in use today.

> **Robert Henry Brown**
>
> Captain
> United States Navy

[2] When more than one official bears the title this is the form that should be followed.

> # Colonel Frank Albert Green
>
> ### United States Army

The wife of an officer places the full name on her card: "Mrs. Robert Henry Brown." The address would appear in the lower right-hand corner.

PROTOCOL — SOCIAL OFFICIAL CALLING PROCEDURES IN THE NATION'S CAPITAL

What changes have come about in social calling procedures in Washington?

Because of the tremendous growth of our government during recent years it has been necessary to revise the rigid calling procedure formerly followed by all officials.

An official should not assume, however, that because of these changes he has no obligations at all to those who outrank him. While the rules have perforce been simplified, there is still a certain procedure to which all officials should rigidly adhere. Not to do so is an inexcusable affront.

Before World War II an official and his wife were expected to present their respects by making a first call upon all those who outranked them. Obviously impossible today, this rule has been simplified, and it is only considered obligatory that first calls be made upon a selected few.

In the past certain days were set aside each week on which it was proper to call upon officials heading the different branches of our government and the Diplomatic Corps. On these regular receiving days wives of the officials were at home. Tea was served, and those calling were personally received. The customary days set aside for these official days at home were: Monday, the Chief Justice of the United States and the Associate Justices of the Supreme Court; Tuesday, members of the House of Representatives; Wednesday, the

Cabinet; Thursday, the Senate; Friday, the Diplomatic Corps. Cards could be left at the White House on any day.

It is obvious that today it would be impossible to observe this form. If official hostesses received upon a definite day at home, their callers might number well into the hundreds.

Therefore it is correct today, for cards to be left upon any official regardless of the branch of the government he represents on any day of the week. This also holds true when calling upon members of the Diplomatic Corps.

Why is an official obligated to call or "leave cards" upon a selected group of officials who outrank him?

It is a courteous mark of respect to those who hold the highest offices in our government.

Is the official himself expected to make the call, accompanied by his wife?

No. The wife of the official performs the amenity, leaving her husband's cards with her own. It is recognized by everyone that the official himself cannot be spared from his important duties to participate in this social custom.

What calls are considered obligatory today?

Upon the President, the Vice-President, the Chief Justice of the United States, the Speaker, Associate Justices of the Supreme Court, and Members of the Cabinet (and their wives, of course).

Should these obligatory calls be made only once during an administration?

No. They should be made once a year, preferably, but not necessarily, during the months of October and November.

Is an official expected to call upon the heads of the Diplomatic Missions?

No. It is left to his discretion as to whether or not he wishes to do so. However, a call upon the dean of the Diplomatic Corps is advisable, while not considered obligatory. Also, officials connected in any way with foreign affairs should leave cards upon all heads of Missions of the Diplomatic Corps.

Should cards be left at any particular time?

Yes. Between the hours of three and six in the afternoon.

How should the cards be presented?

When the servant opens the door at the residence where one is calling, the correct number of cards should be handed to him (not in an envelope), or placed upon the tray which he may present. That is all.

Must cards be left in person by the wife of an official?

It is preferable that she do so, but it is not considered incorrect that they be left by a chauffeur or social secretary. Care must be taken if this form is followed to be sure that the correct number of cards be left at a given residence.

How many cards should be left?

The wife leaves one of her cards for each lady (over eighteen) in the house. Since a woman never calls upon a man (even the President), she will not leave her card for any male members of the family. She leaves one of her husband's cards for each adult, man or woman. It is to be remembered that never more than three of the wife's cards and three of her husband's be left in any one residence.

Can the joint "Mr. and Mrs." card be left?

Yes. In this case, the single card of the husband's would be left for the man of the house and any additional man living therein.

Is it permissible to mail cards when calling upon those who outrank you, rather than leaving them at the residence?

No. To do so is absolutely incorrect. While no attempt is made to see the person upon whom one is calling, the courtesy of delivering the card by hand should be rigidly adhered to.

Is it wise to prepare for an afternoon of leaving cards?

Yes. To save time, list those upon whom you wish to call, placing each name and address on an inexpensive envelope. Enclose therein the correct number of cards to be left at each residence. It is a simple procedure then to route the addresses in accordance with their proximity.

Are the cards left in the envelopes when presented?

No. This is extremely bad form. Always remove them before presenting them at the door. With one exception: When cards are left at an apartment desk or a hotel, they should be enclosed in small envelopes to insure their not being mislaid. In this case, fine-grade envelopes that fit the cards should be used and the names of the person upon whom you are calling (without the address) handwritten in ink on the front of the envelope.

Are these calls returned?

Yes. The official who does not do so is showing an utter lack of the correct procedure to follow. Today, two forms are followed by high-ranking officials when returning calls. One, to send cards by a chauffeur within a week; the other to mail cards to those who have called upon them. Both are correct. It is merely a gracious acknowledgment that the courtesy of your call has been appreciated.

What party calls are obligatory?

In years gone by a personal call (leaving of cards) was considered obligatory after being entertained at luncheon, dinner, or any evening function. If possible to do so, this gracious custom should be followed today. This is particularly true when an official and his wife have been entertained by another official who outranks him.

If, due to circumstances, it is impossible to leave cards, what procedure should be followed?

If this is not possible, some expression of appreciation for the hospitality should be forthcoming. A handwritten note, a gift of flowers, or if one knows the hostess well, a telephoned expression of thanks is sufficient. Never completely ignore such an obligation. It is extremely rude to do nothing.

What is considered the equivalent of a call, or leaving of cards?

Attending a tea, an at home, afternoon reception, or cocktail party to which invitations have been issued, is considered the equivalent of a call. If one has planned to make a first call or owes a dinner call, to attend such a function cancels the debt. Never leave a calling card when attending such a party.

PROTOCOL — COURTESY IN ARMED SERVICES

How do the Armed Services emphasize the importance of courtesy?

"Courtesy among military men is indispensable to discipline" is a statement that is as old as the Armed Services themselves. Since our Army was first founded more than two centuries ago (followed by the Navy and Air Force in later years), these wise words have been the backbone of our military system. The word "courtesy" has two meanings here. One: its usual meaning "consideration for the other fellow"; the other: respect for authority invested in officers with regard to their relationship with one another and the soldiers who follow their leadership. This does not mean servility or bootlicking. Such approach is beneath the standards of conduct followed in all services. It simply means that all men of the Armed Services are expected to follow certain customs that have long been established by usage. The actual way in which these customs are performed may differ in each service, but the basic rule remains the same—"without courtesy there can be no discipline."

What does an officer do upon reporting for new duty?

The procedure followed in all the services is for him to report to the adjutant or executive officer immediately upon his arrival. He will be briefed on what is expected of him both officially and socially.

Are there definite rules of social procedure?

No. This is extremely variable. In former years each service had its own rigid rules, which, while different in performance in each service, were actually based more or less on the same principles. Today it depends entirely upon the commanding officer of an army post, navy yard, or in the Pentagon. It is his decision to decide what procedure is to be followed. Sometimes a fairly formal approach is taken, other times, much less is expected. EXAMPLE: When an officer reports for duty at the Pentagon in Washington he may be instructed that he and his wife must pay a social call at the home of his commanding officer. A certain day may be set, or it may be left to the officer to decide when he should do so. Usually this is done within a short time after his arrival and the call should be made between the hours of four and six, preferably, but not necessarily, on a Sunday afternoon. On the other hand, the commanding officer may wish to forego the social call entirely. The same sort of idea occurs on an army post or at navy yards. At one eastern army post, issued orders are that all officers and their wives call at the commandant's home between four and six on the last Sunday of every month. On another post, the commandant has ordered that the call may be made on any Sunday between the hours of five and seven.

Is anything special expected when making such a call?

On the initial call the officer always accompanies his wife. He himself is used to observing rank and handles himself with dignity and ease. It is the wife who must make every effort to be natural and gracious. If nervous, she should try not to show it. The wife of an officer must always remember that her actions are an extremely important part of her husband's career. As the impression you make means a great deal, it is wise to observe the formalities of regular calling procedure. Make your visit short. Not more than fifteen minutes. Let the commandant's wife start the conversational ball rolling and take it from there. The call is terminated by the wife rising, immediately followed by her husband, and the goodbys being said.

Are calling cards left?

If an orderly greets you at the door with a card tray in his hand place your cards upon it. If not, should there be a tray on a table as you enter, put the cards in this as you pass by. If no tray, it usually indicates that you are not expected to leave cards. (Always be sure you have the cards with you—just in case.)

How does the wife of an officer "learn the ropes"?

There is great loyalty between service wives. Each is anxious to pass on what she has learned to the newcomer. Don't be bashful. Ask questions even if the wife to whom you are talking has a husband who outranks yours.

PROTOCOL — THE AMERICAN FLAG

Why should one follow certain rules in respect to the American Flag?

It is to be hoped that lack of knowledge, rather than disrespect, is behind many people's failure to observe the courtesies—known as "Flag etiquette"—that are the due this symbol of our great country. Self-consciousness too, rather than disrespect or indifference, may come into it. Americans, the general public that is, seem reluctant to make a show of ceremony. It should be known that such an attitude is completely wrong when it comes to the rigid observances that govern our manner of showing respect to our Flag. The following rules should be adhered to at all times. Never deviate from them.

What is required of the observer during the ceremonies of raising or lowering the Flag?

If, for example, you are present at an Armed Force base, and pass at the time the sundown ritual of lowering the Flag is taking place—if walking—stop immediately, face the Flag, and stand still until the ceremony is over. If in a car—stop, get out, and do the same. A man should remove his hat, holding it over his heart. A woman places her right hand over her heart. Members of the Armed Services do not remove their hats if in uniform. They salute while standing at rigid attention.

When the Flag is passing on parade or in review, what then?

Spectators, if walking, should halt. If sitting, rise immediately. Then follow the same show of respect as given above.

What observances are followed when displaying the Flag in front of a residence?

It should not be permitted to fly before dawn or after sundown. When it is raised (briskly) or lowered (slowly), great care should be taken to see that no part of it ever touches the ground.

What about placing it on a vehicle?

Never. It is completely wrong to tie a Flag on the radiator cap or any place on an automobile. This also goes for bicycles.

May the flag be used for interior decoration?

Not for decoration as such. In some circumstances it is permissible to display it, however. EXAMPLE: At a patriotic meeting, the Flag may be placed behind the speaker's rostrum, flat against the wall, with the stars at the left as you face it. Under no conditions should the Flag ever be used as a decoration, such as draping it on a table or in front of a rostrum. Bunting of red, white, and blue may be used for purposes such as these, never the Flag itself.

What should be done when displaying our Flag with those of other countries?

Since there are important differences, depending upon the countries and the occasion, it is wise always to consult an official handbook.

How is a worn Flag destroyed?

Always burn it privately. A Flag should never be desecrated by throwing it in the trash.

PROTOCOL — INVITATION TO THE WHITE HOUSE

What about an invitation to the White House?

Your invitation to the White House could come because of your business or social prominence, because of your outstanding achievements in some particular field, in recognition of your political activities, through friendship, or through your membership in an organization. You could be invited to a tea, a reception, a luncheon or dinner, or an after-dinner musicale. Whatever the reason, the arrival of the white card bearing the seal of the United States and stating "The President and Mrs. Doe request the pleasure of the company of . . ." heralds a memorable and exciting experience. And regardless of rank or worldliness it is understandable that the recipient of a first-time bid to the White House might be in somewhat of a tizzy over knowing how to do, as well as to say, "the right thing." Actually there is little to worry about. White House functions are conducted so smoothly, with every detail worked out in advance, that even the person most unversed in the social graces could hardly make an embarrassing mistake.

What is the correct procedure upon receiving an invitation to the White House?

Invitations to luncheons or dinners must be answered immediately. Formerly these acknowledgments were delivered by hand to the White House. Today, however, it is considered proper that they be placed in the mail on the same day as that upon which the invitation is received.

REMINDER: An invitation to the White House is considered a "command." You should accept unless sickness, a death in the family, or an unavoidable situation occurs.

Form for invitation acceptance (always handwritten):

> *Mr. and Mrs. John Francis Proper*
> *have the honour to accept*
> *the kind invitation of*
> *The President and Mrs. Doe*
> *to dinner*
> *on Monday, November fourth*
> *eight o'clock*
> *The White House*

Invitations to receptions, teas, musicales, and garden parties do not require an answer, unless a response is requested.

How do you know what to wear?

Naturally, for a luncheon or daytime function the woman guest would wear a dressy suit or frock with hat and gloves; a man would wear a dark business suit, never sports clothes. A

White House invitation to an evening function does not state "black tie" or "white tie"—it is taken for granted that only formal evening attire will be worn (except in certain cases such as a stag dinner when "black tie" might be specified for men).

So far as women are concerned, what is the difference between their attire for a White House dinner, reception, or evening musicale?

Many women feel (and they are right) that a long or floor-length gown is the only evening attire suitable for the White House.

Young women sometimes prefer the ballerina length and wear it regardless. There is no restriction on colors—simply choose the most becoming; black is least popular because it does not stand out against the men's dark clothing.

What about the glove situation?

This has become confused because so much has been said about it. If your dress is sleeveless, long (midway between elbow and shoulder) white gloves of kid or doeskin are proper; if your long gloves were designed as a part of your costume, in material and color to complement your dress, wear them.

When do you take them off, and how (if the gloves are long)?

A bare handshake seems more cordial than a gloved one. However, in this one might follow the example of the First Lady, since there is no positive rule. Either way is all right —keep them on; or, if the gloves are short, remove the one from the right hand; if the gloves are long, slip the right hand out of the wrist opening, and tuck the glove inside for the handshake.

How do you handle long gloves at dinner?

If they'll come off without a struggle, remove them and place them on your lap. If they're hard to get out of and hard to get back on, keep them on your arms; tuck the hand part of each glove into the wrist opening. Put the gloves back on after you've had your coffee. If you're attending a reception, you may slip the gloves off your hands and tuck them into the wrist opening while you have refreshments.

What entrance do you go through when invited to the White House?

Your invitation will specify which entrance to use. For a big party it will enclose a sticker for your car and a small admittance card. If the White House has not offered to send a car for you and if you haven't a chauffeured car, either your own or one rented for the occasion, it's better to take a taxi. Upon arrival at the White House, ask the doorman to have a taxi ready for you when you leave. Since he can anticipate your departure time, this is better than waiting till then to order a taxi yourself.

PROTOCOL — SIGHT-SEEING AT THE WHITE HOUSE

Is there any formality, any special observances, that one needs to know about before making a regular White House tour?

Check in advance to learn what hours the White House is open to sight-seers, and on what days and which entrance you may use. This you can find out at any hotel or motel or tourist information center, or by phoning the White House. If you carry a camera, you will be asked to check it at the door— visitors may not take pictures inside the White House for the reason that it slows up the sight-seeing procession and there is danger from broken flash bulbs. Umbrellas must be checked. No smoking, naturally. Simply join the group being shown through the White House, stay in line, don't be boisterous, don't handle things. If you wish any information, ask the guards.

What about clothes?

Shorts and slacks on women are definitely out of place in the White House as well as in the Capitol of the United States; so are shorts, loud-colored open-necked sports shirts or sweat shirts on men. Men and boys should don suits, shirts, and ties for their White House or Capitol tour; their hats should be removed, as in any residence. Women do not necessarily need to wear hats and gloves, but they should be modestly and neatly dressed. Careless attire shows a complete lack of the fitness of things and at the same time a definite disrespect when visiting the shrines that symbolize our great heritage.

INDEX

INDEX

287

ABOUT THE AUTHOR

CAROLYN HAGNER SHAW is the publisher of *The Social List of Washington, D. C.*, which is used by official and social Washington in preparing guest lists, and is the authoritative guide to the complexities of the official and social group which constitute the background of the nation's capital. She has a weekly column in the *Washington Star* entitled "Modern Manners" and also conducts a radio program. Her aunt was White House secretary to Theodore Roosevelt and Woodrow Wilson and her mother founded the Washington Social Bureau of which she is now head.

Stimulating . . .

Educational . . .

Thought-provoking . . .

These distinguished paperbacks are only a few of the exciting Premier and Crest books now in print.

BEST QUOTATIONS FOR ALL OCCASIONS
(new and revised edition) *Edited by Lewis C. Henry*
(Premier d15—50¢)

A complete, comprehensive selection of immortal quotations.

MAN'S EMERGING MIND *by N. J. Berrill*
(Premier d50—50¢)

A dramatic story about the evolution of the human mind and personality by an eminent scientist.

THE LIVING THOUGHTS SERIES
(Premier, 50¢)

The essential philosophies of the world's great thinkers with modern interpretations—*Jefferson* presented by John Dewey (d61); *Thoreau* by Theodore Dreiser (d63); *Emerson* by Edgar Lee Masters (d67); *Machiavelli* by Count Carlo Sforza (d72); *Confucius* by Alfred Doeblin (d74); *Spinoza* by Arnold Zweig (d76); *Darwin* by Julian Huxley (d82).

PHILOSOPHY FOR PLEASURE *by Hector Hawton*
(Premier d75—50¢)

A simple and enlightening book that makes clear the theories of outstanding philosophers.

THE WORLD'S TEN GREATEST NOVELS
(former title: Great Novelists and Their Novels)
Selected by W. Somerset Maugham
(Crest d276—50¢)

Somerset Maugham sets forth brilliantly his choice of the Ten Greatest Novels, with an insight into the lives of the authors. Includes in his list *War and Peace, Pride and Prejudice, Moby Dick.*